ONE PERCENT DEVILS
AND
THEIR SATANIC TOOLS

by Curtis Alan Woods, JD, MSAJ, BA

RoseDog Books
PITTSBURGH, PENNSYLVANIA 15238

RoseDog Books
585 Alpha Drive
Suite 103
Pittsburgh, PA 15238
Visit our website at www.rosedogbookstore.com

ISBN: 978-1-4809-7197-4
eISBN: 978-1-4809-7174-5

Acknowledgments

University of Wisconsin Schools:
History, Psychology, Political Science,
Economics, and Journalism/Mass Media

Seton Hall University School of Law

American University School of Administration of Justice
and
National Criminal Justice Standards and Goals Commission

MSNBC Hosts
(in the tradition of Edward R. Murrow and Walter Cronkite)
Ed Schultz
Chris Matthews
Andrea Mitchell
Rachel Maddow
Lawrence O'Donnell

History Channel
Discovery Channel
and
Public Broadcast System
Time, Newsweek, U.S. News and World Reports

Interdisciplinary Systemic Analysis of Four Disciplines in Crisis

Politics	Religion	New Media	Economics
Anglo-Saxon	Racial, Religious	Repetitive Lies	Trickle Down
New World Order	Gender Prejudice,	and Hitler-Nixon	Myth and Scam
vs.	Hatred, War, Crime	Wedge Issues	v.
Democracy and	vs.	vs.	Keynesian
Moral Capitalism	Morality	1st Amend. Duty	Stimulus Spending

Multi Disciplinary Input

"Theory of Law" -
St. Thomas Aquinas

Natural Law	Eternal Law	Positive Law
Ethics	Morality	Regulations
White-Collar Crime	Thefts, Bribes, Vice	Military-Industrial
Professions and Trades	Products and Services	Science and Tech
Psych-Socio Factors	Family/Friends/Coworkers	School/Religion

Don't Know History and Be Doomed to Repeat Mistakes
Sex, Philosophy, Law, Crime, War,
Pagan, Sumerian, Hebrew, Greek, Roman, Celt, Christian, Muslim,
Emperors, Kings, Democracy, Nazis, Communists, Dictators

Warnings and Advice
Orwell in *1984* and *Animal Farm* and Ike against AS New World Order
Pres. Dwight D. Eisenhower (Ike) about U.S. Military-Industrial Complex
Edward R. Murrow (CBS News) on TV diversions from News
Wendell Oliver Holmes Woods to Parents on December 24, 1945

TABLE OF CONTENTS

INTRODUCTION

During WWII General George C. Patton told the English press, "After the war, the English and Americans will rebuild and rule the world."

Supreme Allied Commander General Eisenhower angrily said, "I can't have one of my generals spouting racism Hitler would applaud. America didn't send a million of its finest men to create an Anglo-Saxon New World Order but to prevent a Nazi New World Order."

During the Nuremburg Trials of crimes against humanity, the defenses of Nazi generals, judges, industrialists and officials were, "I was only following orders" or "I was following the law."

From a legal treatise by the chief Nazi judge evolved the Nuremburg Doctrine. It states, "Everyone owes a higher duty to morality than to the laws of a nation and orders of its leaders."

The Nuremburg Doctrine is international law. Therefore, it applies to every nation, state, county, and municipal government.

However, morality is a relevant term that may vary depending upon one's age, sex, race, culture, religion, education, economic status, etc. How can a universal morality be formulated that can be acceptable to everyone?

The answer comes from "Theory of Law" by St. Thomas Aquinas. That book is based upon democratic socialism as defined by ancient Greek and Roman legal philosophers such as Plato, Aristotle, Cicero, and Caesar.

They identified tests to determine whether laws, orders, words, acts and omissions are moral. Are they consistent with:

- God's plan for mankind

- Natural law civilized by:
  1. Eternal law common to all religions. Judeo-Christians call it:
     a. Fifteen Commandments or laws of Moses;
     b. Golden Rule; and
     c. Nine soul-saving principles or rules of Christ; and
  2. Positive law such as:
     a. Common law principles of legal equity including:
        1) "One should not gain at someone else's expense";
        2) "One should not benefit from one's wrongs";
        3) "All contracts should produce zero sum outcomes"
     b. Greek Constitution and English Magna Charta rights; and
     c. In U.S. positive law includes:
        1) Declaration of Independence;
        2) U.S. Constitution and Bill of Rights;
        3) Regulations of industry, banks, and stock brokers; and
        4) Criminal and civil courts of truth and justice; and
  3. Are laws, orders, words, acts and omissions consistent with mankind's goal of happiness.

In "Theory of Law," St. Thomas Aquinas wrote that God's plan for mankind is a utopia or heaven on earth free of wars and crimes because of a universal covenant (by all peoples on earth) to comply with natural law as civilized by eternal and positive law. A utopia where:

- Everyone has enough food, clothing, shelter, and medical care;
- Everyone who wants more than basis necessities can achieve to their fullest potential in education, training, a trade, business, or profession; and
- Everyone has opportunities to relax and enjoy beauties of nature, art, music, theater, sports, gourmet food, sex, and other gifts from God.

When the world gets to that point, everyone will have reached:

- The pinnacle of mankind's "Hierarchy of Needs" ala Maslow;
- The goal of mankind (happiness) will be achieved;

- There will be no racial, religious, cultural, ethnic, or gender prejudice; and
- According to Democratic President Franklin Delano Roosevelt,

Americans would have achieved Four Basic Freedoms:

1. "Freedom from want," but "One Percent Devils and their Satanic Tools" have caused 33 percent of American children and their families to suffer malnutrition, illness, and death without medical insurance;
2. "Freedom from discrimination," but "Satanic Tools" use of Hitler-McCarthy, Nixon-Trump, and Cruz-Style, Machiavellian, Divide-and-Conquer, Wedge-Issue Tactics to stimulate racial, religious, ethnic, cultural and gender bias, prejudice, intolerance, hatred, and war;
3. "Freedom of speech," but "One Percent Devils and their Satanic Tools" use that freedom to spread Orwellian, *1984*-type, repetitive lies, racial, religious, cultural, and gender prejudice; and
4. "Freedom of religion," but "Satanic Tools" (Republican press, politicians, and preachers) preach racial, religious, cultural, ethnic, and gender prejudice and St. Augustine's "Rules against Sex."

"You can't be spiritual and sexual, so priests and nuns can't marry. Sex is only for procreation. Masturbation, contraceptives, premarital sex, and having fun during sex are sins that lead to a sinful life and hell."

However, St. Augustine's "Rules against Sex" have had tragic, immoral consequences because they violate and repress DNA-engrained natural law human sexual instincts and inclinations. Those rules cause:

- Dozens of psychiatric and physiological sexual disorders (See DSM-IV and The Merck Manual);
- Sixty percent of women to rarely or never have orgasms during intercourse (according to surveys in *Glamour* and *Cosmopolitan* in the mid-1980s, but a *Time* survey [Sept. 8-15, 2014] indicates 72 percent);
- Sixty percent of women when seeking a mate place a higher priority on:

1. A man's potential income, status, and assets (aka gold diggers);
2. Than on romance, friendship, chemistry, mutual interests, and sex;

- And those three bullet points translate into or cause:
1. Forcible rape of 25 percent of women;
2. Rape by false pretense of 50 percent of women; and
3. A 50 percent-plus divorce rate and two or more marriages.

- Divorce has caused U.S. students to drop from number one in education to seventeenth in math, twenty-first in science, and twenty-fifth in reading comprehension and for boys to diminish or de-evolve educationally below girls because:
1. Custody of sons is almost always awarded to mothers, even when they are at fault for divorce and/or are trying to turn children against half of who they are (their fathers);
2. Sons lose daily activities with fathers that involved rudimentary reading, math, and science, such as sports, building dog houses and tree forts, repairing home, cars, boats, bikes and appliances;
3. So instead of boys excelling past girls in high school, college, postgraduate and professional schools, as occurred during the Baby Boomer generation and previous generations, now girls outperform boys in all levels of education because:
   a. Divorced moms make daughters crack the books, so they won't be financially dependent upon a husband; and
   b. Girls don't know how to raise boys to be lawfully motivated men, especially girls who didn't grow up with a father at home:
      - Vengeful ex-wives (whether victims or a primary cause of divorce) add new meaning to "hell hath no fury as a woman scorned";
      - They turn kids against their fathers (or half of who they are) and cause:
        1. Parental alienation syndrome in sons and daughters; and
        2. They acquire:
           a. Memory blackout amnesia of a whole decade of their lives with fun-loving, super dads;

    b.   Identity crises;

    c.   Bipolar Disorder;

    d.   Psycho-Social homosexuality;

    e.   Post Traumatic Stress Disorder (PTSD); and/or

    f.   Other forms of hysteria such as Conversion Disorder.

Later I'll discuss examples of utopian societies that have existed in the past and present. For now the question is: Why has the multiracial, religious, and cultural U.S. stopped moving toward a utopia in America?

The answer is that the only law "One Percent Devils and Their Satanic Tools" honor is natural law unfettered by eternal law and positive law. Natural law is elucidated in books by Ayn Rand that indicate that the rich and strong should take from the poor and weak.

Time is of the essence to save democratic socialism, middle class and moral capitalism. "One Percent Devils and their Satanic Tools" want to replace such institutions by 2032 (when Caucasians will be a minority)with a tyrannical Plutocratic Anglo-Saxon New World Order where the other 99 percent would be brainwashed, mindless, robotic slaves.

George Orwell warned us about Anglo-Saxon New World Order plans in *1984* and *Animal Farm* and revealed immoral means to immoral ends:

- Repetitive lies so voters believe lies are true and truth is a lie; and
- Hitler-McCarthy-Nixon/Agnew- Bully Trump and Anarchist Tea Party Cruz-style Machiavellian, Divide-and-Conquer, Wedge-Issue Tactics:
  1. To stimulate racial, religious, ethnic, and gender prejudice in people with a pathological need to denigrate others to lift their low egos;
  2. To cause them to become afraid and blame their sorry lots in life on:
     a.   Latin-, Asian- and Afro-Americans, Muslims, and working women;
     b.   Leftist, liberal, progressive, socialistic Democrats;
     c.   Or blame victims of "One Percent Devils and Their Satanic Tools";

- Who caused outsourcing, second Great Stock Market Crash/Depression, military-industrial-complex wars, immigration/safety-net problems;
- So people vote for "Satanic Tools" (Republicans) and against their own family, social and economic interests, freedoms, and rights until they repeal the U.S. Constitution and Bill of Rights.

The Da Vinci Code is about "the great con of mankind." This book is about a related con, "The Great Con of American Voters."

"One Percent Devils and Their Satanic Tools" claim to be Judeo-Christian patriots who love America, "strictly construe" the U.S. Constitution, and represent family values, "The Silent Moral Majority," and law and order.

However, every day "One Percent Devils and Their Satanic Tools" violate:

- Democratic socialistic goals of Declaration of Independence;
- All six Democratic socialistic goals of Preamble of U.S. Constitution;
- Enabling clause and a dozen other socialistic clauses of Constitution;
- All ten freedoms and rights in the Bill of Rights;
- Eternal law common to all seven major religions. For Judeo-Christians, eternal law is called:
    1. Fifteen Commandments, aka laws of Moses in Exodus;
    2. Golden Rule; and
    3. Nine soul-saving rules or principles of Christ; and
- Common law principles of legal equity:
    1. "One should not benefit from one's wrongs";
    2. "One should not gain at someone else's expense"; and
    3. "All contracts should result in zero sum outcomes."

The following charts show that "One Percent Devils and Their Satanic Tools" hate 99 percent of Americans, don't believe in the U.S. Constitution, regulations of industry, banks, and Wall Street, or helping children or families. "One Percent Devils and Their Satanic Tools" are:

One Percent Devils and Their Satanic Tools

Against	**For**
Equal gender rights and equal pay	Exploitation of female workers
Afro, Latin, Asian and Native Americans	Only Caucasians ruling U.S.
Muslims, Hindus, Buddhists	Alleged Judeo-Christians
Equality and justice for all	Exploitation of the other 99 percent
Freedom of press	Repetitive lies by 1-percent Devil Press
Social safety nets for victims of "One Percent Devils"	Death of victims so "One Percent Devils" get FICA and income-tax cuts, deductions and subsidies
Democracy	Anglo-Saxon New World Order
Darwin's "Origin of the Species" and and science that's contrary to Bible	Darwin's "Survival of the Fittest" and Ayn Rand rich taking from poor
Fair pay, redistribution of wealth, equal justice, and progressive taxation	Bribes to buy deregulation and rights to exploit and steal from 99 percent of U.S.
Regulation of industry and finance	Unregulated immoral capitalism
Raising minimum wage to $15/hour	Elimination of minimum wage
Labor union rights, benefits, and unemployment compensation	Outsourcing jobs so One Percent Devils can exploit foreign workers and resources
Redistributing income to the	One-Percent Devil income rising
working poor and middle class after income of 99 percent flatlined since 1975	272 percent in last forty years and for more tax cuts for One Percent Devils
One Percent Devils paying taxes for U.S. Military-Industrial Complex (US MIC)	US MIC protecting immoral foreign interests of One Percent Devils
One Percent Devils paying taxes for safety nets for their victims	Victims of One Percent Devils dying without food, shelter or clothing

Infrastructure spending when Democrat is in White House	Infrastructure spending when a Republican is in White House
Food stamps and school lunch	Subsidies to farmers in Congress
Social safety nets for victims	Military-Industrial Complex
Medical research	Military-weapon research
Tax subsidies for research of biofuels and alternatives to fossil fuels	Tax subsidies for oil, gas and coal exploration research
Clean air, water, land, and food	Pollution and global-warming storms
Business regulations	Unregulated immoral capitalism
Funding for pre, grade, and high schools, college grants, and loans	Racially segregated, unscientific charter schools
Abortions and contraceptives	Death by execution, wars, illness
Medicare, Medicaid and Affordable Care Health Insurance to prevent bankruptcy from medical treatment	Elderly, disabled and welfare recipients dying young to reduce FICA taxes and income taxes
Immigration and naturalization	Hiring illegal immigrant workers

"Satanic Tools" (Republican politicians, preachers and press) are bribed by "One Percent Devils" to not honor or comply with eternal law and positive law. Why don't Democrat and independent politicians, press and preachers repeat to "Satanic Tools" the Golden Rule as follows:

"Do unto others what you would have others do unto you" if you were:
- A woman who wants equal rights and pay, contraceptives, or an abortion;
- Afro, Latin, Asian or Native American;
- Jewish, Sunni, or Shiite Muslims, Hindu, Sikh, Buddhists, Protestants, Evangelical, Roman Catholic, or atheist;
- Illegal immigrants who want freedoms and to support family;
- A child who is impoverished, ill, and needs clean air, water, and land;

- Poor, working poor, or middle class;
- Laid off via negligent or intentional torts of "One Percent Devils";
- A victim of outsourcing of U.S. jobs, manufacturing and technology;
- Ill or have a potentially terminal illness but no health insurance;
- Disabled physically and/or mentally;
- Elderly;
- An unwed and uneducated pregnant girl or woman who can't or doesn't want to raise a baby to adulthood; or
- Pregnant due to rape or incest; or
- Raped by false pretense (ala a boy or man said, "I love you and want to make love, but my religion bans use of contraceptives" and after you got pregnant, the man or boy says, "I won't marry you or help raise or support the baby");
- Out of work due to no fault on your part; or
- Broke after banker and broker stole your life's savings/pension through fraud.

Every day "One Percent Devils and Their Satanic Tools" violate commandments or laws that can be found in all religions:

- "You shall not bear false witness against your neighbor" or "utter false reports" so "One Percent Devils and Their Satanic Tools" should not issue Orwellian, *1984*-type repetitive lies that falsely blame Democrats and victims of "One Percent Devils" immorality;
- "You shall not covet your neighbor's house, wife, servants, ox, ass or anything that is your neighbor's" but "One Percent Devils" covet everyone's business, property, stocks, bonds, wives, and daughters;
- "You shall not commit adultery," but after Republican "Satanic Tools" tried to impeach Democratic President Clinton for adultery:
  1. Larry Flint paid millions of dollars to expose adultery by dozens of "Satanic Tool" Republican senators and congressmen; and
  2. When prostitutes in NYC, Philadelphia, Chicago, and L.A. were asked which party's National Convention they'd prefer, they said, "Republican because they are hornier and have more money";

3. Which means they can also pay for high-priced call girls, ala Senator Ted Cruz, ala the Washington Madam and Donald Trump?

4. And eight hundred other politicians in the Washington, D.C., Madam's book;

- "You shall not steal," so "One Percent Devils" shouldn't steal via banker and broker fraud or outsourcing jobs of those who made them rich or steal by exploiting foreign resources and labor;

- "You shall not kill," so "One Percent Devils" who immorally exploit Third World nations' labor and resources shouldn't bribe "Satanic Tools" to have U.S. Military-Industrial Complex invade and kill to protect foreign interests of "One Percent Devils";

- "You shall take no bribe for a bribe blinds officials and subverts the cause of those who are in the right," but an immoral Republican majority on the Supreme Court has legalized bribes through "Citizens United" to "One Percent Devils." One billion dollars of bribes to Super PACs earns Devils seven billion dollars;

- "You shall not join hands with a wicked man," so politicians, Preachers, and press should not join hands with "One Percent Devils" or their Satanic Tools;

- "You shall not afflict widows or orphans" by cutting social safety nets;

- "You shall not wrong a stranger or oppress him" via bias and prejudice;

- "You shall not pervert the justice due to your poor"

- "If you lend money to any of my people with you who is poor, you shall not be to him as a creditor and you shall not exact interest";

- "Those who have more should give more to the poor";

- "If you seduce a virgin you should marry her"; and

- "Honor they father and thy mother," but they are not honored when "Satanic Tools" use Machiavellian, Divide-and-Conquer, Wedge-Issue Tactics to eliminate Social Security and Medicare for those under fifty-five:

1. So they vote to invest their Social Security retirement FICA taxes on Wall Street and lose that investment every twenty years due to massive stock market and banking fraud by "One Percent Devils;" and

2. Use Medicare FICA contributions to buy private insurance that

doesn't cover pre-existing conditions or prevent bankruptcy;

3. So ironically when those who were under fifty-five lose everything on the stock market or go bankrupt from medical costs, they will vote to eliminate Social Security and Medicare for their mothers and fathers.

As such, "One Percent Devils and Their Satanic Tools" also violate the following soul-saving rules or principles of Christ:

- "Judge not lest thee be judged";
- "Let he who hath not sinned cast the first stone";
- "Love thy neighbor" or "enemy as you love yourself";
- "I am my brother's keeper";
- "Help those in need";
- "Those who have more should give more to the poor";
- "The rich may inherit the earth but not heaven"; and
- "If you are slapped, turn the other cheek" (which replaced Old Testament Torah natural law revenge: "An eye for an eye"); and
- "Forgive those who have sinned against you."

Ancient, pagan Greeks replaced King Law with Democratic-Socialistic Law. Founding fathers of the U.S. were Judeo-Christian, Socialistic Democrats. Based upon God-given natural law, the Declaration of Independence says, "We hold these truths to be self evident, that all Men are created equal, that they are endowed by their Creator with certain unalienable Rights, that among these are Life, Liberty, and Pursuit of Happiness – That to secure these Rights, Governments are instituted among Men, deriving their just Powers from the Consent of the Governed."

The Declaration of Independence lists twenty-four ways in which King George violated natural-law rights. The Preamble of the U.S. Constitution declares, "We the People of the United States, in Order to form a more perfect Union, establish Justice, insure domestic Tranquility, provide for the common defense, promote the general Welfare, and secure the Blessing of Liberty...do ordain and establish this Constitution of the United States..."

"Common defense" doesn't mean misusing the CIA and U.S. military to control Mideast oil and gas or to protect foreign interests of "One Percent

Devils" who immorally exploit foreign resources and labor. "General welfare" doesn't mean immoral welfare for "One Percent Devils" through tax cuts, subsidies, and deductions but the general welfare of the other 99 percent.

"To form a more perfect Union, establish Justice and insure domestic Tranquility" is not achieved by allowing "One Percent Devils" to bribe or buy laws that thwart achievement of those goals by the other 99 percent. Later chapters will go into detail about how "One Percent Devils and Their Satanic Tools" violate all six goals of the Preamble of the U.S. Constitution.

The U.S. Constitution gave citizens of the United States "government of the people, by the people and for the people." It gave the U.S. a one-person-one-vote majority rule and a Bill of Rights and the Fourteenth Amendment to prevent majority governments from violating "unalienable" freedoms and rights of individuals and minority groups. However, the U.S. Constitution doesn't mention or endorse:

- Taxes for Military-Industrial Complex and not social safety nets;
- Capitalism, immoral capitalism and elimination of labor unions;
- Outsourcing jobs so foreign resources/workers can be exploited;
- Tax cuts for rich to produce trickle-down-economics benefits that Jesuit Pope Francis calls "the trickle-down-economics myth";
- Taxation of only 99 percent so immorality of "One Percent Devils" is subsidized;
- Keynesian borrowing and economic stimulus spending should only be employed when "Satanic Tool" Republicans are in White House;
- Americans dying without food, shelter, clothing and medical care;

George Washington warned against forming alliances that could draw the U.S. into foreign wars. The Monroe Doctrine told Europe to stay out of the Americas, and the U.S. would stay out of European affairs.

The Civil War created an industrial and financial revolution that replaced Judeo-Christian Democratic Socialism with a nation ruled by "One Percent Devils," aka the robber-baron kings of finance, railroads, mining, timber, industry, ranches and farms, oil, and gas. Those "One Percent Devils and Their Satanic Tools" violated Judeo-Christian eternal law so they could exploit workers and consumers like they are exploited now in communist and Third World nations due to outsourcing of U.S. jobs:

However, every twenty years since the Civil War, fraud by "One Percent Devils" caused stock market crashes, depressions, and millions of Americans to lose jobs, homes, and savings, so they lived and died in abject poverty while "One Percent Devils" became wealthy at their expense.

Immoral capitalism by robber barons caused labor unions to be formed and influenced the U.S. government to create dozens of agencies to regulate services, industries, banks, and Wall Street to protect the other 99 percent.

Rev. Lebbeus B. Woods, attorney-at-law with a PhD in legal philosophy and a 32nd Degree Free Mason was reminded about the Anglo-Saxon New World Order plans by a December 24, 1945, letter from the Office of War Information (OWI).

"I can only say this much about propaganda BS you swallowed hook, line and sinker about war and post-war maladjustments being Hitler's fault. Abraham Lincoln said, 'You can fool some of the people all the time, and all people some of the time, but you can't fool all the people all the time.'

"Honest Abe may have been correct in 1860, but with OWI's sophisticated psycho-socio, cultural, subliminal, and selective incorporation strategies, I might say this much: There are few who don't submit to propaganda if repeatedly subjected to deceiving messages.

"Who is to blame for WWII? Who put Hitler in power? Who financed him? English, French, and U.S. industrialists and financiers. They wanted Nazis and Russian Communists, obvious threats to capitalism, to destroy each other, but Hitler fooled them all and attacked in all directions.

"What is the root of the evil? Industrialists in all countries. A handful of people who go abroad to invest, looking for cheap labor and mineral resources, to the detriment of their own and our country.

"Then when their toes are stepped on, they influence their own governments to come to their aid to protect their selfish interests. Naturally they do and can because aren't they The Ruling Class?

"If people fail to interest themselves in political matters, which is their duty to investigate, someone must stimulate interest as a patriotic citizen. Is it not part of a minister's calling to ascertain whether political institutions and daily practices are in conformity with Christian standards?

"Is not our democratic system based upon Christian Principles? Did it not originate under Christian tutelage, in a Christian era? Then if capitalism and democracy are stepchildren of Christianity, is it not Christianity's duty to give parental advice, or should Christianity allow it's brainchild to become a savage robot with no interference?

"We are moving into a Propaganda World which necessitates a keen observation and study of what is the truth."

Why don't Democratic and independent politicians, preachers and press expose goals and tactics of "One Percent Devils and Their Satanic Tools?" Two relevant and poignant orations are in the movie *The American President*. Annette Benning asked Michal Douglas (the president) about Republicans.

"How do you have patience with people who claim to love America but clearly can't stand Americans?" In a press conference, Douglas said, "For the record, yes, I am a card-carrying member of the American Civil Liberties Union. But the more important question is, why aren't you Bob (Bob Rumson was Douglas' Republican opponent). That is an organization whose sole purpose is to defend the Bill of Rights. So it naturally begs the question why a senator, his party's most powerful spokesman, and a candidate for president chooses to reject upholding of the Constitution...

"America isn't easy. America is advanced citizenship. You've got to want it bad because it is going to put up a fight.

"It's going to say, 'You want Freedom of Speech? Let's see you acknowledge a man whose words make your blood boil, whose standing center stage and advocating at the top of his lungs that which you have spent a whole life time opposing at the top of yours.'

"You want to claim this land is the land of the free? Then the symbol of your country can not just be a flag. The symbol also has to be one of its citizens exercising his right to burn that flag in protest.

"Now show me that. Defend that. Celebrate that in your classrooms. Then you can stand up and sing about 'The Land of the Free.'

"I've known Bob for years. I've been operating under the assumption that the reason Bob devotes so much time and energy shouting in the rain is that he didn't get it. I was wrong. Bob's problem is that he can't sell it. "We have serious problems to solve, and we need serious people to solve them. Whatever your particular problem is, I promise you Bob Rumson isn't the least bit interested in solving it. He is interested in only two things: making you afraid of it and telling you who's to blame for it.

"You (Bob) gather a group of middle-aged, middle class, middle-income voters who remember with longing an easier time. You talk to them about family, American values, and character. And you wave an old flag…and scream about patriotism and who's to blame for your sorry lot in life."

Who do "One Percent Devils and Their Satanic Tools" blame for everyone's sorry lot in life? They falsely blame five groups:

- Victims of their racial, religious, cultural, and gender prejudice tactics;
- Victims of their outsourcing of production, jobs, and technology;
- Victims of their banking and stock-market fraud;
- Those born into poverty because of their economic policies; and
- Oxymoron-leftist liberal socialistic communist Democrats and press.

In 1954 Edward R. Murrow of CBS News was the only reporter who had the guts to attack and end repetitive lies and Machiavellian, Divide-and-Conquer, Wedge-Issue Tactic terrorism by Wisconsin Senator Joseph McCarthy during his anti-Communist witch-hunt hearings. In 1958 Murrow warned about the dangers of television entertainment diverting Americans from the news so they don't become informed voters. However, Murrow didn't foresee ownership of major radio and television stations and Networks, as well as newspapers, by "One Percent Devils."

In 1961 Republican President Dwight David Eisenhower warned about the dangers of the U.S. Military-Industrial Complex when he said, "…The conjunction of an immense military establishment and a large arms industry is new to the American experience. The total influence — economic, political, and even spiritual — is felt in every city, statehouse and office of the federal government.

"We recognize the imperative need for this development. Yet, we must not fail to comprehend its grave implications. Our toil, resources, and livelihoods are involved and at stake. So is the very structure of our society.

"In the councils of government, we must guard against the acquisition of unwarranted influence, whether sought or unsought, by the Military-Industrial Complex. The potential for the disastrous rise of misplaced power exists and will persist.

"Therefore, we must never let the weight of this complex endanger our liberties or democratic process. We should take nothing for granted.

"Only a knowledgeable and alert citizenry can compel the proper meshing of a huge Military-Industrial Complex with our peaceful message and goals, so our security and liberty may prosper together."

However, during campaign ads and speeches in 2010, 2012, 2014 and 2016 Republican "Satanic Tools" proudly advocated elimination of all funding for Social Safety Nets and all other U.S. Government Agencies, except for the U.S. Military-Industrial Complex. They also advocated elimination of all taxes on "One Percent Devils" and their corporations.

Why didn't Democratic politicians, professors, teachers, preachers and press advocate that "One Percent Devils" and their corporations pay:

- One hundred percent of the taxes needed to fund social safety nets for victims of "One Percent Devils and Their Satanic Tools" who outsourced production of fifty thousand U.S. companies and tens of millions of jobs to:
  1. An atheistic, communist Chinese enemy; and
  2. Third-World nations so "One Percent Devils" could exploit their labor and resources in ways they can no longer exploit Americans?
- One hundred percent of the cost of U.S. Military-Industrial Complex that has troops in 109 nations to protect industrial interests of "One Percent Devils?"

The U.S. has labor unions to prevent exploitation of workers. The U.S. has public employee unions because garbage collectors were earning more than teachers, police officers, firefighters, nurses, and social workers.

Why did Democratic politicians, teachers, preachers and press allow:

- Right-to-work laws for a right to work for less money and benefits;
- Unconstitutional voter ID and restricted voting hour laws, as well as gerrymandering, to disenfranchise those who tend to vote Democrat;
- Laws to eliminate collective bargaining of public employees?

What happened to the Baby Boomer generation of morality? Did it sell out moral beliefs in a quest to become "One Percent Devils?"

Multidisciplinary, systemic analysis can save America.
We live in a complex world and rely upon experts. Often they lack adequate knowledge of other academic disciplines that impact their fields.

This book presents a multidisciplinary, systemic analysis of key issues. Several disciplines can help solve contemporary problems and avoid repeating mistakes of the past.

Judge Stern, a U.S. District Court judge, taught attorneys in "Trial Advocacy" to think outside of the legal box to solve problems with facts and theories from other nonlegal academic disciplines.

We must be knowledgeable, alert, and informed.
Goals of the Founding Fathers, democracy, moral capitalism, minority rights and individual rights can be preserved and fostered by alert and knowledgeable voters. However, most voters need to be informed by moral and knowledgeable politicians, teachers, professors, preachers, and press.

Problem is, Democrats have an identity crisis.
After seventy years of Repetitive Lies and Hitler-Nixon-Type, Machiavellian, Divide-and-Conquer, Wedge-Issue Tactics by Republicans, Democrats have forgotten who they represent and moved from progressive, liberal leftists to moderate conservatives without guts to do what is right. They forgot they're supposed to represent the rights of women, minority groups, individuals, working class, middle class, the poor, elderly, ill, disabled, etc.

Before "One Percent Devils and Their Satanic Tools" violate the U.S. Constitution, Bill of Rights, and eternal law they should remember a Golden Rule: "Do unto others as you would have others do to you." By 2032, Caucasians will be a minority. If they persist in exercising immoral natural law rights, such as "rich should take from the poor," Devils and Satanic Tools better hope a coalition of Afro, Latin, Asian and Native Americans are better Judeo-Christians, Buddhists, or Hindus for honoring eternal law.

If such a coalition honors eternal law, the Constitution, Bill of Rights, and legal equity, then Caucasian women, elderly, poor, homosexuals, and college students will join that coalition. It could control all branches of federal and state governments. A 75 percent majority could enact an Equal Rights Amendments for all races, religions, women, elderly, poor, and homosexuals.

Otherwise that coalition could exercise immoral natural law rights to extract vengeance via "an eye for an eye" reverse discrimination laws. If hurt and angered enough, that coalition could execute "One Percent Devils and Their Satanic Tools," ala the French and Russian revolutions.

Goal of book is to make Republican Party moral

When they compete for votes and function as a president, governor, legislator or justice, moral politicians would vote for amendments to ban:

- Secret, unlimited bribes by "One Percent Devils" to Super PACs, ala "Citizen United" and related Supreme Court decisions;
- Labor unions and corporations from giving contributions because that's not freedom of speech. That's bribery or buying of candidates for financial gain at everyone else's expense;
- All taxpayer contributions except via designating 1 percent of income taxes to Democrat, Republican or independent Candidates; and
- Campaigns based on Orwellian *1984*-style, repetitive lies, and Hitler-Nixon-type Machiavellian, Divide-and–Conquer, Wedge-Issue Tactics:
  1. Candidates should be allowed freedom of speech to issue a lie or tactic only once; but
  2. After lies or tactics are exposed, the issuer should be required to apologize and promise not to do it again.

Author's philosophy and ideology

"Honor thy father and thy mother" prevents me from being a Republican or Democrat. As a history, political, law, and religion buff, I evolved into an independent, progressive, liberal, existential libertarian, egalitarian, legalistic Judeo-Christian patriot, if I may be so immodest.

If "One Percent Devils and Their Satanic Tools" reflexively falsely claim I'm a heretic or communist:

- I have a religious writer's fallback position. "Enlightenment came to me in a nighttime or day dream or from a voice in my mind;" and
- "You must have faith in what you cannot see or hear"; so
- **"Don't kill an enlightened, messenger prophet! Act on the issues."**

In the final analysis, "One Percent Devils and Their Satanic Tools" cannot possibly be Judeo-Christian patriots. They lie about what the U.S. Constitution says. They don't represent law and order or family values. They represent "the Silent Immoral Majority" of Americans.

CHAPTER I

Greatest Generations Are WWII Generation
and Baby Boomer Generation of Morality

S ex was on hold five years during WWII for twelve million soldiers and their lovers who worked in war industries. Mother, Ethel Mary Hii, and sister, Aunt Mildred, packed army K rations at American Can in Chicago.

Delayed natural-law human instincts and inclinations to mate and procreate caused a population explosion, aka the Baby Boomer Generation.

My father, Wendell Woods, attorney-at-law, founded the Walworth County Farm Bureau to pass on English farming practices learned while on leave as an agent for OWI/OSS. When asked about English gals, he laughed and said, "They would ask 'When do you want me to knock you up?'"

On Thanksgiving weekend of 1946, Dad met Mom at a dance club on South Shore Drive in Delavan Lake, WI. They were earthy and hot to trot, not just on dance floor. Years later after the club burned down, Uncle Burnise Olsen, legendary investigator and sheriff of Walworth County said, "Club was torched by a rival of the Chicago mob owner, or as an insurance company defense attorney said, 'arson for insurance.'"

Brother Warren was born eight months after Christmas. Either he was premature or a fetal bastard for a month. Eleven months later I was born.

Sister Debra was conceived on a Sunday afternoon after Mom or Dad said, "Time for you boys to go outside and play. Time for us to 'Oh God, Oh God' pray."

1

In the 1950s, we faced two kinds of repression and watched another on television. Sexual repression came from parents who, like regressive Republicans, wanted Boomers to be sexually uptight Victorians. Boomers about to sexually bloom were taught St. Augustine's "Rules against Sex."

After WWII, parents who had been sexually loose tried to repress the irrepressible, natural-law sexual instincts and inclinations of teenage children. However, the Vietnam War was a time when choices were unclear at a time when a military draft notice or death in war could be near.

To many, patriotism, courage, honor, and morality meant fighting atheistic communists in the Vietnam War under a domino-theory myth. If Vietnam fell to communism, the rest of Southeast Asia and continents would fall like dominos.

To others, patriotism, courage, honor, and morality meant opposing U.S. involvement in a Vietnamese civil war that only benefited: U.S. Military-Industrial Complex; oil and gas companies, companies that wanted Vietnamese rubber, minerals, and cheap labor; and stock brokers, banks and insurance companies that invested in the U.S. MIC.

Boys who opposed the war had seven choices. Enlist to fight in Vietnam. Avoid war by enlisting to be stationed in a nation like Germany, Japan or the National Guard. Enlist in the medical corps to avoid killing but risk death or disability. Wait to be drafted into military. Apply for conscientious-objector status to avoid military service. Escape to Canada. Or attend College or post-graduate school and hope the war is over before graduation.

Guys didn't want to die without having sex and/or procreating. Gals wanted to have their boyfriend's baby just in case. Gals and guys said:

- Make love and peace, not war;
- If guys can sew wild oats, gals can have premarital grain;
- However, it's been said "sex without love is second rate";
- Sure wish one of us knew how to make love first rate; and
- Free love wasn't always free before Roe vs. Wade.

Yet despite the damage caused by St. Augustine's "Rules against Sex," in 2012 Republican presidential candidate Santorum repeated St. Augustine's "Rules against Sex" and mistakenly said the Founding Fathers believed in those anti-natural-law mores. However, Puritan founding parents had escaped English sex patrols. They believed, "God intended sex to be fun."

Have you seen anything in Old Testament Torah or New Testament that prohibits premarital sex or sex for fun? Aren't parts of the Old Testament like a Kama Sutra sex manual about how to make love?

Baby Boomers saw racial repression on television. Caucasian state troopers, sheriffs, and police armed with tear gas, water hoses, batons, and guns brutalized peaceful Afro-American civil rights marchers.

When Baby Boomers traveled south of the Mason-Dixon line, they saw "Whites Only" laundries, restaurants, and schools. Gas stations had restroom signs: White Women, White Men and Colored (or the N Word). Afro-Americans didn't have a right to vote, freedom of speech, or a right to peacefully protest. Klu Klux Klan members beat, castrated, shot, hung, and/or burned Afro-Americans. Criminal justice systems were biased against their rights. Peacetime suppression of freedom of speech and press began in the late 1940s. Nixon and McCarthy Republicans were desperate to win control of the White House, Senate, and Congress. They used Orwellian-type repetitive lies and Machiavellian, Divide-and–Conquer, Wedge-Issue Tactics, such as "the press and Democrats are communists." Lies that violated commandments:

- "Thou shall not bear false witness against thy neighbor"; and
- "Thou shall not utter a false report."

By 1948 the Republican Congress was called "The All Talk But No Action, Do Nothing Congress." That history was repeated from 2010-16 when Republicans used lies and wedge issues to do less than in 1948. My dad's 1936 letter to his parents applied in 1948 and 2010-2016. It said, "Republicans don't offer to do anything different. They only promise to do things better or more efficiently run government."

The Do Nothing 2010–16 Congress passed worthless legislation:

- To repeal the Affordable Care Act (over forty times); and
- Dozens of bills to end rights to contraception and abortion; but
- Held dozens of worthless, million-dollar, Congressional hearings (Benghazi embassy attack, IRS after Tea Party, fast and furious guns for drugs, Solyndra solar energy, contraceptives, abortion). Why?

1. To find impeachable offenses by President Obama, and in the case of Benghazi, to prevent former first lady, senator, and secretary of state Hillary Clinton from winning the presidency in 2016. Why?
2. Republicans are not Judeo-Christians because they don't honor the above cited commandments, Golden Rule, and Christian principles but instead are poor losers and bad sports who don't believe in democracy and "The American Way of Fair Play."

In 2008 I mistakenly voted for Republican candidates for president and vice president: war hero Republican Senator John McCain (but the poor boy has since lost his way) and airheaded, Tea Party, two-year Governor Sarah Palin. Imagine if President McCain died. President Palin would apply her lack of knowledge of history, economics, and science to solve crucial problems?

I didn't vote in 2008 for Democratic Senator Barrack Obama because I didn't believe he had enough experience in government or intelligence to be president. I was dead wrong. President Obama may have the highest IQ and knowledge base of all prior presidents.

His solution for every domestic and foreign policy problem was on target and correct. So I voted for him in 2012. How can Republicans have the intellectual dishonesty, gall, and audacity to "bear false witness" otherwise and to try to inappropriately and unjustly impeach President Obama:

- When IRS was auditing Democratic and Republican Super PACs;
- When Republican President G.W. Bush:
  1. Awarded the Solyndra solar energy grant;
  2. Approved fast and furious guns for drugs program; and
  3. Lied about Iraq having weapons of mass destruction and that Saddam Hussein would sell them to anti-American terrorists? Lies that caused:
     a. Over three thousand U.S. Soldiers to get killed and tens of thousands of soldiers to become disabled in Iraq War II;
     b. Hundreds of thousands of Iraqis to get killed and disabled;
     c. National debt to increase by six trillion dollars; and
     d. Billions cut from social safety nets to pay for Iraq War?
- When Republican Congress:

1. Reduced embassy security appropriations for Benghazi; and
2. Never sought to impeach Presidents Reagan, George H. Bush, or George W. Bush after any one of the dozens of attacks on U.S. embassies and embassy staffs; and
3. Never even suggested that President G.W. Bush and Vice President Cheney should be impeached and tried for international crimes against humanity in Iraq; and

- When an end to contraceptives and abortions would:
  1. Put single-parent mothers out of work and on welfare, Medicaid, food stamps, and public-housing assistance, along with their children;
  2. Bankrupt families where both parents must work; and
  3. Cause millions of women to die or become disabled from illegal abortions?

Meanwhile Republicans in Washington, D.C., and states controlled by Republicans aid and abet theft by "One Percent Devils" via unconstitutional:

- Tax cuts, deductions, and subsidies for "One Percent Devils" who evade income and FICA taxes by hiding income in offshore banks;
- Reductions of social safety nets for 47 percent of Americans who are:
  1. Contractually "entitled" to receive Social Security disability or retirement and Medicare because they paid for it through FICA taxes their whole lives; or
  2. Victims of Republican failure to regulate industry, banks, and Wall Street; outsourcing; racial, religious, cultural, and gender intolerance; and bias, prejudice, repression, and suppression by "One Percent Devils and Their Satanic Tools" and the only income and other support for their victims:
     a. Is from Social Security and Medicare; or
     b. Welfare, Medicaid, food stamps, and public-housing assistance.
- Gerrymandering of voting districts, so in states such as Pennsylvania, where 60 percent voted Democrat, only 40 percent of state legislative and federal congressional seats went to Democrats; and
- Voter ID suppression laws to disenfranchise minorities who vote Democrat (elderly, college students, Afro- and Latin-Americans);

- Even though such legislation would waste millions of dollars when state attorney generals defend it in federal court.

How do Republicans get away with "Doing Nothing" to achieve goals in the Preamble of the Constitution? The answer comes in four parts:

- Republican Super Pac CEOs Orville Norquist and Carl Rove spin at least one lie and wedge-issue ploy per week;
- Every Republican president, governor, federal and state legislator or candidate repeat each lie and wedge issue verbatim;
- Rush Limbaugh on radio and Fox News repeats each lie and wedge issue ploy every hour on the hour; and
- Four key groups either don't know U.S. history, or if they do, don't expose lies and wedge-issue ploys by "Satanic Tools":
  1. Democrats and independents;
  2. Newspaper, radio and TV reporters and commentators; and
  3. Preachers, priests, rabbi, clerics, and monks

Baby Boomers grew up in families, churches, synagogues, mosques, or temples where they learned the same eternal law that Judeo-Christians call commandments, the Golden Rule, and soul-saving rules of Christ. In sports Baby Boomers learned "The American Way is Fair Play."

In Scouts, Boomers were taught to be truthful, honorable, just, brave, thrifty, clean, reverent, and to help those in need. Parents also gave Boomers time-tested family socialization or civilizing adages:

- "Fail to learn history and be doomed to repeat mistakes of the past";
- "Fool me once, shame on you. Fool me twice, shame on me";
- "Don't kick a man when he's down";
- "If you can't take it, don't dish it out";
- "Sticks and stones may break your bones but words can't hurt you";
- "Accept what you cannot change and change what you can";
- "Any girl who expects you to fight for her does not love you";
- "Don't have sex with a girl you wouldn't want to marry if you had to";
- "Anyone who asks you to do something wrong is not your friend";

- "A fool and his money are easily parted";
- "Don't bite the hand that feeds you";
- "It's a dirty bird who shits on its own nest";
- "Do not pick on people who are smaller or hit someone with glasses";
- "Treat girls with respect. So don't swear, tell dirty jokes, or hit girls."

In school, Baby Boomers:
- Studied the U.S. Constitution, Bill of Rights, American history; and
- Read "Current Events" (a CIA publication) in civics class and learned that atheistic, communist nations don't have:
  1. Freedom of religion, press, or speech or the right to protest against acts or omissions by the government;
  2. Fourth Amendment rights against wiretaps and mail-opening searches and seizures without a warrant based on probable cause;
  3. Fifth Amendment right not to be forced to testify against oneself;
  4. Marital right not to be forced to testify against a spouse;
  5. Children were forced to testify against parents; and
  6. Political opponents were arrested, tortured, killed, or imprisoned.

However, via TV and newspapers, Baby Boomers saw that women, racial, and religious minorities in the U.S. didn't have equal rights (rights under the Bill of Rights) and were abused for protesting. Baby Boomers became the Generation of Morality because they honored morality learned at home, school, church, sports, and Scouts. Baby Boomers protested and marched for:

- Equal rights and justice for women, Afro-, Latin-, and Native Americans;
- Democratic President Johnson's "War on Poverty" to prevent racial war;
- Reforms of unconstitutional criminal and civil justice systems;
- Medicare and Medicaid;
- Food stamps and Meals on Wheels;

- College grants and student loans;
- Clean air, water, land, and food;
- Contraception and abortion; and
- Against an immoral Vietnam War.

However, President Nixon Republicans issued *1984*-style repetitive lies and Hitler-type Machiavellian, Divide-and-Conquer, Wedge Ploys such as:

- "Civil rights, antiwar, and feminist activists and press are leftist, liberal, socialistic, communist, negative nabobs of nepotism who don't live in the 'real world' and, along with police, shouted at civil rights, antiwar, feminist, and environmental protestors";
- "America: Love it or leave it and return to the homeland of your ancestors";
- Wouldn't that invitation be more appropriate for Satanic Tools who:
- Don't believe in democracy and moral capitalism;
- Can't stand victims of "One Percent Devils" saved by social safety nets: working women, Afro-, Latin-, Asian-, and Native Americans;
- Lie that the 47 percent surviving on social safety nets don't want to work; and
- Want to eliminate all federal departments and agencies except:
    1. The Pentagon and its Military-Industrial Complex; and
    2. The Law Enforcement Assistance Administration, which gives grants to states, counties, and municipalities for drones, tanks, SWAT units, and assault rifles to suppress demonstrations against government acts and omissions.

Nixon's "Law and Order" Republicans unconstitutionally bore false witness that the Warren Court was "soft on crime" or "tied hands of police" with Miranda warnings and the exclusionary rule (Mapp vs. Ohio). Mapp bars evidence at trial from illegal searches and confessions induced by beatings, torture, or sensory, water, food, and cigarette deprivation.

Criticism of the Warren Court primed Northern law enforcement to take a page out of a Southern anti-civil-rights law enforcement playbook. Racial, religious, and gender prejudiced, male-chauvinistic, Caucasian, pro-Vietnam War hawk police hated college students. Their rights were abused like Southern law enforcement abused civil rights marchers, especially at:

- Columbia University in New York City;
- University of Wisconsin, Madison;
- University of California, Berkley;
- Kent State University, where a dozen antiwar protestors were shot to death by National Guard troops also armed with bayonets; and
- Jackson State University, where police shot into dormitory rooms and killed protestors.

In 1967 I was a pro-Vietnam War hawk at UW. One sunny day I walked between antiwar protestors (dressed like hippies and love children). They peacefully protested in front of the Commerce Building because Dow Chemical (manufacturer of napalm for Vietnam), was interviewing students.

Whether planned or pure negligence, Madison police with batons attacked protestors after class bells rang. As hundreds of conservative business students, who supported the war, tried to exit the Commerce Building, they also were beaten by Madison police. We carried seventy-two students (with skull, limb, and rib fractures and lacerations) to the UW Hospital ER. (For more information, go to Chapter VI, pages 229-235 for my editorial titled "July 4, 1967 Assault, Batteries, and Riot by Lake Geneva Police."

My roommate George Bogdanich, with shoulder-length, scraggly hair, made the cover of *Newsweek*. His right hand was out, and he was open-mouthed, shouting "stop" to police. George was so well-read and articulate that my pro-war Republican dogma was no match for his antiwar dovish facts.

I asked George about books on Vietnam. He handed me *The Pentagon Papers* and *Roots of Conflict*. After graduation I was studying for the LSAT when Dad came home from a bad day in court. He shouted, "Get your antiwar and hippie crap out of my house."

I was baffled and asked, "Why?"

"I got a letter from a University of Wisconsin professor that said, 'Communism is being taught in UW classes and communists are behind the civil rights, antiwar, and feminist movements.'"

I replied with disbelief, "I've never heard a professor say communist or communism, even in poli-sci. Probably due to intimidation by Wisconsin Sen. Joseph McCarthy. I'll bet Tricky Dicky's behind that letter."

Dad pointed at the door and shouted, "Get out."

We didn't talk for five years until after President Nixon resigned. On May 1, Law Day, Dad called and said something I'd never heard him say before. He apologized and said, "You were correct. An OWI/OSS colleague who became CIA said the CIA authored the UW prof letter. Are you in law school?"

I said, "Not yet. I told Uncle Burnise I didn't feel prepared for law school but was so angry about being brutalized by rioting Madison and Lake Geneva police that I wanted to reform law enforcement. Uncle Berni said, 'At American University in Washington, D.C., you can earn an MS in administration of justice studying police science, court administration, and correctional science. AU professors are on a massive National Criminal Justice Standards and Goals Commission.'"

While studying police science to determine whether laws could be enforced with respect for suspects and law, I worked:

- During the school year as a store detective at Hecht Company. I had more arrests than Typson Corner Police for all kinds of thefts; and
- During summers I was a special police officer;
- As an intern at U.S. District Court, I watched the Watergate trial.

I also wrote:
- "Police Community Relations – 1975" for the International Association of Chiefs of Police;
- For the New Jersey Governor's Criminal Justice Advisory Committee, I wrote standards and goals for crime prevention, law enforcement, prosecution, defense, courts, corrections, and victim assistance;
- On *Law Review*, I wrote the Portier case note about a mother who, for five hours, watched her son slowly die wedged between an elevator and shaft. The New Jersey Supreme Court recognized claims for negligent infliction of emotional distress;
- For my torts professor Laurence Bershad, I read boxes of research and wrote the first draft of "Discrimination against Women in the

Criminal Justice System." It was published in *Boston Law Review*;
- And in "For the Defense" (1991-2003), the Defense Research Institute published seven of my articles on how to use subpoena and medical research to defeat fraudulent orthopedic, neurological, and neuropsychological injury claims.

After my work was recognized by the medical community, as evidenced by seminars I gave at national medical conferences (National Spine Symposium and American Academy of Disability Evaluating Physicians), powerful enemies and those I trusted caused destruction of a profit-sharing partnership, my own law firm, and a twenty-six state legal medical consulting firm (through which I trained other attorneys).

To preserve my work, I wrote about trials that led to seven articles in a book *Tortious Lies: Medical Myths, Legal Fictions and Junk Science*. By October 2010, I was almost finished writing but had writer's block.

What Caused "One Percent Devils and Their Satanic Tools"?

I had lived for five years like Thoreau's *Walden Pond* in a social and news blackout. After I turned on TV news (October 2010), I was shocked and disgusted by what appeared to be a racial, religious, and gender intolerant political-comedy satire. It wasn't comedy or satire but Fox News.

I scanned networks for objective news and found MSNBC. Its hosts discussed issues with Republicans, Democrats, independents, professors, and authors of books or articles on issues at hand. They rebutted Republican lies and wedge issues aired by Fox, Limbaugh, Beck, Palin, Wallace, etc.

After watching five hours of MSNBC every night for weeks, I realized everything Baby Boomers had fought for and won was on the Republican chopping block. For forty years Republicans have claimed to be patriotic Christians, strict interpreters of the U.S. Constitution, and the "Law and Order Party" even though President Nixon and VP Agnew violated the rights of 200,000 Americans and left office because of crimes.

Thereafter, Republicans claimed to represent "The Silent Moral Majority?" Yet doesn't it seem as though they're unable to obey or honor:

Commandments; Golden Rules; U.S. Constitution; Bill of Rights; Supreme Court decisions; federal laws; or regulations. They want the U.S.

to go back to when female, Afro-, Latin-, and Native American victims of "One Percent Devils" didn't have constitutional freedoms or rights.

Isn't the Tea Party a Pee Party that Urinates on Us and U.S.?

"One Percent Devils and Their Satanic Tools," aka Pee Party Pooper Republicans, have what Nixon wished he had: control of enough news media to pass on enough repetitive lies and Machiavellian, Wedge-Issue Ploy Propaganda that violated natural law, eternal law, and positive law (U.S. Constitution and Bill of Rights):

- So that in 2012, 47 percent voted for a flip-flop, repetitive-lying, Dracula vulture capitalist Romney:
  1. Whose Book of Mormon says Afro-Americans are devils, and that men can be polygamous and wives must be subservient to husbands;
  2. Who outsourced American production, jobs, and technology to an atheistic communist Chinese enemy;
  3. Who, with his lying vice presidential candidate Paul Ryan advocated:
     a. Elimination of all social safety nets for 47 percent of Americans who are retired or victims of "One Percent Devils and their Satanic Tools" (Republican politicians, preachers, and press).
     b. More tax cuts, deductions, and subsidies for "One Percent Devils" outsourcing so they could:
  1. Exploit foreign workers in ways U.S. laws and regulations prevent companies in the U.S. from exploiting workers, but if foreign workers rebel, the CIA and Military-Industrial Complex steps in; and
  2. Destroy American labor unions, but if American workers rebel, Republican "Satanic Tools" can defeat them with:
     a. Five new domestic spy agencies under the Patriot Act;
     b. SWAT teams in large, medium, and small cities;
     c. Backed up by police and National Guard, drones, assault helicopters, and tanks.

As indicated, I wrote standards and goals on corrections. In Fall 2010, I was shocked when Wisconsin gubernatorial candidate Scott Walker said on TV, "After I'm elected governor, no prisoners will be allowed on parole. They will all serve their full sentences."

My letter to Walker said, "There's a state budget deficit, isn't there? Where will you find billions of dollars to build enough prisons? Who wants a prison in their back yard? Will you also fund education, training, and provide job-placement services so ex-cons can work and not recidivate?"

Equally incredible Walker also said, "I'll cut taxes and increase employment." Yet Pope Francis astutely said, "Trickle-down economics is a myth."

I wrote the following to Walker:

- If you cut taxes, you must lay off teachers, police, firefighters, etc.;
- That eliminates their taxable income and spending power;
- So store clerks, factory workers, and service providers will be laid off;
- That eliminates their taxable income and spending;
- So more government workers must be laid off until there's no more government employees to lay off; and
- For governments to effectively and efficiently operate, if inflation is 1 percent or 9 percent, taxes must be increased 1 percent or 9 percent to maintain the status quo.

Didn't Chief Justice Marshall say in Marlboro vs. Madison, "The power to tax is the power to destroy?" Isn't power not to tax, power to destroy federal and state governments? Weren't Baby Boomers raised to believe communists want to destroy the U.S. government? If so, aren't Tea Party Republicans communists because they want to eliminate all federal agencies and spending except for the U.S. Military-Industrial Complex?

Morally, why should a minority group of teachers, police, nurses, firefighters, and social workers lose jobs so a majority of voters (*especially One Percent Devils*) can get tax cuts? Justice William O. Douglas said in 1962,

> "Rights of an individual or minority should not be the subject of a majority vote, including rights of: public employees; poor; working poor; middle class; children; women; racial; and religious minorities."

Since the 1929 Stock Market Crash and Great Depression, every president employed Keynesian borrowing and economic stimulus spending to bring the U.S. out of depression. Yet Gov. Walker rejected an $800 million federal grant to build a high-speed rail line from Milwaukee to Madison.

Taxable income and spending generated by construction of rail tracks, engines, cars, stations, and adjacent businesses would've reduced Wisconsin's unemployment to 3 percent. Instead Gov. Walker repaid the owner of Southern Wisconsin Railroad Co. (for illegal campaign contributions) by giving him $200 million of state funds to build a line from O'Hare to Milwaukee.

Gov. Walker should've accepted the $800 million and spent that $200 million for a high-speed line from Madison to the Wisconsin Dells, aka Disney World of the North. That would've created an economic boom in southeastern and central Wisconsin. Instead of American and foreign vacationers getting stressed out, hurt, or killed driving from all corners of America, they could fly to O'Hare, get on a high-speed train for the Wisconsin Dells, and read a book or newspaper during the three-hour trip.

There they could rent cars, camping, fishing, hunting, and skiing Equipment, and/or take a taxi cab to one of the gambling casino hotels. Imagine the billions of more dollars that would've been spent at the Dells and supporting businesses. Increased vacationers would result in expansion of businesses, building of new businesses, and hiring of tens of thousands of workers. That would cause a budget surplus and lower tax rates.

Did Walker Fail Economics, Poli-Sci, and History 101?
I'm embarrassed that Walker graduated from my high school, DDHS.

Doesn't he know that historically, Wisconsin's been a progressive, liberal state?

- In 1848 Wisconsin was the first moral state to ban death penalties;
- The equal racial rights Republican Party of Lincoln and Gov. Lafollette's Progressive Party were founded in Wisconsin;
- Wasn't Wisconsin the first state to enact legislation for:
  1. Collective bargaining (but Gov. Walker severely curtailed rights of public worker unions);
  2. Minimum wage (but Walker's against it) and maximum hours;
  3. Worker's compensation for injuries on the job;

4. Child labor laws and laws to protect pregnant workers?

During previous depressions and recessions, haven't Wisconsin governors employed Keynesian borrowing and economic stimulus?

Walker violated commandments, Golden Rules and the general-welfare provision of the Constitution by not helping the poor, sick, and uninsurable by:

- Not setting up an insurance exchange system to take applications for Affordable Care Health Insurance;
- "Bearing false witness" that the federal enrollment system was ill conceived when in fact he and other Republican governors caused an overload of the federal system by not setting up state systems;
- Refusing to accept Medicaid expansion even though coverage would've cost Wisconsin taxpayers zero. When Wisconsinites pay more federal taxes than they receive in federal aid for social safety nets, education, law enforcement, etc; and
- Didn't Walker also sign voter ID and reduced-voting-time legislation to disenfranchise elderly, college students, Afro- and Latin-Americans?

When he ran for governor in 2010, didn't Walker promise to increase employment in Wisconsin by 250,000? Yet as a result of his cutting of taxes and state funding to counties and municipalities, tens of thousands of teachers, police, firefighters, nurses, and social workers lost their jobs.

Didn't Gov. Walker say tax cuts for companies would enable them to expand production plants, build plants, and increase employment? Yet of the ten states in the Rust Belt, didn't Wisconsin have the lowest increase in jobs because Walker caused layoffs of thousands of government employees?

In 2014 Gov. Walker's campaign commercials had six people claim they got jobs. Yet ads didn't say what jobs and with what companies, so reporters couldn't determine whether those in ads really got jobs. Why didn't his opponent reveal how many in private and public sectors lost jobs?

Didn't Republican President Teddy Roosevelt break up vertical and horizontal monopolies of "One-Percent Devil" robber-baron kings of finance and industry: J.P. Morgan (Wall Street and banking); Rockefeller (oil and gas); Carnegie (steel); and Vanderbilt (railroads)?

However, haven't Republicans from Nixon to Walker helped facilitate A re-emergence of horizontal and vertical monopolies so kings of industry and finance are again too powerful; threats to democracy and moral capitalism; and too big to be allowed to fail? Hasn't Gov. Walker taken huge bribes from the Koch brothers, who want open-pit iron mining and fracking of Wisconsin until there are earthquakes and water pollution?

I Won't Take Tea Party Pooper Republican BS Anymore!
Remember that movie where a guy was so frustrated, he threw open a window and shouted "I have had enough. I won't take it anymore"?

For me, the Straw that broke the camel's back was the thirty-seventh repetitive lie, Wedge-Issue Oxymoron for Morons. It psychologically projected immorality and illegality of treasonous Republicans against President Obama. The most ludicrous Oxymoron for Morons was that he "was born in Kenya and is a colonialist, European socialist, communist, Nazi traitor."

An Oxymoron for Morons because:

- President Obama produced a Hawaiian birth certificate;
- Only colonialists in America are "One-Percent Devil" industrialists;
- European socialistic austerity is what Republicans want even though it had caused high unemployment/economic depression in Europe;
- Republicans employ Hitler-style, Machiavellian, Divide-and-Conquer, Wedge-Issue Tactics to stimulate racial, religious, and gender bias, prejudice, and intolerance so people vote Republican and against their own social and economic interests; and
- Aren't Nazis and communists mutually exclusive opposites?
- Don't Republicans want an Anglo-Saxon New World Order?
- Wouldn't an antidemocracy, antimoral capitalism, Anglo-Saxon New World Order (NWO) be similar to a Nazi or communist NWO? Why do Republicans use such Oxymorons for Morons?
- They know most Americans aren't intelligent and knowledgeable;
- They're neo-Nazi racists who hate their Afro-American president;
- They have low self esteem and need to denigrate President Obama to elevate their egos; and
- Satanic Republican Tools take "Citizen United" bribes from:
  a. Atheistic Communist Chinese companies; and

  b. One Percent Devils who believe in:
      1. Darwinian "Survival of the Species";
      2. Ayn Rand "The strong should take from the weak"; and
      3. An immoral quest to end democracy and moral capitalism;
      4. So they can create the kind of Anglo-Saxon New World Order:
          a) General and then-President Eisenhower opposed; and
          b) George Orwell warned about in *1984* and *Animal Farm*.

Republicans add new meaning to "look who's calling the kettle black." Speaker of the House Boehner (Webster's pronounces Boehner as Bone-er) literally and/or figuratively pulled a boner by psychologically projecting Republican sins of obstruction by lying that President Obama caused:

* Budget deficit and crisis;
* Increases of deficit;
* U.S. credit rating to drop (August 2012);
* Government shutdown (October to December 2013);
* High unemployment and increasing unemployment; and
* Only 2 percent economic growth.

How could 47 percent of Americans who voted for Republican Romney to be president and a majority of Americans voted for Republican U.S. senators, congressman, governors, and legislators of twenty-six Republican states, not know or not care that Republican President G.W. Bush caused all that by:

* Giving away the $400 billion budget surplus left by Democratic President Bill Clinton;
* By borrowing six trillion dollars from an atheistic Communist Chinese enemy instead of raising taxes to pay for wars in Iraq and Afghanistan;
* Failing to regulate banks and Wall Street, which caused the second greatest stock-market crash and economic depression; and
* A Republican majority in the House of Representatives:

1. Refused to pass infrastructure legislation to put Americans back to work; and
2. Refused to do their job by refusing to develop a budget by compromise, held the budget hostage, and used it to blackmail or extort what they wanted from Democratic President Obama.

Educational Philosophy and Goals of Founding Fathers

"The History of Whately, Mass, 1661-1891," begins with a narrative history and ends with trunks and branches of Founding Father family trees that migrated to the Connecticut Valley of western Massachusetts. Grandma Lydia Little Smith Woods's first Smith ancestor in Whately was Lieutenant Samuel Smith in 1634. During the 1600s and 1700s, Smiths procreated with spouses of twenty-three families (most noteworthy: Hamilton, Foote, Dickinson, Hurd, Howard, Kellogg, Barnes, Morrison, Johnson, and Wible).

In the chapter on education it says,

"The Puritan fathers had a broad and true conception of what education is, and among the earliest acts passed, was one requiring the selectmen of towns to see to it that parents and master train up their children in learning and labor and other employments which may be profitable to the Commonwealth. *For the learning and habits of industry and knowledge of some profitable employment, here enjoined, not only fitted the child to become a useful member of the state, but at the same time fitted him/her for individual excellence and happiness.*"

(Note: Aquinas said, "the goal of mankind is happiness," and the Declaration of Independence says we have an unalienable right to pursue happiness.)

"The proper aim of school instruction, as of all instruction of children, is to fit them for efficient duty. There is need of knowledge, need of culture and need to learn the dangers of life and how to shun them, as well as the best way to use its advantages. The child needs to get a true idea of his dependence on others for his happiness and influence, and to believe in and respect the rights of others, as well as to believe in his personal independence and claim his own rights. He needs to have his wits sharpened early if he is to be a successful competitor for position and power.

"Our public schools, where all classes mingle and where *courses of study are adapted to the various capacities and where restraint and liberty are wisely adjusted* and where parents and teachers co-operate, as they do in every successful school, and home and school discipline supplement each other, our public schools, thus administered, furnish the best *preparation for practical life*. Probably parochial and patronage schools and private tutors would insure a higher standard of merely scientific attainment to particular classes in the community, but true education of the people is, beyond question, best promoted by our free school system" (pages 187-188 of Chapter XI).

Sophia Smith founded Smith College (which became the elite school for daughters of the rich and famous). Her father Gad "...was very prominent in town and business affairs, giving employment to many men. He kept a large country store, a hotel, ran a large farm, carried on an extensive slaughtering house and coopering works for making beef barrels for shipping beef to the West Indies" (page 566).

So Why Do U.S. Students Rank Seventeenth in Math, Twenty-first in Science, and Twenty-fifth in Reading Comprehension

The following is a comparison of education when Baby Boomers ranked number one in Industrial Nation Educational Attainment. After Boomers:

- Students didn't have to take home two to four novels and biographies per semester to read for literature classes;
- Students didn't have to memorize addition/subtraction or multiplication/ division tables or use slide rules. They were allowed to use calculators and then computers; and
- Without competence in math, competence in science is impossible;
- Educational goals don't strive to accomplish underlined goals above to garner education such as math and science by applying it to:
  1. Problems children face and will face at work and home in the future;
  2. To sharpen competition wit to succeed; or
  3. To fit children for duties in practical life and future employment;
- Teachers don't motivate students to learn math and science by showing how it will help them succeed in their potential future career choices (baseball, football, basketball, shot put, discus thrower, musical artist, attorney, doctor, engineer);
- Cognitive problem solving and deductive reasoning diminished when schools shifted from a final examination with long and short essays to only a multiple-choice format and answers requiring only a yes or no.

- No parent home after school or post-school study option in school until parents get back home from work;
- A psycho-socio compulsion of students to be constantly on cell phones, texting, playing computer games and movies, sending emails, Twitter, Facebook, online gambling and shopping; and
- Several other reasons are set forth in the introduction.

Republicans: A Primary Cause of Poor Performance

Isn't it amazing how the Republican Party has flip-flopped from its antislavery and Fourteenth Amendment equal-racial-rights roots. In 1869 cousin Anson P.K. Safford, a Lincoln Republican, was appointed by President Grant to be the first governor of the territory of Arizona (which included New Mexico). Seven out of ten citizens were Mexican.

Anti-Mexican Caucasians in Arizona don't seem to know or are morally oblivious to the fact that Mexicans in the 1860s were moral Roman Catholics. They welcomed and helped Euro-Caucasian immigrants and didn't demand green cards, work permits, or an electrified fence with a moat and alligators on the eastern border of the territory to keep Caucasians out.

Gov. Safford learned Spanish to understand what Mexicans needed. He created the first statewide public school system. Safford believed Mexicans should learn to speak and read English so they'd understand their rights under the U.S. Constitution and read news on issues before voting.

However, Republicans since Nixon have "bore false witness" that professors, experts, and other intelligent people were "Ivy Tower intellectuals who didn't live in the 'real' world." That's part of an antiscience, research and education agenda of the Republican Party.

A regressive agenda that ignores the facts that:

- U.S. students rank seventeenth in science, twenty-first in math, and twenty-fifth in reading comprehension in part because Republicans are unwilling to raise property, income, and sales taxes to pay for more educational equipment, facilities and better-qualified teachers; and
- U.S. needs educated/trained workers in a global, high-tech world;
- Republicans don't want educated and intelligent voters who recognize repetitive lies and Hitler-Nixon-style, Machiavellian Tactics cons;

- Republicans ignore the "general welfare" mandate in the Preamble and enabling clause (Article I, Section 8.[1] and [8]) of the U.S. Constitution "to promote the progress of science and useful arts." As such Republicans are antiscience and education when it comes to:
  1. Global warming, polluted land, air, water, and food because of bribes from "One Percent Devils" of fossil fuels;
  2. Darwin's "Evolution of the Species" and carbon dating because they expose myths in Genesis; and
  3. Medical science and research but Republicans are for military-weapons research because they'd rather kill than cure people:
     a. So those receiving benefits from social safety nets die young;
     b. So FICA, income, and sales taxes can be cut.

That's consistent with Republicans clapping and cheering during Republican presidential debates (in 2012) at the thought of:

People without health insurance dying in the ER from lack treatment;

Gov. Perry signing death warrants for 232 people, most of whom were Afro- or Latin-American, because the wealthiest state would rather kill than help them move out of a life of poverty and crime; and

Elimination of Medicare, Medicaid, and Affordable Care Health Insurance so those on Social Security retirement or welfare die young so FICA taxes can be cut for "One Percent Devils."

Are charter schools racial segregation reincarnated? Do they teach global warming and "Evolution of the Species" or promote immoral capitalism and insider trading? If so, should taxes fund charter schools?

Didn't the U.S. Council of Bishops and nuns on a bus say that my congressmen Paul Ryan's budget is immoral? Didn't Pope Francis say that Republican "trickle-down economics is a myth" because nothing trickles down to help the poor, working poor, and middle class from tax cuts for the rich? Isn't that because companies don't expand plants, build plants, or hire more employees unless demand for products exceeds supply?

Didn't Pope Francis also preach against growing income disparity between "One Percent Devils" and the other 99 percent? Didn't he preach for moral capitalism and redistribution of wealth from Devils to their victims?

CHAPTER II

Law and Morality to Prevent Anglo-Saxon New World Order Starts with Nuremberg Doctrine

During the Nuremberg War Crimes Trials, cousin Col. John Oscar Woods, aka "The Fighting Chaplain of the 80th Airborne" (who was awarded four Battle Stars, the Legion of Merit, and Bronze Star), counseled:

- Nazi generals, industrialists, administrators, and judges whose defenses were "I was following orders" or "I was following the law"; and the
- Chief Judge of War Crimes Tribunal couldn't find legal authority in international law to convict Nazis for crimes against humanity;
- Col. Woods contacted his uncle, my Grandpa Lebbeus, who said, "Legal authority can be found in a treatise on morality of law by the chief Nazi judge, Hans Yanning"; and
  1. Thereafter, the Nuremberg Doctrine held that: "Everyone owes a higher duty to morality than to the laws of a nation and orders of its leaders"; and
  2. Since that doctrine is international law, it's applicable to all nations, states, counties, and municipal governments.

How One Percent Devils and Their Victims, the Other 99 Percent, Define Morality

Morality, or more accurately, immorality of "One Percent Devils and Their Satanic Tools" is caveman natural law based on unfettered human nature

23

instincts, inclinations, and rights. They have replaced Torah, Old Testament, New Testament, and Koran with:

- Charles Darwin's "Survival of the Fittest"; and
- Ayn Rand saying "the strong and rich should take from weak and poor."

However, morality for the other 99 percent is based on:

- Natural law civilized by eternal law and positive law; and
- Morality varies depending upon whether one is:
  1. Female or male;
  2. Heterosexual, homosexual, bisexual, trisexual or transgender;
  3. Caucasian, Asian-, Latin-, Afro- or Native American or immigrant;
  4. Buddhist, Hindu, Sikh, Muslim, Jewish, or Judeo-Christian;
  5. Upper class, upper-middle class, middle class, working class/poor;
  6. Functioning at 100 percent or physically and/or mentally disabled;
  7. A baby, youngster, teenager, middle-aged, senior, or elder.

It's been said, "Morality is a relative term depending upon your moral perspective." How do we determine when laws, orders, words, acts, or omissions of politicians, teachers, preachers, and press are moral or immoral?

So How Can a Universal Morality
That's Acceptable to Everyone Be Deducted?
"Theory of Law" by St. Thomas Aquinas discusses three tests for determining whether laws, word, acts, and omissions are moral or immoral. Are they consistent with:

- God's plan for mankind;
- Natural law civilized by:
  1. Eternal law common to all religions such as:
     a. Commandments or laws of Moses, Buddha, Muhammad;
     b. Golden Rule; and

    c.   Soul-saving principals, laws, or rules; and

2. Positive law such as:

    a.   Declaration of Independence;

    b.   U.S. Constitution and Bill of Rights; and

    c.   Principles of legal equity such as:

       1) "One should not gain at someone else's expense";

       2) "One should not benefit from one's wrongs"; and

       3) "Contracts should produce zero-sum outcomes"; and

- The third test for determining morality of laws, words, acts, or Omissions: "Are they consistent with mankind's goal of happiness?"

Aquinas said, "The goal of mankind is happiness" and "God's plan for mankind is a utopia or heaven on earth, free of wars and crimes." That can be achieved via a universal covenant (by all peoples) to comply with natural law civilized by eternal law and positive law.

A utopia where:

- Everyone's basic needs for food, clothing, shelter, and medical care are met;
- Those who want more can achieve to their fullest potential in education, training, a trade, business, or profession; and
- Everyone has opportunities to relax and enjoy beauties of nature, art, music, theater, sports, sex, and other gifts from God.

When the world gets to that point, everyone would have reached:

- The pinnacle of mankind's "Hierarchy of Needs" ala Maslow;
- The goal of mankind (happiness) would have been achieved;
- There would be no racial, religious, cultural, or gender intolerance; and
- People would have what President Roosevelt called four basic freedoms: "Freedom from want, discrimination, of speech and religion."

Utopias have existed throughout history and some exist today:

- Tibetans in Shangri-La were considered the most spiritual and moral people on earth but equally moral and spiritual were and are:
- Cherokee, Potawatomi, Piute, Anastasia, and Hopi Indian nations;

25

and
- Quakers, Amish, and Mennonites.

Yang negativists will say "a worldwide utopia is an impossible dream." That's true in a world controlled by "One Percent Devils and Their Satanic Tools":

- Who ignore and violate eternal law and positive law;
- Who employ natural law rights, "strong should take from weak";
- Who bribe for negative laws to facilitate outsourcing of U.S. jobs:
    1. To an atheistic Communist Chinese enemy that's creating a Chinese New World Order of economic domination; and
    2. To Third World nation so "One Percent Devils" can immorally exploit labor and resources in ways that are illegal in the U.S; and
- "One Percent Devils" are free to do so because "their Satanic Tools" will vote for war to protect their industrial and financial interests.

That happens for two reasons:
- Twenty-five percent vote Republican because they are white-collar criminals who bribe for laws so they can become "One Percent Devils"; and
- Twenty-five percent vote Republican because they're white trash:
    1. Who are uneducated and believe repetitive lies are true; and
    2. Their self concepts or egos are low and need to be elevated via Hitler-Nixon-type, Machiavellian, Divide-and-Conquer, Wedge-Issue Bias, Prejudice and Intolerance that insults, belittles, puts down, and blames for their sorry lot in life:
        a. Working women who get jobs, promotions and bonuses that Caucasian men would have gotten;
        b. Afro-, Latin-, Asian-, and Native Americans, whether they have jobs or are benefiting from social safety nets due to repression and suppression by Caucasians or outsourcing of jobs; and
        c. Jews, Muslims, Hindu, Sikh, Buddhists and those of other faiths because Republicans don't believe in freedom of religion.

Most baffling are "One Percent Devils" (Donald the Duck Trump and Koch Brothers) who didn't earn but inherited vast wealth "and their Satanic Tools" (Mitt Romney who inherited wealth, Congressmen Boehner, Cantor, Ryan, and Senator Mitchell), who get rich from insider trading tips, Fox News and preachers, who are highly educated, some at the best universities. One would think their egos would be high enough that they wouldn't have a pathological need to denigrate, put down, or repress others.

An appeal must be made to the 25 percent who want to be "One Percent Devils" because most of their relatives and descendants won't be members of the "One Percent Devils" ruling class of an Anglo-Saxon New World Order. Most relatives and descendants would be among the 99 percent who'd be brainwashed, mindless, robotic slaves, spied on with two-way televisions by Big Brother, ala *1984*. A majority of people on earth have five choices:

- Agree to obey a proper balance between natural law, eternal law, and positive law to create a world without poverty, war, and crime; or
- Become mindless robotic *1984*-type peasant slaves of an atheistic:
  1. Anglo-Saxon New World Order;
  2. Russian New World Order; or
  3. Chinese New World Order; and become
- Victims of overpopulation, starvation, disease, crime, civil wars, or international wars (there are thirty-two ongoing wars now) and WWIII; or
- Victims could rebel, as in the French and Russian revolutions where:
  1. "One Percent Devils and Their Satanic Tools" were French and Russian royalty, noble families, and government officials; Except in the U.S., "One Percent Devils" (industrialists, financiers, retailers, and service providers) and their "Satanic Tools" (Republican politicians, preachers, and press) would have their heads chopped off or shot in the back of the head;
  2. However, history reveals those who take over control of nations are just as tyrannical plutocratic and autocratic as predecessors; or

- Nuclear holocaust Armageddon. Incredibly, many alleged Christians want Armageddon because they believe that like magic in three days:
    1. Skeletons would be raised from the dead and bodies reconstituted with a brain, nervous systems, muscles, organs and skin;
    2. Radiation poisoning of land, water, and air would disappear; and
    3. The earth would be replenished with vegetables, nuts, fruit, and meat.

Elements of Natural Law

According to "Theory of Law" by Aquinas, the first laws were God-given natural laws based on God-given human instincts and inclinations:

- Instincts for:
    1. Survival, self defense, defense of family and community;
    2. Hunting, fishing, and exploring new lands by men with Yin;
    3. Gathering by women with Yang:
        a. Vegetables, fruits, nuts, and berries; and
        b. Herbs to:
            1) Relieve pain, stress, sorrow, and fight infection; and
            2) Elevate mood, sexually stimulate, and create enlightenment;
    4. Sexual attraction (smells, sounds, and movements), romance, mating, and procreation;
    5. Nurturing and socializing children; and
    6. For children to care for parents when they become disabled;

- Inclinations to:
    1. Build a better life, have more, and do more through:
        a. Education or training in a profession, business, or trade; and
        b. Study, work hard, and employ trial and error;
    2. Explore new lands for food, minerals, timber, and gold;
    3. Gamble, sell sex, buy sex, and use God's herbal gifts:
    4. Consume beer, wine, and receive Four H's of marijuana: happiness, hilarity, horniness, and hunger; and

a. For stronger relief of pain/sorrow, coca leaves and poppy juice (opium); and

b. Break problem-solving mind blocks to achieve enlightenment.

What Happens When Laws Are Contrary to
God-Given Natural Law Human Instincts and Inclinations?

Natural law is based upon God, angel or alien DNA-engrained instincts and inclination (via cloning and/or aliens, angels and/or God's procreating with apes and then humans), combined with DNA-engrained human instincts and inclinations that evolved from apes into humans (according to the History Channel and "Evolution of the Species" by Darwin).

The three oldest professions are prostitution, gambling, and herbal healing. Natural law human instincts and inclinations cannot be controlled by laws. When laws make those professions illegal, victimless crimes they:

- Create psychiatric disorders;
- Turn otherwise law-abiding citizens into criminals;
- Create criminal subcultures for protection and to get what is needed;
- Create and fuel organized crime;
- Cause bribes and corruption of police, prosecutors, and judges; and
- Enable Judeo-Christian police, prosecutors, and judges to suppress and imprison racial, religious, and cultural minorities to the extent that even though the U.S. has 5 percent of the world's population, 25 percent of the world's prisoners are in the U.S., and most of them are in for possession or sale of drugs (*Time*, Sept. 8-15, 2014);
- That forces early parole of murderers, robbers, burglars, rapists; and
- Those in prison for possessing or selling drugs, prostitution, and gambling learn new criminal trades in prison.

Don't victimless crime laws create more harm than good? Wouldn't it be more healthy and moral to legalize those professions again, regulate them, and tax their income? Wouldn't law enforcement allocations to vice squads be better spent by retraining vice-squad detectives to fight white-collar crime that steals many times more than all other crimes of theft? Wouldn't prisons serve society better and reduce violent-crime recidivism by releasing drug dealers, users, prostitutes, and gamblers and keeping violent criminals in prison for their entire sentence?

St. Thomas Aquinas said, "The goal of mankind is happiness." However, preachers, priests, rabbi, and clerics:

- Have had laws passed to ban gambling, prostitution and social drugs because they don't want followers to be happy; and Scare followers into complying with commandments by claiming that natural disasters (earthquakes, volcanoes, lightning, pestilence, plagues, droughts, and floods) are God's means to punish sinners;
- Because they want people to be frightened and miserable so they:
  1. Attend religious services;
  2. Ask God to forgive sins for happiness and relief from pain; and
  3. Put 10 percent of what you earned or stole in offering baskets.

Why'd St. Augustine Destroy Sex as a
Spiritual Path to Godliness, Heaven, Paradise, Shangri-La, Valhalla

Pagan Celts believed a woman was La Sacre Femme (The Sacred Feminine) and sex was a spiritual experience that brought a couple closer to God, godliness and heaven. Is that why lovers say "Oh God! Oh God!"?

However, on or about A.D. 400, St. Augustine spent six months having every kind of sex. Then he wrote the following "Rules against Sex":

"You can't be spiritual and sexual. Therefore nuns and priests can no longer get married. Sex is only for procreation. Masturbation, contraception, premarital sex, and sex for fun are sins that lead to a sinful life and hell."

One wonders whether Republicans who espouse those rules (former congressional representatives Rick Santorum, Michelle Bachmann, and Sen. Pat Robertson) have normal human sexual instincts? Robertson also said, "If women can't control their libido, Affordable Care Health Insurance shouldn't pay for their birth control."

Didn't they and their spouses ever:

- Awaken with an erection or swollen clitoris and nipples?
- Have wet pajamas from a wet dream?

- Think about sex at least seven times a day, as surveys reveal is the average number of sexual fantasies people have per day?
- Get so horny they turned to Master Bates or took a cold shower?
- Have a psychiatric sexual disorder that blocks sexual instincts?

Fact is, libido is controlled by DNA, hormones, and food eaten. As indicated, St. Augustine's unnatural law "Rules against Sex" have caused:

- Psychiatric/physical disorders. (See DSM-IV and Merck Manual);
- *Cosmo* and *Glamour* surveys in the 1980s, which revealed:
    1. Sixty percent of women never or rarely have orgasms. *Time* said in the Sept. 8-15, 2014, issue that only 29 percent of women reach orgasm during sex compared with 75 percent of men;
    2. Sixty percent of women when seeking a mate place a higher priority on a man's assets, income, career, and/or status than on love, friendship, chemistry, mutual interests, and a good sex life; and
    3. *Time* (Supra) said that married couples only have sex sixty-six days out of 365 days a year — or about once a week. Yet another survey recently revealed that the happiest people on earth are in Scandinavia because they have sex much more often.
- Divorce rate of 50 percent-plus with many having two or more marriages;
- Forcible rape of 25 percent of women;
- Rape by false pretense of 50 percent of women; and
- Pedophilia, even by Roman Catholic priests.

There's nothing in eternal law (Commandments in Old Testament/ Torah and Christ's teachings in New Testament) that bans sex for fun, premarital sex, prostitution, contraceptives, masturbation, gambling, marijuana, hashish, opium, or coca. Thus laws banning those activities not only are unnatural laws but negative laws that cause more harm than they could possibly prevent.

Victimless crimes aren't just used by racial-, religious-, and gender-biased law enforcement to suppress women, Afro-, and Latin-Americans. During the Vietnam War, it was used to suppress antiwar protestors.

However, "One Percent Devils and Their Satanic Tools" (Republican politicians, preachers, press, and their spouses) can:

- Rig political system to allow "One Percent Devils" of banks and Wall Street to gamble and steal billions via scams, cons and schemes:
    1. Paper money and junk bonds (when Republican Reagan was president);
    2. Predatory lending, mortgage bundling, pyramid schemes, and other derivatives caused by:
        a. Democratic President Clinton:
            1) Bringing a wolf into the chicken pen by appointing former Goldman Sachs Vice Chairman Robert Rubin as secretary of treasury; and
            2) Joined hands with wicked Republican men to eliminate federal law and regulation protection created by Democratic President Roosevelt to protect us and U.S. from unregulated banker and Wall Street broker greed; and
        b. Republican President G.W. Bush appointed Goldman Sachs Chair Henry Paulson as secretary of treasury to further deregulate;
    3. And that group of conspirators caused history to repeat itself:
        a. In 1920s lack of regulation of banks and Wall Street caused:
            1) Economic "Roaring Twenties" from Wall Street cons and scams;
            2) Massive October 29, 1929, stock-market crash;
            3) Twenty-five million to lose jobs and homes; and
            4) Great Economic Depression of the 1930s;
        b. In the 1990s and 2000s, Presidents Clinton and G.W. Bush and Goldman Sacks men who became secretaries of treasury caused:
            1) Economic Roaring 1990s and 2000s from scams and cons;
            2) Massive stock market and banking crash of 2008;
            3) Twenty million to lose jobs, homes, pensions, health insurance;
            4) And the Second Great Depression; and

- "One Percent Devils and Their Satanic Tools" (Republican politicians, Preachers, and press) and their spouses also don't get busted for:
  1. Paying high-class hookers and for sex with sexual slaves and underaged girls or boys;
  2. Bribing a doctor to get prescriptions for uppers, downers, narcotics, and medicinal marijuana;
  3. Gambling other people's money on stock swindles and scams; and
  4. Dozens of types of white-collar crime.

Fact is, governments cannot ban or prohibit God-given natural law human instincts and inclinations. Thus laws that prohibit prostitution, gambling, and social drugs are antinatural laws and negative laws.

Wouldn't it be better to legalize social drugs, prostitution, and gambling, regulate those activities, and make them taxable events to balance government budgets, reduce tax rates, and fill prisons with violent criminals?

Why not let American farmers grow and sell marijuana. Farmers work from 6 A.M. to 10 P.M., but most years family farms barely break even. Farm kids who don't want to farm can sell marijuana in stores that are vacant.

As to narcotics, why not set up stores to sell heroin and cocaine to people who have it in blood or urine? Those who are addicted won't have to steal or sell their bodies to get hundreds of dollars necessary to buy it.

Natural Law Is the Basis for Declaration of Independence
Note the underlined portions of the first paragraphs of the Declaration of Independence, which are God-given natural law entitlements of mankind, ala "Age of Enlightenment" by Thomas Paine and "Theory of Law" by St. Thomas Aquinas:

"When in the Course of Human Events, it becomes necessary for one People to dissolve the Political Bands which have connected them with another, and to assume among the Powers of the Earth, the separate and equal Station to which the Laws of Nature and of Nature's God entitle them, a decent Respect to the Opinions of Mankind requires that they should declare the causes which impel them to the Separation.

"We hold these Truths to be self-evident, that all Men are created equal, that they <u>are endowed by their Creator with certain unalienable Rights, that among these are Life, Liberty, and the Pursuit of Happiness,</u> that to secure these Rights, <u>Governments are instituted among Men, deriving their just Powers from the Consent of the Governed,</u> that whenever any Form of Government becomes destructive of these Ends, <u>it is the Right of the People</u> to alter or to abolish it, and <u>to institute new Government, laying its Foundation on such Principles, and organizing its Powers in such Form,</u> as to them shall seem <u>most likely to affect Safety and Happiness."</u>

Eternal Law

Hindu, Sikh, Buddhist, and Muslim eternal law is essentially the same as Commandments, Golden Rule, and soul-saving Christian principles (set forth in the introduction). However, after each religion was founded, subsequent misguided religious leaders didn't honor eternal law when they "bore false witness" or "uttered false reports" that God wanted them to kill, plunder, rape, and enslave godless, savage, and heathen people in cities and nations who worshiped one God and have the same eternal law.

When kings wanted to conquer and plunder cities and nations of other religions, religious leaders aided and abetted crimes against humanity by "bearing false witness" and "uttering false reports" that God wanted heathen, godless savages in those cities and nations killed. Why?

- So kings wouldn't have religious leaders assassinated or replaced;
- So popes, cardinals, bishops, priests, clerics, or monks could become powerful and wealthy from:
  1. A percentage of the loot and land stolen by the king; and
  2. Ten-percent tithes in offering baskets for:
     a. Safe return of loved ones from war; and/or
     b. Speedy assent of souls to heaven of those who fell in battle.

Positive Law

King's law didn't cover injury due to negligence or breach of marital or business contracts. So the Church of England, other Protestant churches, and the Roman Catholic Church established courts of equity. They gave the United States of America common-law principles of legal equity:

- "One should not benefit from one's wrongs";

- "One should not gain at someone else's expense"; and thus
- "Transactions should produce zero-sum outcomes."

The U.S. Constitution is a positive law that gave Americans the following that "One Percent Devils and Their Satanic Tools" violate every day :

- One vote per person, majority rule democracy "of the people, by the people and for the people";
- All six goals in the Preamble of the Constitution;
- Enabling Clause and a dozen other clauses of the Constitution;
- Nine of the ten rights and freedoms in the Bill of Rights;
- Amendments and laws that gave equal rights for all races; and
- Rights of women to vote, equal pay, contraceptives, and abortion.

The Bill of Rights was based upon real or perceived abuses of American colonists by the British crown's troops. Those rights are supposed to prevent a majority party in U.S. governments from abusing rights of individuals and minority groups. The Fourteenth Amendment is supposed to prevent state, county, and municipal governments from abusing rights of individuals and minorities.

Codes of ethics for doctors and attorneys are positive laws. Business laws and regulations are positive laws enacted because "One Percent Devils" violated Commandments, Golden Rule, soul-saving principles of Christ, principles of civilized humanity and legal equity.

Those "One Percent Devils and Their Satanic Tools" couldn't be trusted to do what was legal, moral, or in the best interests of employees, consumers, pregnant workers, families, and children. So the U.S. has the following regulatory agencies and laws to protect Americans:

- Federal: Security Exchange Commission and Banking Commission (to protect investors from fraud by banks and stock brokers);
- Federal Food and Drug Administration and USDA (safe food and drugs);
- Consumer Product Safety Commission (safe toys, cars, appliances);
- Environmental Protection Agency (clean air, water, and land);
- Federal Aviation Administration (safe flying); and

- To end exploitation of workers by One-Percent Devil Kings of Industry:
  1. Child labor laws and pregnant worker laws;
  2. Minimum wage and maximum hour laws;
  3. OSHA (Occupational Safety and Health Administration);
  4. Worker's compensation and Social Security disability;
  5. Collective bargaining and National Labor Relations Board;
  6. Unemployment compensation, etc.

The progressive income tax is a positive law aimed at taxing more those who financially benefit most from the U.S. economic system. "Satanic Tools" are bribed by "One Percent Devils" to enact regressive tax negative laws:

- Sales tax and property tax laws are negative law regressive taxation where 99 percent pay a much larger portion of their income paying such taxes than "One Percent Devils and Their Satanic Tools;"
- Tax cut, deduction, and subsidy laws for "One Percent Devils" are regressive negative law and reverse Robin Hood-ism of taking taxes from working poor and middle class and taking away social safety nets for the poor to provide such cuts, deductions, and subsidies;
- Laws allowing "One Percent Devils" to evade taxes by hiding income in offshore accounts is negative taxation; and Negative taxation includes deductions and subsidies so "One Percent Devils" can evade or violate Commandments, Golden Rule, soul-saving principles of Christ, and the above cited positive law regulations by outsourcing production of fifty thousand U.S. companies, tens of millions of jobs, and technology to:
  1. An atheistic communist Chinese enemy that intends to:
     a. Gain world economic dominance every way possible; and
     b. Create a Chinese New World Order that violates eternal law and has none of the above positive law protections; and
  2. Third World nations to immorally exploit laborers who have none of the above positive law protections.

Haven't "One Percent Devils and Their Satanic Tools" turned every taxpayer into an accomplice to outsourcing crimes against humanity when their taxes are given to "One Percent Devils" via tax cuts, deductions, and subsidies for outsourcing exploitation of foreign workers? When we buy products made in China and Third World nations, aren't we accomplices who aid and abet outsourcing crimes against humanity?

When comparing natural, eternal, and positive law with Republican politics, questions, ironies, and oxymoron's come to mind. How can Republican politicians, preachers, and press claim to be patriotic Judeo-Christians who represent "The Silent Moral Majority" when their words, acts, and omissions violate so many Commandments, Golden Rule, soul-saving rules, Constitutional provisions, rights in the Bill of Rights, principles of legal equity, and The American Way of Fair Play?

Why aren't most Americans knowledgeable and alert about threats and dangers "One Percent Devils and Their Satanic Tools" present to: moral capitalism and democracy; middle class, working poor, and poor; elderly and disabled; racial, cultural, and religious minority groups and women?

Why don't newspapers, radio, and TV news begin by discussing each political issue and indicate who's telling the truth and who's lying? Why don't preachers, priests, rabbi, and clerics do the same during sermons? Why don't teachers and professors do the same?

If Republican trickle-down economics theory is a myth, regressive taxation is immoral, and Republican President G.W. Bush's failure to regulate banks and Wall Street caused the second greatest stock-market crash and depression, why did voters in 2014 give Republicans a majority in Congress and Senate? If the 47 percent on social safety nets are victims of "One Percent Devils" why'd 47 percent vote for Dracula-vulture capitalist and flip-flop, lying Republican Mitt Romney, who outsourced to China and Third World nations?

CHAPTER III

Etiology of "One Percent Devils and Their Satanic Tools"
and Significant Warnings about:
• An Anglo-Saxon New World Order;
• U.S. Military-Industrial Complex; and
• Television Diverting People from News.

Many Founding Fathers and presidents were Thomas Paine "Age of Enlightenment" Freemasons. My grandfather, Lebbeus Bigelow Woods, was a Lutheran minister and attorney-at-law with a PhD in legal philosophy and a 32nd Degree Mason.

In the 1930s, a 33rd Degree Freemason Grand Master informed Gramps about plans by "One Percent Devils" to:

- Replace democracy and moral capitalism with an Anglo-Saxon New World Order, as morally bankrupt and tyrannical as Hitler's Nazi New World Order and Russia's Communist New World Order;
- But before that, English, French, and U.S. industrialists and financiers had to get Nazis and Communists to destroy each other. So:
  1. Financiers like J.P. Morgan financed Hitler's rise to power;
  2. Racist Henry Ford had his engineers teach German VW engineers how to design rapid-moving production assembly lines;
  3. IBM scientists helped German engineers develop unbreakable military codes, and during WWII IBM developed a massive computer to break those codes;

4. AT&T cooperated with the FBI's illegal wiretapping of presidents, senators, congressmen and those running for office;

5. U.S. Post Office allowed illegal mail openings by FBI;

6. U.S. Military-Industrial Complex had plans to:

   a. Create an interstate highway system for rapid movement of U.S. troops to suppress revolution in U.S. by the other 99 percent;

   b. Strategically place war industry R&D, production plants, military bases and National Guard to suppress revolution; and

7. In the late 1960s, "Satanic Tool" Republicans created the Law Enforcement Assistance Agency to pour billions of dollars into federal, state, county, and municipal law enforcement agencies:

   a. For hiring tens of thousands of law enforcement officers, training and heavily arming them with M-15 military assault rifles, sniper rifles, Apache gunships, tanks, armored personnel carriers;

   b. To create SWAT teams in large, medium, and small cities; and

   c. Under the guise of a Republican "Law and Order" Platform;

   d. But in reality, they were ordered to suppress civil rights, antiwar, and feminists movements, peaceful protest marches, and sit-down strikers who were exercising First Amendment rights of freedom of speech and to peacefully assemble to protest government acts and omissions;

   e. "Satanic Tool" Republican President Nixon also ordered:

      1) Military and civilian intelligence agencies to illegally wiretap and open mail of fifty thousand civil rights, antiwar, and feminist activists and 150,000 of their friends and family; and

      2) Other federal departments to deny or frustrate receipt of federal benefits for those fifty thousand, such as student loans, farm subsidies, welfare, Medicaid, Medicare, Social Security disability and retirement and even veterans benefits to Vietnam soldiers who became antiwar advocates; and

f. Thanks to the Patriot Act, the U.S. government:
    1) Can legally violate those rights from the Bill of Rights; and
    2) Now there's seven more domestic spy agencies to assist; and
    3) For fifty years, FBI Director J. Edgar Hoover:
        a) Illegally wiretapped, eavesdropped on, and opened mail of labor unionists, communists, neo-Nazis, Klu Klux Klan members, as well as movie, music, sports, and news stars who Hoover felt were immoral influences on children;
        b) He even listened to audio tapes of them and politicians making love or having various kinds of sex;
        c) When he wasn't engaging in homosexual pedophilia;

g. So what's to stop a president from using Patriot Act powers to secretly declare that Tea Party evangelists are Antichrist communists who want to overthrow the U.S. government by eliminating every federal government agency and department except the Pentagon and Law Enforcement Assistance Agency?

h. If that happed, Tea Party evangelists would also be tracked via GPS, satellite, and audiovisually seen in the dark having sex with a condom. Kind of like the Church of England's sex patrol snoops that forced Puritans to sail the Atlantic Ocean to America;

i. Quite frankly my greatest fear from 2000 to 2008 was that Republicans would use their control of the White House, Senate, Congress, and Supreme Court to execute an Anglo-Saxon, New World Order coup d'état; and

j. That's why the U.S. Supreme Court must be reconstituted with three Democrats, three independents and three Republicans; and

k. Voters should make sure that no party should control the White House and both houses of Congress;

l. Because "power corrupts and absolute power absolutely Corrupts"; and

    m. Perhaps it's time for amendments:

        1) Putting term limits for congressmen and senators; and

        2) Banning "One Percent Devils" from owning any form of news media;

        3) Banning repetitive lies and Machiavellian tactics in politics;

        4) Enforcing the doctrine of separation of church and state by banning churches from turning St. Augustine's "Rules or Mores against Sex" into laws; and

        5) Making all victimless crime laws unconstitutional;

8. President Nixon also ended the military draft and created a volunteer military for two reasons:

    a. To prevent protests against future wars; and

    b. eliminate college-educated officers who would:

        1) Question orders; or

        2) Refuse to comply with orders they considered:

            a) Too risky, dangerous, or futile; or

            b) Immoral, such as:

                1)) Vice President Cheney's Spanish Inquisition or Salem Witch Hunt torture chambers;

                2)) Carpet bombing civilian areas by President G.W. Bush; or

                3)) Drone attacks that kill civilians due to inaccurate intelligence;

9. Two of the goals of protracted Iraq II and Afghanistan wars were:

    a. To train U.S. soldiers to fight house-to-house to suppress future revolutions or rebellions in the U.S. against "One Percent Devils and their Satanic Tools;" and

    b. To train special forces and drone operators in the United States of America what they are doing in the Mideast; and

10. Because control of knowledge is power, "One Percent Devils's" plan included creation of a propaganda mechanism called:

    a. The Office of War Information (OWI); and a

    b. Sister agency of spies, aka Office of Strategic Services (OSS), (which became the Central Intelligence Agency after WWII); but

c. During WWII, the OSS and FBI joined hands with the U.S. mafia who:

    1) Controlled dock worker unions to get them to prevent sabotage of U.S. shipping; and

    2) Got Sicilian mafia to collect intelligence and do sabotage during the Allied invasion of Sicily; and

d. After WWII:

    1) The CIA got mafia to commit assassinations; and

    2) J. Edger Hoover didn't order FBI to go after mafia until President John F. Kennedy ordered Hoover to destroy mafia; and

    3) That's one reason JFK and RFK were assassinated;

    4) Other reasons are that:

        a) Their father got rich smuggling booze to mafia during Prohibition;

        b) Marijuana, heroin, and cocaine were criminalized so police could suppress Afro-, Latin- and Asian-Americans; and

        c) Mafia was allowed to set up drug networks to feed those minority groups to get them deported or imprisoned;

        d) President Kennedy had:

            1)) Refused to support Bay of Pigs Invasion of Communist Cuba so mafia didn't get casinos back;

            2)) Busted the CIA Air America, Thailand, and U.S. mafia drug connection; and

            3)) Ordered withdrawal of all U.S. Troops from Vietnam; and

11. Because knowledge is power, "One Percent Devils" own so many television and radio stations/networks and major newspapers:

a. To facilitate use of repetitive lies and Hitler-McCarthy-Nixon-Machiavellian, Wedge-Issue Tactics so Americans vote against their own family, economic and social interests, freedoms and rights; and

b. Traitorous "Satanic Tools" on U.S. Supreme Court say:
1) Bribes to Super PACs, is freedom of speech?; and
2) Orwellian *1984*-style repetitive lies and Machiavellian Tactics are constitutional even when they are gradually eroding democracy, middle class, and moral capitalism;

12. In 1951 Republicans passed the Twenty-second Amendment to limit presidents to two, four-year terms in office because Democratic President Franklin Delano Roosevelt won four terms; but
a. Before impeachment hearings, Republicans were moving to repeal the Twenty-second Amendment so Nixon could remain president for the rest of his life as a dictator; and then
b. Republicans wanted an amendment so Arnold Schwarzenegger (born and raised in a Communist Austria?) could be president; he couldn't keep his pants on
c. Republicans elected movie star Ronald Reagan, whose jokes whittled down Democrats but he:
1) Was a C-student at a small Illinois college;
2) Had senile dementia; and
1) Didn't make decisions without consulting a fortune teller;

13. In 2000 Republicans elected G.W. Bush because he had qualities Republicans wanted in a president in 2012;

14. During the 2012 presidential campaign, Carl Rove or Orville Norquist proclaimed, "All a President Romney would have to be able to do is sign Republican legislation";

15. Replacing the Bill of Rights, democracy, and moral capitalism with a tyrannical Anglo-Saxon New World Order dictatorship;

16. U.S. doesn't need ignorant presidents or ignorant Tea Party senators, congressmen or Supreme Court justices who are pawns or "Satanic Tools" of "One Percent Devils;"

17. A complex, multiracial, religious, ethnic, and cultural United States requires the most intelligent and moral people to be in the White House, Senate, Congress, and Supreme Court; and

18. Quite frankly right now the only politicians who fit those qual-

ifications to be president are Joe Biden, Hillary Clinton, Elizabeth Warren, and Bernie Sanders; and also

19. Quite frankly every Republican candidate for president is:
    a. A repetitive liar and an immoral Hitler-McCarthy-Nixon, Machiavellian, Divide-and-Conquer, Wedge-Issue Purveyor;
    b. Unintelligent and/or uniformed;
    c. Intellectually and morally dishonest; and/or
    d. Doesn't believe in democracy or moral capitalism;

20. A good example is the Pennsylvania Republican chairman, who proudly proclaimed that unconstitutional gerrymandering and voter suppression laws would enable Republican Mitt Romney to win the White House; and

21. Traitorous Roberts' Supreme Court made it easier to disenfranchise Afro-, Latin-, and Asian-Americans, elderly, and college students who tend to vote Democrat; and

22. That begs a question: Which lying, immoral, oxymoron for morons dumbass will Republicans try to put in White House in 2016? That would be funny if it wasn't so sad;

23. Because after an Anglo-Saxon New World Order coup d'état by "One Percent Devils and Their Satanic Tools," mafia drugs will medicate the other 99 percent of Americans; and then the

24. Anglo-Saxon New World Order will take over drug distribution via repetitive lies and Machiavellian, Divide-and-Conquer Tactics to stimulate mafias and neo-Nazis to destroy each other; and

25. History repeats itself after "One-Percent Devil" capitalists tried to get German Nazis and Russian Communists to destroy each other.

After Pearl Harbor, Wild Bill Donavan, the director of OSS (and first director of the CIA), recruited educated agents fluent in European languages, such as Joseph Kennedy Jr. His OSS plane was shot down over France.

My father, Wendell Woods, signed letters Wendell Oliver Holmes Woods after he wrote something prophetic. He wasn't fluent but had workable knowledge of French and German and was mentored in positive and negative reinforcement tactics by their author, Professor Pavlov.

Dad's paper "Selective Incorporation Tendencies" revealed how good facts can be turned into bad facts or bad facts turned into harmless or good facts. For example, progressive, liberal Democrat is a good person but add the words socialist or communist, and a progressive, liberal Democrat is a traitor or aider and abettor of communism.

I knew Dad as a hardcore Republican who voted a straight ticket.

However, his paper explained how Republicans had defeated many of President Franklin Delano Roosevelt's New Deal legislation bills using:

- Repetitive lies so voters believed lies were true and truth was a lie; and
- Machiavellian, Divide-and-Conquer, Wedge-Issue Tactics.

That paper and political connections got Dad on a train to the Office of War Information (OWI) in Washington, D.C. Connections included cousin Charles Plumley, a Republican congressman from Vermont, and Gramps had known President Teddy Roosevelt and his cousin FDR for years.

In a letter to his parents about the train ride to D.C., Dad commented about insults to Negros and Northern Yankees by Southern soldiers. He said, "How ironic. Southern racists are going to fight racist Germans?"

Dad stayed with cousins Alida and David Smith (sister and brother), who were also descendants of Sophia Smith, founder of Smith College, the elite school for daughters of the rich and famous. They practiced law before the U.S. Supreme Court.

When not working on cases, they accumulated several post-graduate degrees. When Dad asked how they would turn good facts into bad facts and vice versa in pro-Allied and anti-Axis propaganda, Alida and David did it by employing multidisciplinary systemic analysis. Similar to the way the Warren Court did during Brown v. The Board of Education.

OWI/OSS agents were supposed to take priority flights to England, but the same storm that delayed D-Day by a month grounded their planes. So they traveled by train to New York City and left for England on a supply ship. However, the convoy was too slow. So the captain broke away and miraculously got through wolf packs of German submarines.

Dad, a lieutenant/agent of the Office of War Information, was stationed in the basement coding and decoding room of the U.S. Embassy in London

— ground zero for thousands of German V-I cruise missiles with one thousand pounds of TNT and V-II rockets with two thousand pounds of TNT.

When off duty at night, OWI agents went to Hyde Park to listen to orators on soapboxes and watch hundreds of floodlights and antiaircraft artillery shooting down V-Is. During the day, they watched British jets chase and shoot down V-I cruise missiles, aka Pilotless Buzz Bombers.

OWI had several functions:

- Creation and broadcast of pro-Allied and anti-Axis propaganda;
- Decoding intelligence from European underground resistance units;
- Coding orders for sabotage of bridges, trains, and telephone lines; and
- When cousin Col. Lebbeus Bigelow Woods was planning for the D-Day invasion of France, Dad took observation flights over France.

During one flight, a waist gunner was shot up. Dad grabbed his 50-caliber machine gun. It was like shooting skeet. Tracers from the gun led to the engine of an ME-109 and "pop." However, Dad was glad when the pilot's parachute opened because he could have been a Waltz/Woods cousin. The B-17s in which Dad flew observation missions were:

- Piloted by lifelong friends Roger and Donald Nash of Sharon, WI; and
- Manufactured by Boeing in Seattle because great-uncle Rufus Woods convinced President Franklin Delano Roosevelt to build two hydroelectric dams on the Columbia River and cheap electricity brought Boeing to Seattle:
  1. Behind the Grand Coulee Dam is Franklin D. Roosevelt Lake; and
  2. Behind Chief Joseph Dam is Rufus Woods Lake.

Col. Lebbeus Bigelow Woods of the 9th Air Force Division was awarded the Legion of Merit, Luxembourg Croix de Guerre, and Belgian Fourragere. In 1946 he was director of supply and maintenance at the Bikini Island atomic bomb tests. Radiation caused leukemia. He died in 1953. Woods Reservoir at the Arnold Engineering Development Center in Tullahoma, Tennessee, is named after Col. LB Woods.

How Dad Met Key Players in This Book

After Dad handed Supreme Allied Commander General Eisenhower intelligence from European underground, Chief of Staff General Smith entered with a copy of the *London Times*. General Patton had said to the press, "The English and Americans will rebuild and rule the world after the war."

Dad said, "An Anglo-Saxon New World Order" and explained what his father said. Gen. Eisenhower ordered Gen. Patton to HQ and said, "I can't have one of my generals spouting racism Hitler would applaud. America didn't send a million of its finest men to create an Anglo-Saxon New World Order but to prevent a Nazi New World Order."

Later I will relate President Eisenhower's warning about the dangers of misplaced power in "One Percent Devils" of U.S. Military-Industrial Complex and dangers it presents to democracy, freedoms, livelihoods, and peaceful goals. Dad's liaison activities for OWI led him to others who would work together on the same counter-goals and tactics:

- Dad's best friend in London was Ben Gunn, who looked and walked bent over like Gandhi after a forty-day fast:
  1. He was a genius who helped break German military codes; but
  2. When I knew Ben, he was an anthropologist staying on our farm while he visited Beloit College and University of Wisconsin anthropology museums:
     a. To compare Mideast and American Indian artifacts; and
     b. Seven-to-nine-foot-tall Nephilim skeletons from Mideast and Wisconsin;
     c. In 1911 fourteen Nephilim skeletal remains with disproportionately large skulls were excavated from a water/airtight cobblestone grave on what is now the Lake Lawn Lodge Golf Course on Delavan Lake:
        1) Oneida Indian Nation migrated from Siberia to Delavan Lake and Lake Geneva eight thousand years ago when there were woolly mammoths (elephants), bison, lions, and wolves;
        2) Potawatomi Indian Nation lived there and on other lakes and rivers of the Midwest from 1641 to 1833.

Their ancestors:

a) Were Indo-European Aryans who migrated from India to Europe thirteen thousand years ago:

b) Some, like my Baron Waltz ancestors, settled in Germany and Switzerland and became known as Celts;

c) Others migrated from there and across the Atlantic glacier to the Americas and became Potawatomi who were known as:

    1)) "The Original People," ala descendants of Adam and Eve. Note: A Discovery Channel DNA study found that everyone of every race has a common DNA that could only come from an Adam and Eve ; and

    2)) "Keepers of the Sacred Flame."

d) The Bible, scriptures from other religions, and Legends of Potawatomi, Cherokee, Piute, Anastasia, and Hopi Indian Nations indicate:

    1)) Nephilim were seven-to-nine-foot giants with disproportionately large heads and curly red hair and beards. They were procreated by gods or their angel messengers and human women, which in the Americas were Indian squaws; and

    2)) Gods or messenger angels gave humans:

        a) Natural law civilized by eternal law and positive law;

        b) Science and math so humans could solve their own problems and not waste time praying for help; and Discovery and History Channel indicate:

            • Procreation with aliens, thought to be gods, supplied the missing DNA link between apes and humans; and

• Gave humans that 75 percent of their brains that few know how to employ:

1. Extrasensory perception to communicate with animals and birds that "Hiawatha" (in Longfellow's poem below) called brothers;
2. Telepathic communication between human brains;
3. Mind reading of human thought; and that's
4. Why humans believed gods were all-knowing beings;

- The History Channel indicates divine intervention inspired Sir Isaac Newton, Da Vinci, Jules Verne and Albert Einstein to evolve mankind's knowledge base to a point where humans were moral and competent enough to learn how to use the other 75 percent of their brains;
- I deduct or derive several conclusions:
  1. Gods and their angel messengers haven't wasted more time establishing religions since Muhammad;
  2. Because misguided religious leaders of each religion caused followers to violate eternal law against people of other religions;
  3. Because of what Grandpa Lebbeus felt as:
     a. Divine interventions that twice saved his life; and
     b. Mystical experiences upon death of his:
        1) Mother, Mary Morrison Woods, who died of the same disease for which she was caring for neighbors until exhaustion weakened her immune system; and
        2) Wife Lydia Little Smith Woods;
        3) Both never drank alcohol, smoked, cussed, or had a bad word to say about anyone but always helped those in need.

Because I had used up my nine cat lives by age twenty-one, I wondered, "Is God saving me for something important? Did God turn on my multidisciplinary systemic analysis brain and selective incorporation memory that remembers things that will enable me to achieve goals. Have ideas, concepts, and theories been telepathically communicated to me via nighttime dreams, daydreams, and nightmares?

- Ben Gunn introduced Dad to Ian Fleming of British military intelligence, aka MI-5. After WWII he wrote James Bond 007 books about MI-5's tactics and technologies;

- Ian introduced Dad to Arthur Blair, who, under the pen name George Orwell, warned English and Americans about "One Percent Devils's" plans for an Anglo-Saxon New World Order, achievable via the Ministry of Truth issuing:
  1. Repetitive lies until voters believe lies were true and truth is a lie;
  2. Hitler-McCarthy-Nixon-type, Machiavellian, Divide-and-Conquer, Wedge-Issue Tactics;
  3. So English and Americans vote for "Satanic Tools" and against their family, economic and social interests, freedoms and rights.

In 1948 Arthur Blair wrote *1984* and later wrote *Animal Farm* under the pen name George Orwell to prevent being charged as a communist traitor for revealing top-secret plans for an Anglo-Saxon New World Order. He wrote about what could happen in the future, but OWI and MI-5 had *1984*, Ministry of Truth brainwashing capabilities in 1948.

Dad knew Edward R. Murrow, the most trusted man in America. An icon of journalism for CBS Radio, London, and CBS News's *See it Now*. They met when Murrow broadcast from the roof of the U.S. embassy.

Ten years later they met with playwright Arthur Miller at that NYC restaurant where walls are filled with cartoon caricatures of the rich and famous. Miller wanted to write a play to expose Wisconsin Senator Joseph McCarthy's communist hunting terrorism tactics.

Miller couldn't risk McCarthy branding or labeling him as a communist. He'd be blackballed from Hollywood and Broadway. Dad said, "In the 1680s, Rev. Cotton Mather wrote that my grandfather Philip Smith "died from a hideous witchcraft." Don't McCarthy's tactics mirror or parrot the Salem Witch Hunt terrorism tactics?"

Miller wrote *The Crucible* and let audiences draw the correlation.

Edward R. Murrow felt something was missing from McCarthy's quote from Shakespeare's play *Julius Caesar* where Brutus said, "The fault, my dear Caesar, is in our stars" (aka astrology). McCarthy then stimulated selective incorporation tendencies of people and added, "The fault lies with our communist stars of news like Edward R. Murrow."

In other words, McCarthy didn't address Murrow's criticisms of McCarthy's unconstitutional tactics. He tried to "kill the messenger," kind of like when Shakespeare said, "kill all the lawyers."

Murrow knew Dad had studied Shakespeare's plays and enjoyed watching them when English Shakespearean players performed at the University of Wisconsin and in London during the war. Dad said, "If McCarthy had read on, he would have read Caesar saying, 'The fault, my dear Brutus, is not in our stars but ourselves.'"

During his next *See it Now* show, Murrow started with the quotes from *Julius Caesar* and said, "The junior senator from Wisconsin didn't cause communist Hysteria, but he has exploited it and done so quite well. No one familiar with the history of this country can deny that congressional hearings are useful. It is necessary to investigate before legislating. But the line between investigation and persecuting is a very thin one, and the junior senator from Wisconsin has stepped over it repeatedly.

"We must not confuse dissent with disloyalty. We must remember always that accusation is not proof and that conviction depends upon evidence and due process of law.

"We will not walk in fear, one of another. We will not be driven by fear into an age of unreason if we dig deep in our history and doctrine and remember we are not descended from fearful men. Not from men who feared to write, to associate, to speak, and to defend the causes that were for the moment unpopular.

"This is no time for men who oppose McCarthy's methods to keep silent. Or for those who approve.

"We can deny our heritage and history, but we cannot escape responsibility for the results. We proclaim ourselves as defenders of freedom wherever it exists in this world. But we cannot defend freedom abroad by deserting it at home.

"The actions of the junior senator from Wisconsin have caused alarm and dismay amongst our allies abroad and given considerable 'comfort to our enemies.' And whose fault is that? Not really his.

"He didn't create this situation of fear. He merely exploited it — and rather successfully."

"Cassias was right. 'The fault, dear Brutus, is not in our stars but ourselves.' Good night and good luck."

Hasn't Congressman Assi, I mean Issa, used McCarthy tactics during dozens of hearings where he stacked the deck of witnesses but failed to find impeachable offenses by President Obama? Ironically then and now, McCarthy said a decade before Murrow cut him down to size, "Americans realize this cannot be a fight between America's two great parties. If this fight against communism is made a fight between two great parties, the American people know that one of those two great parties will be destroyed. And America cannot endure very long with a one-party system."

(See the movie *Good Night and Good Luck* for the story.)

However, isn't that what "One Percent Devils and Their Satanic Tools" want? Don't they want to destroy the Democratic Party to create tyrannical, plutocratic, autocratic control of all three branches of federal and state governments? Don't they want to destroy labor unions and collective bargaining for that purpose, to eliminate their campaign contributions so there's no major counter-force to billions of dollar of "Citizens United" bribes to Super PACs?

Is Texas Tea Party Republican Ted Cruz, Joe McCarthy reincarnated? Doesn't Cruz look like McCarthy (with a locket of hair curled down over the middle of forehead), whine like McCarthy, and espouse McCarthy poison?

Yet aren't Tea Party Republicans trying to eliminate funding for social safety nets, education, medical research, regulation of industry, business, and finance? Weren't Americans raised to believe atheistic Russian and Chinese Communists wanted to destroy the U.S. government to create Communist New World Orders? Thus aren't Republicans by definition communists because they want to destroy democracy, moral capitalism, and the U.S. government except the U.S. Military-Industrial Complex?

Doesn't Article III, Section 3. Cl. [1] of the U.S. Constitution say, "Treason against the United States, shall consist of ... adhering to enemies, giving them Aid and Comfort?"

Are not Tea Party Republicans giving "aid and comfort" to communist and Muslim enemies when Tea Party Republicans:

- "Bear false witness" that Pope Francis, President Barrack Obama, and other opponents are communists, ala Joseph McCarthy?
- Disenfranchise Latin- and Afro-Americans, elderly, and college students who are Democrats via:
  1. Voter ID laws?
  2. Restricted voting day and hours laws? and
  3. Unconstitutionally gerrymandering voting districts?

- Conning Americans into voting Republican and against their own economic interests, ala Orwellian *1984* and *Animal Farm* via:
  1. Repetitive lies? and
  2. Hitler's Machiavellian, Divide-and-Conquer, Wedge-Issue Tactics?
- Vote to cut and eliminate social safety nets for victims of "One-Percent Devil" crimes against humanity?
- Vote to give tax subsidies and deductions for outsourcing U.S. production, jobs, and technology to:
  1. An atheistic Communist Chinese enemy; and
  2. Third World nations so U.S. companies can exploit foreign workers like slaves (paid twenty cents to a dollar per hour, work twelve to eighteen hour days, seven days a week, without protection from OSHA, EPA, worker's comp, and other laws that protect U.S. workers?
- Vote to send in the CIA and U.S. troops to protect resources, industrial and financial interests of "One Percent Devils" when workers in Third World nations rebel or their leaders try to stop such exploitation?

Doesn't all that "aid and comfort" enemies of the U.S. by showing it can be just as immoral as atheistic communist and Muslim nations. Didn't Karl Marx write against exploitation of workers by Russian and U.S. capitalists like robber barons Rockefeller, Carnegie, Vanderbilt, and J.P. Morgan?

Haven't Americans been raised to believe communists want to destroy U.S. government? Since Tea Party Republicans want to destroy all departments of federal government except Military-Industrial Complex, doesn't that by definition mean Tea Party Republicans are communists?

Weren't hundreds of thousands of Americans killed or disabled fighting to prevent a Nazi New World Order? Since WWII hasn't the U.S. fought a Cold War to prevent Russian and Chinese New World Orders that would be just as immoral?

Why don't half of Americans realize "One Percent Devils and Their Satanic Tools" (Republican politicians, preachers, and press) are trying to create an Anglo-Saxon New World Order? Didn't American students after the Baby Boomer generation of morality read Orwell's warnings about an Anglo-Saxon New World Order in *1984* and *Animal Farm*?

Edward R. Murrow's Warning Re: Diversions from News

Murrow was also concerned about the mesmerizing power of television to divert people from reading the news, listening to it on radio, or watching it on television. Who was it who said, "Americans need to be knowledgeable and informed when they walk into a voting booth"?

The CBS news executive who introduced Edward R. Murrow at the 1958 Radio and Television News Director Association Meeting said, "On his show *See It Now*, Murrow threw stones at giants:

- "Segregation";
- "Exploitation of migrant farm workers";
- "Apartheid";
- "FBI Director J. Edgar Hoover"; and
- "An historic fight with Joe McCarthy."

Then Edward R. Murrow said, "Our history will be what we make it. If there are any historians in fifty to one hundred years from now, there should be preserved the kinescope of one week of all three networks (CBS, NBC, and ABC). They will there find recorded in black and white and in color evidence of decadence, escapism, and isolation from realities of the world in which we live.

"We are currently wealthy, fat, comfortable, and complacent. We have a built-in allergy to disturbing and unpleasant information. Our mass media reflects this. But unless we get up off our fat surpluses and recognize that television, in the main, is being used to distract, delude, amuse, and insulate us, then television, those who finance it, those who look at it, and those who work at it, may see a totally different picture too late.

"I began by saying, 'Our history is what we make it.' If we go on as we are, history will take its revenge. Retribution won't limp in to catch up with it. Just once in a while, let's exalt the importance of ideas and information.

"Let's dream to the extent of saying that on a given Sunday night, a time normally occupied by the *Ed Sullivan Show*, is given over to a clinical survey on the state of American education, and a week or so later, a time normally used by Steve Allen is diverted to a thorough study of American politics in the Mideast.

"Would the corporate image of their perspective sponsors be damaged? Would shareholders rise up in their wrath and complain? Would anything happen but a few million people would have received a little illumination on subjects that may determine the future of this country and therefore the future of the corporation.

"To those who say people wouldn't look, be interested, or are too complacent, indifferent, and insulated, I can only reply, 'There is, in one reporter's opinion, considerable evidence against that contention. But even if they are right, what have they got to lose? Because if they are right, and this instrument (television) is good for nothing except to entertain, amuse, and insulate, then in the tube (TV) that is flickering now, we will soon see that the whole struggle is lost.

"This instrument can teach, illuminate, and it can inspire, but it can do so only to the extent humans are determined to use it toward those ends. Otherwise, it is only wires and lights in a box. Good night and good luck."

For more on Murrow's dilemma read, *The Medium is the Message* by Fred Friendly, the producer of Murrow's show *See it Now*.

Edward R. Murrow was blessed to have William Palely as CEO of CBS (Columbia Broadcast System). He didn't interfere with Murrow's editorial content even when it would offend corporate sponsors. Paley also didn't interfere in the 1960s with editorial content of CBS anchor Walter Cronkite and his editorialist Eric Severide. As I recall, ABC and NBC News anchors like Huntley and Brinkley also had editorial freedom.

However, that can't be said about NBC now. It's owned by General Electric, a huge corporation that hides billions in profits in offshore accounts to evade paying income taxes. Thank goodness, however, for MSNBC. Their hourly news hosts appear to be in the mold of Murrow and Cronkite, who were considered the most credible men in America.

At the time of Murrow's 1958 speech, there were only three networks: CBS, ABC, and NBC. Now there's over two hundred networks to divert us from news. Some reporters, as on Fox News, are "Satanic Tools" of "One Percent Devils." CNN used to set the standard for reporting, but now its news anchors and reporters also sound as if they're unintelligent or informed.

Then there's the Koch Brothers, who own a newspaper empire of dozens of major newspapers. I doubt those papers say anything against Koch Brother immorality and illegality (see Chapter IX on freedom of press).

They say "most Americans learn news from late-night comedy shows."

The following letter from Dad sums up this discussion.

Office of War Information
United States Government
December 24, 1945   American Embassy, London

Dear Folks,

I can only say this much about propaganda BS you swallowed hook, line, and sinker about war and post-war maladjustments being Hitler's fault.

Abraham Lincoln said, "You can fool some of the people all the time and all of the people some of the time, but you can't fool all the people all the time."

Honest Abe may have been correct in the 1860s, but with OWI's sophisticated psycho-social, cultural, selective incorporation, and subliminal messaging, I might say this much: There are very few who don't submit to propaganda if repeatedly subjected to deceiving messages.

Remember that snake oil salesman at the Walworth County Fair. He passed truth and selectively incorporated lies but said enough truth to make his claims appear credible? So who is to blame for WWII? Who put Hitler in power? Who financed him?

English, French, and U.S industrialists and financiers. They wanted Nazis and Communist Russians, obvious threats to capitalism, to destroy each other, but Hitler fooled them all and attacked in all directions.

Now in your criticism of any country, do not blame the people, do not blame the English and German masses. *What is the Root of the Evil?*

It is not the individual but industrialists throughout the world in all countries. A handful of people who go abroad to invest, looking for cheap labor and mineral resources to the detriment of their own and our country.

Then when their toes are stepped on, they influence their own governments to come to their aid to protect their selfish interests. Naturally they can and do because aren't they the ruling class?

You haven't seen this in newspapers, but you must read between and see through the lines. Why didn't capitalistic nations go to the aid of China when Japanese slaughtered Manchurian or help Ethiopians when attacked by Italians or the Fins after Russians invaded? Because U.S. industrialists and financiers had no interests in those countries.

If people fail to interest themselves in political matters, which is their duty to investigate, then someone must make it their task to stimulate such an interest as a patriotic citizen. Who can better bring it to their attention than the minister. Is it not a part of a minister's calling to try to ascertain whether political institutions and daily practices are in conformity with Christian standards?

Is not our democratic system based upon Christian principles? Did they not originate under Christian tutelage and in a Christian era? Then if capitalism and democracy are stepchildren of Christianity, is it not Christianity's duty to give parental advice to its offspring? Or should Christianity allow its brainchild to become a savage, brainwashed robot with no interference.

If you haven't been using this analytical approach, it probably will be hard to change, but remember, we are moving into a propaganda world, which necessitates a keen observation and study of what is the truth.

Your Loving Son,

Wendell Oliver Holmes Woods

P.S. I'm bringing my Jewish, African fiancé home.

Dad wanted sermons on Commandments, Golden Rules, democracy and capitalism — not St. Augustine's anti-natural law "Rules against Sex."

Father would've been heartened to hear "Nuns on the Bus" and the U.S. Council of Bishops proclaim the budget of the congressman of his district, Roman Catholic Republican Paul Ryan, is immoral. It's a first step to eliminate social safety nets for victims of "One Percent Devils and Their Satanic Tools" and leaves on budget only appropriations for U.S. Military-Industrial Complex. (The next page is General and President Eisenhower's U.S.-M.I.C. warning).

As a lover of sex and a minor in economics, my hardcore Republican father would also applaud Pope Francis's:

- Declaration that Republican trickle-down economics is a myth;
- Advice to priests:
  1. To avoid espousing St. Augustine's "Rules against Sex"; and
  2. To preach about how to achieve moral capitalism.

Like me, Dad's in heaven's waiting for the Lutheran Church of America:

- To do the same; and
- To condemn Republican use of Hitler-type, Machiavellian, Divide-

and-Conquer, Wedge-Issue Tactics that primed Germans for WWII and a Nazi New World Order:

1. To stimulate racial, religious, and gender intolerance and hatred in the weak minded and unintelligent with low self-esteem;
2. So they vote Nazi or Republican and thus against their own economic and social interests;
3. So "One Percent Devils and Their Satanic Tools" can create an Anglo-Saxon New World Order that would be just as evil and immoral as a Nazi or Communist New World Order?

Didn't a priest, Martin Luther, nail on the door of Nuremburg Cathedral ninety-five proclamations of church immorality? Didn't proclamations cause reformation that altered European politics and economics?

Wasn't Nuremburg the capital of the Nazi Party? Didn't the Nuremberg Doctrine of international law hold that "generals, industrialists, politicians, judges, and administrators owe a higher duty to morality than to laws of a nation and orders of its leaders?"

Republicanism = Oxymoron for Moron Propaganda Spins

After the keynote address at the Republican National Convention in Chicago in 1936 (Dad attended with Great-Uncle Rufus of the *Wenatchee Daily World*), Dad wrote his parents, "Senator Styver used the symbol 'Americanism' exactly fifty-seven times in his keynote. What is Americanism? There never was a more abstract, elusive symbol than Americanism."

Webster's Dictionary defines Americanism as a custom, trait, or thing peculiar to the United States of America; and devotion to or preference for the U.S. and its institutions. During Baby Boomer generation of morality, Nixon Republicans spun two equally elusive symbols in campaign advertisements and speeches — "Patriotism" and "Law and Order" — in ways similar to Hitler Nazis.

To Nixon Republicans, patriotism meant the U.S. fighting in a Vietnamese civil war. Law and Order meant it's legal to break the law to suppress civil rights, antiwar, feminist, and environmental activists.

Since 2010 Tea Party Republicans spun even more elusive symbolic words such as "welfare." They believe:

- "Welfare" for victims of "One Percent Devils and their Satanic Tools" is "immoral;" but
- "Welfare" for "One Percent Devils" in terms of tax cuts, deductions, and subsidies is "moral" according to:
  1. Natural law human instincts and inclinations;
  2. Darwin's "survival of the fittest;" and
  3. Ayn Rand's "the strong should take from the weak."

Ironically Tea Party Republicans (TPRs) labeled President Obama "The Food Stamp President" and "The Welfare President." However, Republican President G.W. Bush's lack of regulations of banks and brokers caused the second-greatest stock-market crash, economic depression, and thus caused a greater need for food stamps and welfare. Ironic because TPRs tried to draw a nexus between Afro-Americans and welfare, but there have always been more Caucasians than Afro-Americans on welfare and food stamps.

Tea Party Republican also tried to turn the word "entitlement" into an immoral or dirty word. They believe "One Percent Devils" are entitled:

- To foster racial, religious, cultural, and gender intolerance that suppresses and leaves 40 percent of Americans in poverty;
- To outsource production of fifty thousand companies and jobs of millions who then lost pensions, savings, homes, health insurance, etc.;
- To use American soldiers to protect their foreign industrial interests;
- To deregulate Wall Street and banks so they can steal billions from 99 percent of Americans via cons, schemes, and scams;
- To bailouts when banks and Wall Street immorality caused stock-market crashes, depression; and
- To not pay FICA and income taxes so they don't have to pay for social safety net compensation for their:
  1. Military victims;
  2. Stock-market victims;
  3. Outsourcing victims; and
  4. Victims of racial, religious, cultural, and gender discrimination.

Doesn't the word "entitlement" by definition mean that people who receive entitlements are entitled to them? Black's Law Dictionary defines entitlement as "right to benefits, income or property which may not be abridged without due process and equal protection of the law. Webster's defines entitlement as the state of being entitled and the right to guaranteed benefits under a government (for more see Chapters III – VII).

Gen. and Pres. Eisenhower's Warning about Dangers of U.S Military-Industrial Complex to Democracy, Our Liberties, and Peaceful Goals

Dad was promoted to supervisor of code machine operators (who were bilingual European women) because he always had a smile and calmed them down with jokes and funny stories as V-Is and V-IIs rained down around London's government district.

Sometimes when Gen. Eisenhower was at the U.S. embassy, he went with Dad to a basement pub nearby. In one photo, they look like a dad and son. Both were half-bald chain-smokers. Dad always had a smile, jokes, and funny stories. Earthy humor was often based on OWI propaganda spins such as, "Germans are so anal retentive they must have been potty trained at the point of a Luger or Mauser."

I asked Dad whether he knew Ike's most difficult decision? Dad said, "I delivered an urgent message from the Polish underground resistance. They pleaded for Gen. Eisenhower to divert troops to concentration camps before all Jews, Roman Catholics, Gypsies and Slavs were exterminated. Ike was caught in a catch-22 or between a rock and a hard place.

"If he diverted troops to concentration camps, Stalin's Russian Communists would beat the U.S. to Germany's rocket and atomic bomb technology and use V-II rockets with nuclear warheads to obliterate England, the East Coast of the United States, and Poland to create a nuclear-contaminated buffer between Germany and Russia, which meant Slavs, Gypsies, Roman Catholics, and Jews would die no matter which decision General Eisenhower made.

"If Russian Communists got V-II and nuclear bomb research first, all we would have achieved was to replace a Nazi New World Order with an equally immoral or amoral atheistic Communist Russian New World Order."

In his 1961 final farewell address, Pres. Eisenhower warned about the dangers of One-Percent Devil industrialists, financiers, and the U.S. Military Industrial Complex. He said, "Good evening, my fellow Americans. This evening I come to you with a message of leave taking, farewell, and to share a few things with you, my fellow countrymen.

"We now stand ten years past the midpoint of a century that's witnessed four wars among great nations. Three of those involved our own country.

"Until the latest war, our nation did not have an armaments industry. Upon war we had time to turn plows into swords. We can no longer risk emergency improvisation.

"We have been compelled to create a permanent armaments industry of vast proportions. Added to this, 3½ million men and women are directly engaged in the defense establishment.

"Now the conjuncture of an immense military establishment and a large arms industry is new to the American experience. The total influence — economic, political, and even spiritual — is felt in every city, statehouse, and office of the federal government.

"We recognize the imperative need for this development. Yet we must not fail to comprehend its grave implications. Our toil, resources, and livelihoods are involved and at stake. So is the very structure of our society.

"In the councils of government, we must guard against the acquisition of unwarranted influence, whether sought or unsought, by the Military-Industrial Complex. The potential for the disastrous rise of misplaced power exists and will persist.

"Therefore, we must never let the weight of this complex endanger our liberties or democratic process. We should take nothing for granted. Only a knowledgeable and alert citizenry can compel the proper meshing of a huge Military-Industrial Complex with our peaceful message and goals. So our security and liberty may prosper together."

More on George Orwell's *1984* and *Animal Farm*
Books about a Futuristic Anglo-Saxon New World Order
Eric Arthur Blair (whose pen name was George Orwell) could have written *1948* instead of *1984*. By 1948 German, U.S., British, and Russian governments had capabilities to compel citizens to vote against moral capitalism, the U.S. Bill of Rights, the Constitution and democracy. "One Percent Devils and Their Satanic Tools" wanted to replace democracy with an Anglo-Saxon New World Order that would be just as ruthless and morally corrupt as Nazi and/or atheistic Communist Russian New World Orders.

Orwell's initial sources of information on propaganda brain washing tactics and strategies came from propaganda experts in British military intelligence (aka MI-5) and the U.S. Office of War Information. Then Orwell studied propaganda strategies and tactics used by:

- Hitler to turn Germans against democracy, Jews and non-Aryans;
- Muslim clerics and Sunni and Shiite royalty to divert anger of Muslim masses toward a common enemy (Israel, Jews, and the U.S.) by "Bearing False Witness" that Allah or Muhammad wanted a jihad:
  1. Shiite and Sunni royalty endorsed jihad to divert anger of the Muslim masses away from royalty:
     a. Who didn't share oil and gas wealth with the masses; but
     b. Spent half on jets, tanks and police to suppress the masses; and
     c. Left the masses in lives of poverty;
  2. False jihads diverted anger of masses away from clerics who told Muslims the only book they needed to read was the Koran. As a result:
     a. Male Muslims were jealous and resentful of male Jews who were highly educated military strategists, farmers, scientists, engineers, doctors, and attorneys; and
     b. Female Muslims were jealous of female Jews who could:
        1) Fight and be officers in the military, doctors, scientists, etc;
        2) Vote, hold public office, inherit, buy, and sell property;
        3) Pick their own mates instead of Muslim fathers selling daughters to the highest bidder; and
        4) Let their hair blow in the wind and wear shorts, short-sleeve shirts, and bikini bathing suits and didn't have to be dressed in black from head to toe.
- British Conservatives lied about Labor Party members being socialists or communists and significantly contributed to post-WWII depression;
- Republicans who "bore false witness" that Democrats or opponents in the press were communists, including but not limited to:

1. War hero and anti-gender equality Republican Richard Nixon:
   a. In 1948, he won a U.S. congressional seat by "bearing false witness" that a female congresswomen was a communist;
   b. In 1962 he fraudulently set up "Democrats for Nixon" to con Democrats into giving Nixon campaign contributions; and
   c. *Selling of the President* is about how Nixon in 1968:
      1) Used Hitler-type propaganda tactics to create campaign platforms of patriotism and law and order; and
      2) "Bore false witness" that:
         a) Elitist (code word for Jewish) press were communists;
         b) Civil rights, antiwar, feminist, and environmental activists and protestors were communists
2. Wisconsin Sen. Joseph McCarthy's anti-communist witch hunt began during hearings by his Un-American Activities Committee;
- And Blair (aka Orwell) knew when Wild Bill Donavan became director of the Central Intelligence Agency in 1948 he'd bring to
- CIA, OWI's sophisticated propaganda strategies and tactics. (See my father's letter about OWI's capabilities after Ed Murrow's speech.)

Brain washing propaganda strategies and tactics of Hitler, Muslim clerics, royalty, Whigs, and Republicans in 1948 were explained in *1984*:

- Repetitive lies until people believe lies are true and truth is a lie; and
- Machiavellian, Divide-and-Conquer, Wedge-Issue Tactics:
  1. To stimulate racial, religious, and gender bias, prejudice, Intolerance, and hatred;
  2. So people vote Whig or Republican and against social and economic interests of themselves, family, and friends.

Propaganda strategies and tactics so powerful that Dad's letter said, "There are very few who don't submit to propaganda if repeatedly subjected to deceiving messages... .If people don't exercise their duty to be knowledgeable and alert to dangers to democracy and moral capitalism, then preachers should inform their congregations."

However, in order to prevent being labeled as a communist and charged with revealing U.S. and British top secret propaganda tactics, Eric Arthur Blair used a pen name George Orwell and wrote about a fantasy, futuristic "1984." That book and *Animal Farm* elucidate what life would be like in an Anglo-Saxon New World Order. See Chapter XIII for more details.

More on Alien Gods, Humans, and 75 Percent of Brain Most Humans Never Learn How to Use

What is the unused 75 percent of the human brain for? Perhaps Longfellow's poem about a Wisconsin Chippewa boy has part of the answer.

"Hiawatha"
Then the little Hiawatha
Learned of every bird its language,
Learned their names and all their secrets,
How they built their nests in summer,
How they hid themselves in winter,
Talked with them whenever he met them,
Call them Hiawatha's chickens.
Of all beasts he learned their language.
Learned their names and all of their secrets,
How the beavers built their lodges,
Where the squirrels hid their acorns,
How the reindeer ran so swiftly,
Why the rabbit was so timid,
Talked with them whenever he met them,
Called them Hiawatha's brothers.

Did an alien, thought to be a god, messenger angel, or Nephilim telecommunicate into Hiawatha's brain the ability to communicate with animals and birds and consider them his brothers and chickens? In Babel did a god open that 75 percent of brains of Noah's grandsons and telecommunicate a different language, and when they talked to each other, it sounded like Babel or they babbled a different language?

Chippewa were known as "Keepers of the Faith." Their Ottawa cousins were "The Trader People." Potawatomi cousins were "Keepers of the Sacred Flame." Lithographs of Potawatomi chiefs in the 1830s tie together my genealogy research and confirm Ben Gunn's theory that thirteen thousand years ago, Aryan, Indo-European Gypsies migrated from India:

- To a fortress of mountains now called Waltz:
  1. In what is now western Germany and eastern Switzerland; and
  2. After Christ it was ruled by a Templar Knight, Baron Jacob Waltz, who survived the Friday the Thirteenth massacre of Templar Knights; and
  3. Baron Jacob Waltz's descendants are my grandfathers;
- Some Aryan, Indo-European Gypsies settled in Waltz and became Celts who would rule Europe until defeated by Roman legions led by Julius Caesar and pagan Celtic King Clovis of the Frankish Kingdom of France defeated pagan Germanic tribes and converted both nations to Christianity; and
- Other Indo-European, Aryan Gypsies continued on and crossed the Atlantic glacier to the eastern shore of the Americas:
  1. Delaware Gypsies settled down in Delaware;
  2. Cherokee Gypsies went south to the Carolinas; and
  3. Potawatomi/Chippewa/Ottawa ancestors settled in New England.

As the North American glacier receded northward, Ottawa, Potawatomi, and Chippewa ancestors migrated into Canada, where they called themselves "Neshaname" (original people), who descended from an Adam and Eve:

- Discovery Channel's worldwide DNA study confirms that every race descends from the same Adam and Eve; and
- Clovis arrowheads are not only found in Clovis, France, but my own back yard in Lyons Township, Delavan, and Lake Geneva, Wisconsin. Potawatomi Chiefs in the 1830s looked European, had mustaches and goatees, and wore European-style clothing. In a bronze statue in Fontana Bay of Lake Geneva, Chief Bigfoot, in buckskins and a coonskin hat, looks like a tall, thin Daniel Boone. Chief Shabbona looks like a plump pope or mafia godfather. Chat-O-Nis-See

looks like a Turkish prince, and Sun-a-Get looks like a Viking with a horned crown.

However, American Indians who migrated from China to Siberia to Alaska and to Wisconsin, such as the Oneida Nation, didn't have facial hair and look more like Siberian Chinese.

Buddha also communicated with animal and bird brothers. Buddhists won't even kill a cockroach. Rama, founder of the Hindu faith, believed in upward and downward mobility of souls via reincarnation because:

- Rama died and saw a bright white tunnel of Reincarnation. Many people who died walked through a bright, white tunnel until resuscitated:
    1. Ancient pagan Indian Vedas Sanskrit says that after Rama died in Noah's flood in 5000 B.C., God restored his life;
    2. After which Rama glowingly talked of walking through a tunnel of bright white light and seeing a ghostly image of a God who did a cost benefit analysis of descendents passing through by reading their minds, which revealed whether they did good or evil and gave a thumbs-up for reincarnation to a higher species or thumbs-down to a lower species; and
    3. Isn't that eerily similar to St. Peter at the bright, pearly gates issuing thumbs-up to heaven and thumbs-down to hell?

Reincarnation evolved from gods altering DNA to create beings with human bodies and heads of birds or animals. Those beings are depicted in ancient statues and drawings in India, Southeast Asia, Egypt, and the Americas.

Indian Vedas Sanskrit says a god procreated with a pagan Vedas La Sacre Femme. Their daughter procreated with Rama. In the fifth century, Revji founded the Sikh faith because Hindus were violating eternal law.

In the sixth century, Muhammad's Persian, Indo-European, Aryan son, Ali, founded the Shiite faith so his followers could go to war and conquer the world. However, after Ali's army conquered Spain, the unused 75 percent of King Charlemagne's brain was opened by God. Charlemagne summoned:

- Assistance of the four elements (water, wind, fire, earth); and

- Like Hiawatha was able to communicate with his bird and animal brothers. Charlemagne solicited assistance from his brothers; and
- Soundly defeated Ali's Shiite forces in southern France. Thereafter, King Charlemagne was anointed pope, not just because of his victory. He was a descendant of Sarah, the daughter of Jesus Christ and Mary Magdalene, and they were descendants of King David, who violated commandments "You shall not bear false witness" or "utter false reports" when he declared that god had given him divine sovereign authority to violate eternal law against Semite cousins.

After Sarah married into the Merovingian family, it became a dynasty, as her descendants married into the royal and noble families of Europe, so European kings would inherit King David's divine sovereign authority to violate commandments such as "Thou shall not kill" or "steal."

Frankish King Clovis was a descendant of Sarah. Charlemagne was a descendant of Celtic pagan King Clovis, who promised his Christian wife, Clothide, that he'd convert to Christianity if he defeated Germanic tribes.

Since an ancient Baron Waltz married a descendant of Sarah, that brings us full circle to my brother, sister, and I, who would have the blood of Christ and Mary Magdalene. I have no doubt that a sizeable percentage of Americans also have their DNA and blood in their veins, in part because kings and princes were constant procreators with wives, concubines, other men's wives, and via rapes during wars. One cousin says we're descendants of a bastard procreated by King Louis XIV.

In the final analysis, no Caucasian American or European can claim to be pure French, German, English, etc. Every European nation was conquered a dozen or two times. Winners raped losers and eventually merged into new cultures. They say "there's only six degrees of separation between all human beings. So why don't we try acting like God's Wanted?

Which brings us full circle to my brother, Warren, and me. I can't remember the number of times one of us said, "I knew that was going to happen" or "I had a dream about that."

We were both strong, fast, and agile and either had the luck of the Irish, incredibly developed natural law human instincts and inclinations to survive, or perhaps we benefited by divine intervention. However, those dreams or flashbacks ended during our late teens:

- In one year of constant combat in Vietnam with the legendary First Infantry Division that was mirrored in the movie *Platoon*, my brother rose from PFC to staff sergeant with a Silver Star, Bronze Star, Purple Heart, and a lifetime of Post Traumatic Stress Disorder, sweat-producing, nightmare, war Dreams; and
- I've survived marital and divorce-court horror stories; but
- After those stresses began, Warren and I have never said, "I dreamt that would happen" or "I knew that would happen."

So that begs some questions. Does that 75 percent of our brains we don't use include extrasensory perception or Nostradamus abilities to predict the future. Or was Nostradamus so good at deductive reasoning that he took facts known to everyone and listed logical chains of events that led to an Antichrist Hitler?

CHAPTER IV

Goals of Preamble and Enabling Clause of Constitution and Keynesian Economics vs. Trickle-Down Economics Myth

For fifty years I didn't think Republicans really expected or wanted to abolish Medicare, Medicaid, welfare, contraceptives, and abortion or cut taxes and balance the budget. I thought Republicans put those items on platforms merely to sucker unintelligent and uninformed Americans to vote Republican. However, Tea Party Republicans are gradually turning their platforms into state and federal laws that violate goals of the U.S. Constitution.

Vice President Hubert Humphrey ran against former Vice President Nixon in 1968. Humphrey's response to Nixon's demands for tax cuts for the rich to stimulate economy and create jobs coined a platform called "Trickle-Down Economics."

However, economists say tax cuts for "One Percent Devils" don't create jobs, but significant tax cuts for working poor and middle class would stimulate economic growth because they would use the extra money to purchase Made in America. However, as will be indicated, every president since Franklin Delano Roosevelt, whether Republican (except G.W. Bush) or Democrat, used Keynesian borrowing and economic stimulus spending to create jobs and bring the U.S. out of economic depressions and recessions.

Republicans Violate All Goals of U.S. Constitution
Almost everything Republicans stand for violates the goals of the Preamble of the U.S. Constitution:

1. "We the People of United States, in order to form a more perfect union;
2. "Establish Justice;
3. "Insure Domestic Tranquility;
4. "Promote the General Welfare;
5. "Provide for a Common Defense; and
6. "Secure the Blessings of Liberty to ourselves and our Posterity;
7. "Do establish this Constitution for the United States of America."

Black's Law Dictionary provides definitions. A preamble explains reasons for the Constitution and objects sought to be accomplished. It is helpful in the interpretation of ambiguities. General welfare describes the government's concern for the health, peace, morals, and safety of its citizens.

Capitalism isn't mentioned in the Preamble or provisions of the Constitution. Founding Fathers were business gentlemen whose word and handshake was their bond, and they believed in "The American Way of Fair Play." Given the nature of Preamble goals, if Founding Fathers anticipated future capitalists, such as robber barons (of railroads, steel, mining oil and gas, timber, and cattle) and "One Percent Devils," after "Promote the General Welfare," they would have added "Promote Moral Capitalism."

Gentlemen businessmen Founding Fathers never fathomed that:

- Capitalists would become "One Percent Devils" who got rich from:
  1. Infrastructure, trained employees, and tax incentives so U.S. companies could do business and become wealthy; and
  2. They'd be so grateful for that and the American economic system that enabled them to become rich;
  3. They'd outsource production of fifty thousand plants and tens of millions of U.S. jobs and technology to:
     a. An atheistic Communist Chinese nuclear enemy which intends to gain world economic dominance via a Chinese New World Order;
     b. Third World nations so "One Percent Devils" can exploit their labor and resources in all of the ways they can no longer exploit within the borders of the United States; and

    c. When people in those nations rebel, the CIA and U.S. Military Industrial Complex step in to protect their immoral interests;

    d. While tens of millions of Americans who lost jobs due to outsourcing also lose homes, pensions, life savings, and medical insurance, and many homes become broken homes after divorce;

- "One Percent Devils and Their Satanic Tools" would add salt to their wounds by reducing and trying to eliminate social safety nets:
  1. For their victims of outsourcing; and
  2. Victims who have been socioeconomically suppressed as a result of Hitler-Nixon-type, Machiavellian, Divide-and-Conquer, Wedge-Issue Tactics and campaign advertising and speeches that stimulate racial, religious, cultural, and gender bias, prejudice, and intolerance;

- "Satanic Tools" (Republican politicians, preachers, and press) would add insult to injury by having the utter audacity to blame their victims by uttering false reports that they are lazy and only want to mooch on social safety nets; and

- Incredibly, independent and Democrat politicians, preachers, and press let them get away with it, day after day and month after month because they've been too intimidated by Republican propaganda that "bore false witness" and "uttered false reports" that anyone who disagrees is an unpatriotic socialist or communist.

As my father's December 24, 1945, letter said, "Is not our democratic system based on Christian principles? Did it not originate under Christian tutelage and in a Christian era? Then if capitalism and democracy are stepchildren of Christianity, is it not Christianity's duty to give parental advice to its offspring? Or should Christianity allow its brainchild to become a savage robot with no interference? "

The Declaration of Independence, U.S. Constitution and democracy were based upon natural law and Judeo-Christian principles (see introduction):

- "Thou (Satanic Tools - Republicans) shall not join hands with a wicked man" (i.e. "One Percent Devils);

73

- "You shall take no bribe for a bribe blinds an official and subverts the cause of those who are in the right";
- "Thou shall not steal (by paying bribes for laws and tax benefits)";
- "You shall not pervert justice due to the poor";
- "You shall not wrong a stranger or oppress him";
- "You shall not afflict any widow or orphan";
- "I am my brother's keeper";
- "Help those in need"; and
- "Do unto others as you would have others do unto you."

Four goals of the Preamble of the Constitution ("to establish Justice, insure domestic Tranquility and promote the General Welfare in order to form a more perfect Union") are:

- Consistent with those Judeo-Christian principles;
- Inconsistent with outsourcing and social safety net bullet points;
- Inconsistent with what "One Percent Devils and Their Satanic Tools" are for and against (see introduction); and
- Inconsistent with rights of individuals and minority groups.

General Welfare Enabling Clause of Constitution

Art. 1, Sec. 8 Cl. 1, of the U.S. Constitution is called the General Welfare Enabling Clause. It declares that, "[1] Congress shall have Power to Lay and Collect Taxes for the Common Defense <u>and</u> General Welfare;

"[2] To borrow money on the Credit of the United States;

"[3] To regulate Commerce with foreign nations, and among the several States, and with Indian Tribes;

"[4] To establish an uniform Rule of Naturalization...;

"[7] To Establish Post Offices and Postal Roads;

"[8] To Promote Progress of Science and Useful Arts; and

"[9] To constitute Tribunals inferior to the Supreme Court;

"[10] To define and punish Piracies and Felonies committed on the high seas, and Offenses against the Laws of the Nation;

"[12 – 16] To provide for an Army, Navy and Rules of War."

Given General George Washington's difficulty in getting Congress to fund his army during the American Revolution, the Founding Fathers knew there would be times when the United States would have to borrow money. Contrary to Tea Party "Satanic Tool" Republicans, there's nothing in the U.S. Constitution:

- Forbidding borrowing money and federal budget deficits;
- Enabling Republican President G.W. Bush to eliminate $400 billion budget surpluses he inherited from Democratic President Clinton by giving rebates and tax cuts (primarily for "One Percent Devils" to buy re-election) when the national debt was trillions of dollars; or
- Going to war in Afghanistan and Iraq II without raising taxes but borrowing six trillion dollars from an atheistic Communist Chinese enemy to pay for those wars:
  1. Especially since Article III, Section 3. [1] defines treason as "adhering to… Enemies, giving them Aid and Comfort"; and
  2. Thus China could bankrupt the U.S. by calling in the debts; and
- There's nothing in U.S. Constitution about paying off national debt by cutting social safety nets and other federal funding assistance to states, to the detriment of 99 percent of Americans;

The General Welfare Enabling Clause authorizes Congress to "Regulate Commerce." Accordingly, during the last one hundred years, Congress has passed laws to create dozens of federal agencies to regulate industry, banks, Wall Street, and service industries to protect 99 percent of Americans. There's no constitutional basis for "One Percent Devils and Their Satanic Tools" to demand elimination of all regulation of commerce.

The General Welfare Enabling Clauses authorizes Congress to "establish uniform Rules of Naturalization." Founding Fathers were Caucasian Judeo-Christians who gave us First Amendment freedom of religion. There's nothing in the U.S. Constitution banning immigration and naturalization of Latin-American, Irish, or Italian Roman Catholics, Asian Buddhists, Jews, or Muslims.

There's nothing in the preamble or General Welfare Enabling Clause to suggest that "in Order to form a more perfect Union, establish Justice, insure Domestic Tranquility, promote the General Welfare and provide a Common Defense" means:

- Elimination of all social safety nets for 47 percent of Americans who:
  1. Paid FICA taxes and are contractually entitled to Social Security disability or retirement and Medicare; or
  2. Received unemployment compensation, welfare, and Medicaid because they're victims of "One Percent Devils" who:
     a. Exploited them as employees, and after they got rich, outsourced their jobs;
     b. Perpetrated fraud, scams, cons, and schemes that led to the 2008 Stock Market Crash and caused:
        1) Twenty million to become unemployed and underemployed;
        2) Depletion or elimination of pensions, IRAs, 401Ks, mutual funds, stocks, and bonds; and
        3) Millions of people to lose homes and medical insurance; or
  3. Are impoverished and economically suppressed because of:
     a. One hundred and fifty years of racial, religious, cultural, and gender bias, intolerance, prejudice, and suppression by Republicans: and
     b. Bribes by "One Percent Devils" to Secret Super PACs for use by "their Satanic Tools" (Republican politicians, preachers, and press) to spread:
        1) Repetitive lies so voters think lies are true and truth's a lie;
        2) And Hitler-Nixon-type, Machiavellian, Divide-and-Conquer, Wedge-Issue Tactics of racial, religious, cultural, and gender bias, prejudice, intolerance, and suppression.

Leaving as the only item on the federal budget, the Military -Industrial Complex:

1. So it can fight wars to protect foreign interest of "One Percent Devils;" and
2. They're so grateful to the soldiers, they bribe "their Satanic Tools" to reduce and ultimately eliminate Veterans Hospitals and Affairs; and

3. There's nothing in Constitution to privatize medical care of vets; contrary to "One Percent Devils and Their Satanic Tools," Preamble and Enabling Clause don't just authorize Congress to collect taxes and borrow to pay for U.S. Military-Industrial Complex and wars to protect interests of "One Percent Devils." It has power to tax and borrow money to:

- "Regulate Commerce with foreign Nations, and among the several states" but not the power to authorize U.S. businesses to outsource U.S. jobs, production, and technology so those who got rich from U.S. economic system get even more immorally rich exploiting foreigners;

- "Establish uniform Rules of Naturalization…" and illegal immigrants is another problem Founding Fathers didn't anticipate and give guidance. Either Republicans don't know history and Golden Rule or conveniently ignore them:

  1. When Puritan Protestant English landed at Plymouth Rock and John Smith's immigrants landed on Roanoke Island, American Indians didn't hand out green cards and work permits;

  2. "History of Whately, Mass. 1600s to 1900" indicates initially English purchased land from Indians. Homes were next to wigwams. Indians helped English hunt, fish, plant, and reap crops. However, that changed when alcohol was introduced and English stopped paying for land, killed Indians, and stole their land;

  3. In 1869 Mexico ceded Arizona (which included New Mexico) to the United States, and it became a territory. Seven out of ten citizens were Mexican. However, they didn't demand a wall with an electrified fence and alligators be built on the eastern border to keep Euro-Americans out of the territory so they couldn't take land from Mexican citizens;

  4. "History of New Haven, Connecticut" reveals:
     a. When millions of Irish Roman Catholics immigrated due to a potato famine, Protestant Americans abused, exploited, and suppressed the Irish with biased and prejudiced police, prosecutors, courts, and corrections;
     b. When millions of Italian Roman Catholics immigrated, Irish Americans entered civil service and soon controlled

77

police departments, prosecutors, and judges. They exploited, abused, and suppressed Italians; and

c. When millions of Jews immigrated, they were abused, exploited, and suppressed by Protestants and Roman Catholics.

So Jews entered civil service and soon controlled schools.

As much as English Protestants and Irish and Italian Roman Catholics hated and tried to control each other, no one demanded that English, Irish, Italians, or Jews be sent back to their native lands. However, when it came to Asians and Latin Americans, immigration laws were changed:

- A limit was set for the number of Asian and Latin Americans who could legally immigrate each year; and
- Only those who were educated, skilled, or had family in America could legally immigrate;
- Except when lives of people of any nation or race are threatened and need political or racial asylum.

That begs some questions. When people illegally immigrate to the U.S. from Mexico, Central America, and South America out of natural law instincts and inclination to get a job so they can support their families in their homelands, wouldn't the humanitarian solution be to allow them to stay and work in the U.S? Congress also has power under Enabling Clause to:

- "Promote General Welfare and Establish Justice" through funding of:
  1. Social safety nets for victims of "One Percent Devils and their Satanic Tools;"
  2. Criminal and civil justice systems; and
  3. Laws and regulations for industries, Wall Street, and banks;
- Promote more than progress of military science but also for general welfare by promoting through research and education funding for:
  1. Medical, environmental, product, food, and other sciences; and
  4. Useful arts, such as liberal arts and fine arts;
- "To Establish Post Offices and Postal Roads:"

1. Which doesn't mean Congress can eliminate the U.S. Postal Service and privatize the postal service by forcing the U.S. Post Office to pay for seventy-five years of future pensions for postal workers in five years:

    a. To force U.S. Post Office into bankruptcy;

    b. So FedEx and UPI (who didn't exist when the Constitution was written) can take over the Postal Service and gouge Americans with monopolistically inflated postal rates; and

    c. since there would no longer be postal workers to use seventy-five years of pension funds, "Satanic Tools" would transfer pension funds to U.S. Military-Industrial Complex; and

2. Building postal roads (roads, railroads, bridges, and airports) infers infrastructure spending to keep them safe and efficient; and

- There's nothing in Enabling Clause or Sixteenth Amendment (which establishes an income tax) about:

    1. Not raising taxes to keep pace with inflation;

    2. Cutting taxes for "One Percent Devils" under a trickle-down theory that's a myth. "One Percent Devils" and companies:

        a. Don't hire or expand production or services because of tax cuts;

        b. They hire and expand production when demand exceeds supply;

        c. And they don't use tax cuts, deductions, and subsidies:

            1) To purchase not Made in America but foreign cars, yachts, vacations, vacation homes, furs, jewelry, wine, and caviar;

            2) They outsource U.S. production, jobs, and technology to:

                a) An atheistic Communist Chinese enemy; and

                b) Third World nations so their labor and resources can be immorally exploited by means that are against the law in the United States;

    3. Laying off a minority group of government workers so:

        a. Taxes don't have to be raised; and/or

  b. Ninety-nine percent of Americans can get tax cuts; and

  c. "One Percent Devils" get huge tax cuts; or

 4. And there was nothing in the Enabling Clause about paying for wars to protect interests of "One Percent Devils" by shifting funding from social safety nets to Military-Industrial Complex budget.

Baby Boomer generation of morality Daughters and Sons of the American Revolution can now say, "We hold these Truths to be Self-Evident" during the past forty years:

 1. "One Percent Devils":

  a. Income has risen 272 percent; and

  b. Their share of national wealth increased from 40 percent to 72 percent;

 2. While they caused income for the other 99 percent to flatline at zero:

  a. Their incomes haven't kept pace with inflation for forty years and:

   1) Either both parents must have jobs; or

   2) Single parents need two or three jobs; and yet the

  b. Share of assets by 99 percent dropped from 60 percent to 28 percent in forty years;

 3. While "Satanic Tools" want women out of the workforce and home as housewife mothers, which is the "best for children," class warfare that started forty years ago by "One Percent Devils and Their Satanic Tools" forces both parents to have jobs and single parents to have two jobs and that leads to unsupervised children getting into trouble;

 4. There's nothing in Constitution precluding women from having jobs;

 5. "Satanic Tools" (Republican politicians, preachers, and press) are bribed by "One Percent Devils" to ignore five of six goals of Preamble and not:

  a. Provide for General Welfare of 99 percent of Americans;

  b. Establish Justice for 99 percent of Americans;

    c.   Domestic Tranquility for 99 percent of Americans;

    d.   Form a More Perfect Union for 99 percent of Americans; and

    e.   Secure Blessings of Liberty for 99 percent of Americans;

6.   "Satanic Tools" have been bribed by "One Percent Devils" to:

    a.   Vote for tax cuts, deduction, and subsidies, so "One Percent Devils" can outsource U.S. jobs, production and technology to:

        1)   An atheistic Communist Chinese enemy; and

        2)   Third World nations to immorally exploit foreign workers;

    b.   Vote only for U.S. Military-Industrial Complex budget to:

        1)   Protect foreign industrial interests of "One Percent Devils";

        2)   Spy on the other 99 percent of Americans; and

        3)   Control 99 percent via surveillance drones, wiretaps, SWAT teams and National Guard;

    c.   Vote against funding for:

        1)   Social safety nets for:

            a)   Female, non-Judeo-Christian, Afro-, and Latin-American victims of Hitler-Nixon-type, Machiavellian, Divide-and-Conquer, Wedge-Issue Tactics by "Satanic Tools";

            b)   Outsourcing victims of "One Percent Devils and their Satanic Tools";

            c)   Veterans of wars for "One Percent Devils";

            d)   Children born into poverty due to "One Percent Devils";

            e)   Unwed and uneducated female victims of rape, incest, and rape by false pretense of love induced by:

                1))   Sexually suggestive advertising by "One Percent Devils"; and

                2))   Viagra from "One Percent Devils" advertisements;

        2)   Aren't the following consistent with the goals of the Preamble?

            a)   Pre- and post-natal care, public housing, food stamps, school lunches, health insurance, clean air, water, land, and food;

            b)   Grade schools, high schools, college grants, and student loans;

    c) Medical research and research into alternatives to fossil fuels;

7. And also during last forty years, as cost of living rises, cost of governments rises;

8. During the last forty years, as unemployment increased, government tax deficits and social safety net costs increased;

9. During the last forty years, manufacturers and service providers:
   a. Hired employees when demand exceeds supply; and
   b. Fired or laid off workers when:
      1) Supply exceeds demand;
      2) Jobs were outsourced to China and Third World nations; and
      3) Corporations purchased other corporations, so remaining workers:
         a) Do the work of two to five people and work longer hours;
         b) But without a pay raise, so they work for fewer dollars per hour;

10. Lack of regulation of Wall Street and banks caused stock-market crashes and economic depressions every twenty years since the Civil War:
    a. Junk bond and paper money fraud under Republican President Reagan;
    b. Stock-market crash/recession under Republican President G.H. Bush;
    c. Mortgage/derivative market fraud recession by President G.H. Bush;
    d. Yet Republicans have tried to extort deregulation by President Obama;

11. Keynesian borrowing and economic stimulus spending has been employed by every president, whether Republican or Democrat, to geometrically increase economy via:
    a. Spending for infrastructure jobs and government-worker jobs;
    b. Which increased taxable income, reduced deficits, and created government budget surpluses; and
    c. Increased spending and demand for products and services;

    d. Which increased hiring of industrial and service workers;

    e. Which created more taxable income, spending, and hiring, etc;

12. Tax Cuts:

    a. From Republican President George W. Bush in 2001 and 2003 tax cuts only enabled 99 percent of Americans to purchase two pizzas per week;

    b. Republican Wisconsin Gov. Scot Walker's tax cut only put one pizza on the table per week for Wisconsinites; and

    c. Caused layoff of thousands of government workers; but

    d. Cuts gave multimillion dollar windfalls to the "One Percent Devils" who caused depression by outsourcing and Wall Street fraud; and

    e. That bought more bribes via insider trading tips and secret campaign contribution bribes to Super PACs and offshore accounts of "their Satanic Tools";

13. The problem with the tax-cut, trickle-down-economics theory myth is that tax cut legislation:

    a. Didn't require industries and service providers to hire new employees, expand production, or build new plants; but

    b. Caused layoffs of hundreds of thousands of government workers and loss of their;

        1) Taxable income and worsened deficits;

        2) Spending power;

        3) Rights to life, liberty, and pursuit of happiness;

        4) Savings, pensions, medical insurance, homes, and families; and

        5) Caused former government workers to use social safety nets: unemployment compensation, disability, welfare, food stamps, public housing, and hospital ERs for medical care;

14. Trickle-down theory of "Satanic Tools" that tax cuts, deductions, and subsidies for "One Percent Devils" will stimulate economy is a myth because they don't use tax cuts to:

    a. Purchase Made In America but to purchase foreign homes, cars, yachts, vacations, furs, jewelry, wine, and caviar;

    b. Hire workers and expand production but to:

        1) Outsource U.S. jobs; and/or

2) Buy other companies, lay off their workers, and force remaining workers to do the work of two to five former employees but without a pay increase to compensate for extra work; and

3) That's why:

    a) U.S. Council of Bishops and Nuns on a Bus said Republican budgets are immoral; and

    b) Pope Francis said:

        1)) Tax-cut, trickle-down theory is a myth;

        2)) There should be a redistribution of wealth from rich to poor, working poor and middle class; and

        3)) Priests should preach about moral capitalism;

History of Keynesian Borrowing and Stimulus Spending and Democratic President Franklin Delano Roosevelt

Thirteen million workers (10 percent) lost jobs during the Great Depression. What did it take to bring United States out of the Great Depression?

President Franklin Delano Roosevelt employed Keynesian borrowing and economic stimulus spending to fund New Deal legislation for the following (much of which is from "Quick Study Academic American History 2" by Bar Charts, Inc.):

- (1932) Reconstruction Finance Corporation (RFC) to provide loans to banks, insurance companies, railroads, and state and local governments;
- (1933) Agricultural Adjustment Act (AAA) to control overproduction and pay farmers for losses;
- (1933) Tennessee Valley Authority (TVA) was established to build hydroelectric dams and control flooding;
- (1933) In Washington State, the Grand Coulee Dam and Chief Joseph Dam were built to provide:
  1. Hydroelectric power that attracted Boeing to Seattle, and it built thousands of B-17, B-25 and B-29 bombers for WWII; and
  2. Irrigation turned desert into gardens, farms, and orchards;

- (1933) National Industrial Recovery Act (NIRA) set standards for business administration, established fair trade practices and ensured unions the right to collective bargain;
- (1933) Prohibition was repealed, and the alcohol industry boomed;
- (1934) Wheeler-Howard Act (Indian Reorganization) restored Indian lands to tribal ownership and forbid further division of Indian land;
- (1935) Emergency Relief Appropriation Act (ERA) authorized president to provide public-works programs for the unemployed:
  1. Works Progress Administration (WPA);
  2. Resettlement Administration (RA);
  3. Rural Electrification Administration (REA);
  4. National Youth Administration (NYA); and
  5. Programs to build national parks, roads, bridges, etc.;
- (1935) National Labor Relations (Wagner) Act granted workers the right to organize and bargain collectively and established the Labor Relations Board to ensure democratic union elections and eradicate unfair labor practices by employers;
- (1935) Social Security Act was passed;
- (1937) Farm Security Administration is established to aid migratory farm workers;
- (1937) Memorial Day Massacre: Chicago police open fire on striking steel workers and others who were peacefully picketing;
- (1938) Fair Labor Standards Act is passed to:
  1. Forbid child labor;
  2. Establish minimum wage;
  3. Establish forty-hour work week; and
  4. Provide for unemployment compensation when unemployment was down to 10.4 million;
- (1941) Fair Employment Practice Committee forbid discrimination in war industries and government.

As to the 1936 presidential and congressional elections, my father wrote his parents, "Republicans don't promise change but only to do things better." Yet Republicans did what they could to reverse New Deal legislation:

- Republican majority in U.S. Supreme Court held as unconstitutional:
  1. National Industrial Recovery Act in Schechter vs. U.S (1935);
  2. Agricultural Adjustment Act in U.S. vs. Butler (1936); and
- Republicans in Congress and Senate demanded tax increases to pay off the New Deal national debt and balance the budget. However, a Republican tax increase had a reverse Keynesian effect:
  1. It reduced family income for buying products and services;
  2. That reduced the need for production and service workers;
  3. That caused the loss of their taxable income and purchase power;
  4. That caused more layoffs and increased the national debt; and
  5. Prevented a return to full employment before WWII.

Unfortunately, Republicans didn't learn an important lesson. It is unwise to balance a budget during economic depression. In 1944 FDR:

- Proposed an economic bill of rights for everyone to have decent jobs, food-shelter-clothing, and financial security during unemployment, illness, or old age; and
- Signed a GI Bill of Rights (see GI Bill below).

Democratic President Harry Truman
After WWII President Truman's Twenty-one point economic message urged:

- Extension of unemployment benefits;
- Increase in minimum wage;
- Permanent farm price supports;
- New public-works projects; and
- President Roosevelt's economic bill of rights.

At the end of WWII, twelve million men and women were in uniform. Millions of women worked in war industries. Several transitions occurred:

1. As industries stopped manufacturing war goods and retooled to produce consumer goods;
2. Women workers were laid off and most married returning soldiers;

3. Millions of male and female veterans either:
   a. Went to college under the GI Bill; or
   b. After retooling, former soldiers were employed in manufacturing.

The U.S. was the only industrial nation that still had factories intact. High unemployment in Europe and Japan led to a threat that those nations would end democracy and capitalism and become communist nations.

Democratic President Harry ("If you can't stand the heat, get out of the kitchen") Truman employed Keynesian borrowing and economic stimulus:

- In 1946 inflation had reached 18.2 percent;
- The Unemployment Act of 1946 said the U.S. government would use its resources, including deficit spending, to assure "maximum employment, production, and purchasing power";
- The GI Bill had two effects:
   1. It took two million former soldiers out of the job market, paid for their college, medical, and law school education, and stimulated growth of a highly educated middle class;
   2. GI loans stimulated the growth of economy by giving veterans low-interest loans to purchase cars, homes, and build homes; and
   3. Both effects created a geometrically expanding economy;
- Pentagon Chief of Staff General George C. Marshal's Marshall Plan had positive and negative effects:
   1. It rebuilt war-ravaged industries of Europe and Japan; and
   2. Employed millions in those nations;
   3. But those nations got modern technology for producing products such as steel that allowed those nations to produce steel and other products more cheaply than in the U.S., which had older technology; and
   4. German, Italian, and Japanese companies committed industrial espionage to steal more technology;
   5. German, Italian, and Japanese governments:
      a. Illegally subsidized industries; and
      b. Banned imports of many U.S. products.

However, in 1946 Republicans won a majority in the U.S. Senate and House of Representatives. They passed the Taft-Hartley Act to prohibit "closed shops" (companies that could only hire union members) and allowed state's "Right to Work" laws. The history of "Right to Work" laws has been that workers have a right to work for less in those states than in states with "closed shops," where workers earn union wages and fringe benefits.

Republicans won both houses of Congress on a platform aimed at reversing all of President Roosevelt's New Deal legislation. Yet ironically Republicans threw the poor a bone when it passed the National Housing Act in 1949 to provide reasonably priced housing for all Americans. That spawned the creation of low-cost communities, such as in Levittown, PA, and created many construction-worker jobs.

Otherwise the 1946 and 1948 Republican Senate and House were known as the "Do Nothing Congress."

Republican President Dwight David Eisenhower

As indicated, when Republicans are in power, and the economy is weak, they will employ Keynesian borrowing and economic stimulus spending. After the Korean War ended, the U.S. entered a recession:

- In 1956 a Republican Senate, House, and president authorized the Highway Act to build a National Defense Highway System (aka Interstate Highway System (IHS)), to permit rapid transit of U.S. troops in case of invasion. IHS created an economic boom:

    1. Building of IHS directly and indirectly employed millions of construction workers, engineers, supervisors, and businesses that provided them with food, housing, clothing, and medical care; and

    2. That infusion of money into the U.S. economy:

        a. Increased taxable income to rapidly pay off loans for IHS;

        b. Increase in purchase power of all of those workers resulted in U.S. companies building production plants and stores and hiring industrial workers, managers, and clerks, who also then had taxable income and purchase power; and

        c. This, combined with GI Bill benefits for WWII and Korean War veterans, enabled millions of Americans:

      1)   To build homes in suburbs; and

      2)   Buy cars to drive from suburbs into cities for work;

  d.   IHS also stimulated a boom in travel industry, enabling:

      1)   Travel to federal and state parks, ski resorts and distant relatives and friends;

      2)   And that caused production of hotels, motels, camp-grounds, camping trailers, camping, fishing, hunting, and ski equipment;

- In 1958 Republicans provided two means that stimulated research and development through science and math:

    1.   National Defense Act (NDA) provided funding for upgrading education in science, math, and foreign languages; and

    2.   National Aeronautics and Space Administration (NASA) was established; and

    3.   Both NDA and NASA would result in creation of many new defense and consumer products and supporting industries; and

- In 1961 President Eisenhower warned about the danger of a Military-Industrial Complex getting the U.S. into wars for profit.

Democratic President John Fitzgerald Kennedy

Democratic President Kennedy's infusion of money into the National Aviation Space Administration had several economic effects:

- College students switched majors to math, engineering, and science;
- Thousands of engineers, scientists, mathematicians, managers, and construction workers were hired;
- Hundreds of industries were built to support NASA programs;
- Extensive high-tech research and development advanced science;

    1.   Consistent with Article I, Sec. 8, Cl. 8 of U.S. Constitution to "Promote Progress of Science;"

    2.   U.S. leaped ahead of Communist Soviet Union in development of computers and intercontinental ballistic missiles, which was consistent with a goal of the Preamble for "Providing for the Common Defense";

    3.   U.S. economy exploded with hundreds of new military and consumer products, plants, and workers to manufacture them; and

    4.   Again significant increases in:

   a.   Taxable income to pay off NASA loans and appropriations; and

   b.   Purchase power to buy products and services.

Democratic President Lyndon Baines Johnson

Democratic President Johnson employed Keynesian borrowing and economic stimulus to achieve goals of Preamble and Enabling Clause via:

- A "War Against Poverty" to prevent racial war;
- Medicare and Medicaid to give thirty million uninsured people an ability to get medical treatment without going bankrupt;
- College grants and student loans to:
  1. Reduce unemployment by taking high school graduates out of job market; and
  2. Increase female, Afro, and Latin American college attendance; and
  3. Just as GI Bill increased middle class by paying for veterans to go to college, business and professional schools, student grants, and loans also expanded middle class;
- Voting Rights Law so Afro-Americans could vote;
- Equal Rights Law for females, such as Title X, which gave girls equal rights to sports and other activities in schools.

Republican President Richard Millhouse Nixon
President Nixon paid for Keynesian stimulus by borrowing from:
- Social safety net funds (Social Security, Medicare, and Medicaid);
- Payments to American Indian tribes for oil, gas, and minerals; and
- By transferring President Johnson's War on Poverty funds to President Nixon's Law and Order program because Republicans would rather arrest, kill, and imprison Afro and Latin Americans than to help them rise out of a life of poverty and crime. Nixon's net result was:
  1. Funding of federal Law Enforcement Assistance Administration to give grants to state, county, and municipal governments to:
     a.   Hire more troopers, sheriffs, and police officers; and
     b.   Arm them with sidearms, shotguns, M-15 assault rifles, Tazers, tear gas, pepper gas, and batons; and

    c. Create SWAT Teams in every large, medium, and small city;

2. But they turned liberal, progressive Democrats into anarchistic revolutionaries (Students for a Democratic Society, Black Panthers, and Symbionese Liberation Army). They robbed banks, sold drugs, and prostituted themselves to get money to buy guns and make bombs; and

3. State troopers, sheriff officers, police, U.S. intelligence agencies (CIA, FBI, NSA and military intelligence) illegally spied on fifty thousand civil rights, antiwar, and feminist activists, as well as the press and 150,000 of their family or friends via illegal, warrantless:

    a. Opening of mail; and

    b. Wiretaps on home and work telephones; and

4. There were so many arrests that prosecutors, courts, and corrections were so overwhelmed that LEAA had to give grants to expand prosecutors offices, courts, and corrections;

5. So that now 25 percent of everyone in the world who is in prison is An American even though America only has 5 percent of the world's population (according to *Time* (Sept. 8, 2014)):

    a. Afro and Latin Americans serve longer sentences than Caucasians for the same crimes; and

    b. A disproportionately higher number of Latin- and African-Americans are executed than Caucasians; and

    c. Streets are no safer now than when Nixon was president;

6. In part because Nixon changed correctional philosophy:

    a. From rehabilitation and education and training in prison; halfway houses to help reassimilate ex-cons back into society; and help them get and maintain jobs; and

    b. To "Just Desserts" — punishment that befits the crime:

        1) But because there are so many victimless-crime drug users and dealers in prison, there's not enough room to keep murderers, robbers, burglars, rapists, pedophiles, pickpockets, and con artists in prison for full sentences; and

        2) Few of them are in prison long enough to get GEDs or complete carpentry, plumbing, or electrician training.

How Else Did President Nixon "Stimulate" U.S. Economy?

Republican President Nixon stimulated the economy by signing legislation to:

- Create the Environmental Protection Agency to end and clean up pollution of air, water, land, and food for the General Welfare:
    1. Then universities established environmental-science schools;
    2. Their research and development provided methods and machines to prevent pollution and clean up polluted air, water, and land;
    3. Which created new industrial and service industries;
    4. Environmental-science graduates were hired by:
        a. U.S. Environmental Protection Agency;
        b. State EPAs; and
        c. U.S. industrial corporations, especially industrial polluters;
- Expand Vietnam War from 150,000 to 500,000, he:
    1. Took 350,000 men out of the workforce;
    2. Which reduced unemployment by that many; and
    3. Stimulated Military-Industrial Complex production and profits;
- Wasn't President Nixon a superb capitalist in grain commodities?
    1. When there was a severe drought in the Ukraine, President Nixon sold Russia wheat and corn from U.S. grain reserves for ten cents on the dollar; but
    2. The following year when the U.S. Midwest had a drought, Russia sold The U.S. back its own grain at the very high commodity market price?
    3. Does that mean Russian Communists were better capitalists?

How Nixon Caused Four-Dollar-Per-Gallon Gas Prices

Republican President Teddy Roosevelt filed a Sherman Antitrust Act lawsuit to break up into thirty companies Rockefeller's Standard Oil of New Jersey, which had a horizontal and vertical monopoly in the U.S. By breaking Standard Oil into thirty companies, competition created lower gas prices.

President Nixon ignored the Sherman Antitrust Act and allowed major oil and gas companies to drive mom-and-pop gas stations, small- and medium-sized oil and gas companies into bankruptcies so large oil companies could buy them for ten cents on the dollar. President Nixon also pushed through tax subsidies to help oil companies drill for more gas.

By Senate hearings in 2012 on the $400 million subsidies to oil and gas companies:

- The U.S. only had five U.S. oil and gas companies;
- Each CEO said they put gas on the market for eighteen cents per gallon and didn't need the $400 million in subsidies; and
- Yet Republicans:
  1. Won't eliminate unneeded subsidies for oil and gas companies;
  2. But eliminated subsidies for production of gas from biofuels. However, let's back up a bit to other ways President Nixon benefited oil and gas prices at the expense of Americans. With the Vietnam War winding down, President Nixon had two problems:
- A gas-price war declared by major U.S. oil and gas companies had driven prices down to twenty-three cents per gallon in 1971;
- The U.S. would no longer be paying U.S. oil and gas companies for a million gallons of fuel per day for the Vietnam War:
  1. That would create a glut of oil and gas on the market and drive gas prices lower;
  2. Lower than twenty-three cents per gallon; and
  3. It cost eighteen cents to produce and sell each gallon; and

President Nixon had a surplus of U.S. tanks, jets, and other military equipment and supplies:

1. So the U.S. Military-Industrial Complex would have to lay off workers; and
2. Five hundred thousand soldiers would be discharged and unemployed.

President Nixon wanted to keep Military-Industrial plants pumping out war materials and sell the surplus to Mideast nations. However, gas prices were so low they couldn't afford to buy tanks or jets. The Koran prohibited borrowing.

So President Nixon had Secretary of State Kissinger (was he born in Communist Russia?) secretly work with Mideast oil producing nations to create OPEC (Organization of the Petroleum Exporting Countries) to:

- Reduce production of oil and gas worldwide;
- So gas and oil prices were forced high enough that Mideast nations could afford to buy U.S. tanks, jets, artillery, rockets, etc; and
- Eventually those Mideast nations would either use those weapons against the U.S. or threaten to do so.

Ironically President Nixon wanted to win a Nobel Peace Prize and go down in history books as The Great Peacemaker. To achieve that, he did something no Democrat would have dared to do or else they'd be called communists or aiders and abettors of communism.

President Nixon gave Russia and China favored trade status with the U.S., allegedly so U.S. companies could sell products in those countries. However, another goal was an Anglo-Saxon New World Order goal of allowing U.S. companies to outsource U.S. production, jobs, and technology:

- To give atheistic Communist Russia and China a stake in capitalism so they wouldn't try to destroy it;
- So U.S. companies could exploit Russian, Chinese and Third World nation workers in ways they couldn't exploit U.S. workers;
- Allegedly to put cheaper Russian and Chinese products on the U.S. market to force U.S. companies to lower prices;
- But the hidden agenda was to eliminate U.S. production by labor union workers and to make all U.S. production done by low-cost, non-union labor;
- However, there was a glitch. By eliminating production in the U.S. by outsourcing production, jobs, and technology of fifty thousand companies, they eliminated a huge part of the middle class, and thus a huge sector of America could no longer buy products made anywhere.

Democratic President Jimmy Carter

President Nixon stimulating the creation of OPEC, wars in the Mideast, and Iranians taking over the U.S. embassy caused two periods of severe shortages of gas in the late 1970s. No one could fill tanks full. Every gas station had long lines of cars waiting to refuel. Many went from one gas station to another in order to get a full tank. Then came fuel rationing.

Democratic President Carter put $750 billion into research and development of alternatives to fossil fuels such as:

- Passive and active solar energy;
- Energy efficient cars, homes, appliances, and businesses;
- Electric, hydrogen, and biofuel cars; and
- All that created new industries, products, and jobs.

Jimmy Carter didn't win re-election because he was set up to fail by Republican Pentagon generals. The Vietnam War was over. A majority of voters wanted taxes to go down by cutting the budget for the U.S. Military-Industrial Complex. So President Carter did what Americans voted for him to do. He reduced the size of the military and eliminated many military bases in the U.S.

After Iranians took over the U.S. embassy in Iran and captured ninety embassy employees, Republican Pentagon generals setup the Iranian embassy hostage rescue operation to fail. Thus they politically punished President Carter. They designed a rescue plan that violated principles of military strategy and tactics. The Pentagon should have sent in three times as many helicopters and transport planes. It knew those planes were not tested to make sure they could withstand a sandstorm.

So what happens when you send in a bar minimum of helicopters and transport planes and a sandstorm causes one helicopter and transport to crash? A failed mission, and the Pentagon got away with destroying a second term for President Carter — one of the few really moral men who have been president.

Republican President Ronald Reagan

In part for the U.S. oil and gas industry, Republican President Reagan transferred President Carter's alternative to fossil fuel funds to "Star Wars" to develop a missile defense shield. However, while that:

- Put thousands of former NASA engineers and managers back to work;
- And produced dozens of consumer products that led to building production plants, expanding plants, and hiring;

1. Star Wars missiles still can't hit the broad side of a barn; and
2. The U.S. is still too dependent upon Mideast oil and gas; and- President Reagan also got the U.S. into wars in Grenada, Panama, Bosnia, and Somalia. Wars that benefited:
   a. One Percent Devils of U.S. Military-Industrial Complex; and
   b. U.S military captured Panama President Manuel Noriega, the kingpin of the infamous Iran-Contra Affair:
      1) CIA got drugs from Guatemalan rebels (Contras);
      2) CIA gave drugs to Noriega;
      3) Noriega transported drugs to U.S. mafia;
      4) Col. Oliver North took mafia money to Iran to buy weapons;
      5) CIA transported weapons to Contras.

President Reagan was like the three monkeys: "I said nothing. I heard nothing. I saw nothing." When President Reagan said, "I don't recall," that may be true because he had senile dementia memory loss.

What is it with the love affair Republicans have with President Reagan, a C student from a small Illinois college? A president who couldn't make a decision without consulting a fortune teller. A movie star president who only had to tell funny jokes and read what speechwriters wrote:

- His secretary of treasury waited months for President Reagan to give economic policy directives:
  1. So the secretary had his staff read Reagan's campaign speeches in order to formulate economic policy; and
  2. That included "Do not enforce SEC and bank commission regulation, which caused the paper money/junk bond fraud that caused a massive stock-market crash where:
     a. Millions lost jobs, savings, pensions, IRAs, and 401(k)s;
     b. "One Percent Devils" used insider trading knowledge to:
        1) Get rich selling short as the stock market plunged; and
        2) Get richer buying stocks cheap as they bottomed out; and
        3) Those "Devils" who caused the stock-market crash were bailed out so they wouldn't go bankrupt because

      their corporations were too big to allow to fail and bring down the U.S. and world economies even further;

- When Gov. Reagan ran for president, he promised to cut federal spending and taxes. However, as president:

    1. He employed Keynesian borrowing and economic stimulus spending for infrastructure repairs to bring the U.S. out of a recession caused by a stock-market crash because his administration didn't enforce banking and Wall Street regulations;

    2. He asked Congress to raise the debt ceiling twelve times; and

    3. Increased taxes six times by eliminating deductions people could take on tax returns. but no:

        a. They weren't tax-rate increases that took money out of pockets;

        b. They only reduced tax refunds to take money out of pockets;

        c. The worst deduction eliminated was interest on credit cards:

            1) Credit card interest deductions were intended to get people to borrow and buy more at stores to stimulate the economy;

            2) Then after Americans got hooked on spending more than they could afford by charging to credit cards;

            e) President Reagan took away credit card interest deductions;

- And according to the book by Chris Matthews of MSNBC, *Tip and the Gipper*, Republican President Ronald Reagan (Gipper) had no problem "compromising" with Democrat Sen. Tip O'Neil:

    1. However, Republicans in 2010-2016 believe "compromise" is a dirty word;

    2. Even though the Founding Fathers anticipated that "comprise" would solve or eliminate political disputes.

So I ask again: what's with the Republican love affair with Reagan? Why has every Republican legislator in Washington, D.C., from 2010 to 2016 claimed to be a Reagan Republican? Haven't Republicans during the last six years voted against everything that President Reagan would have done because President Obama is not just a Democrat but a Caucasian, Afro-American Democrat President?

Democratic President Bill Clinton

Republicans are elephants because they don't forget who hurt them. Still smarting from Democratic Senate Watergate and Iran Gate hearings, Republicans mercilessly tried to impeach President Clinton about real estate investments and lying about sex with Monica in the Oval Office.

News reporters in other countries (especially France and Italy) said world leaders laughed about Republican Senators going after President Clinton about sex. Why? Because many people want to become world leaders so they can have all the sex they want or can handle.

Republicans defeated President Clinton's efforts to get Affordable Health Care Insurance. They wanted there to be individual initiative or contribution by insureds. Republicans said that's why they opposed a national health insurance program. Ironically President Obama gave them their individual initiative, but Republicans still voted against the Affordable Health Care Act.

Nevertheless, even though Republicans tried to stop Clinton's every effort, Democratic President Clinton's economic plan led to low unemployment and something "balance the budget" Republicans have never done. He left Republican President G.W. Bush with a $400 billion budget surplus.

What Should Be Done with Budget Surpluses?

There have been two primary causes of depressions or recessions:

- After the Civil War, WWI, WWII, Korean War, Vietnam War, and Gulf War (Iraq I), discharge of soldiers, unemployment, and recession; or
- Lack of enforcing regulations or deregulation of Wall Street and banks caused banking and investing fraud, stock-market crashes, layoffs, depression, or recession.

As a result, starting with the end of the Civil War, the U.S. had economic depressions every twenty years. They're almost as predictable as earthquakes. California has an earthquake trust fund to rebuild without raising taxes.

When federal and state governments have budget surpluses they have four choices about what to do with surpluses:

1. Put surpluses into economic trust funds so during the next depression or recession, government workers don't have to be laid off to balance budgets and cause worsening of recession or depression;
2. Spend surplus to pay down budget deficits and pay off loans;
3. Give surplus back to taxpayers in the form of rebates and tax cuts;
4. Redistribute surplus to poor, working poor, and middle class by increasing social safety net benefits.

Trickle-Down Economics and Republican President G.W. Bush

There are good reasons why the *London Times* headline in November 2004 said, "How Could Americans be So Stupid?" to re-elect Republican President G.W. Bush. Instead of using Clinton's budget surplus to pay down the budget deficit, President Bush gave two tax cuts in order to get "One Percent Devils" campaign-contribution bribes so he would be re-elected.

After the 2008 stock-market crash caused by his administration's failure to properly regulate banks and brokers, President Bush and Republicans opposed:

- The Dodd-Frank Legislation to prevent another 2008-type stock-market crash and depression;
- Bailout of GM and Chrysler and saving a million U.S. jobs because they wanted to outsource production of U.S. cars to an atheistic Communist China;
- Bailout of banks and brokers who gave Republicans the most campaign-contribution bribes; and
- Keynesian borrowing and economic stimulus through infrastructure spending to put construction and industrial workers back to work; but
- There's no scientific evidence that 2001 and 2003 Bush tax cuts:
  1. Caused even one company to expand production capacity or build new production plants; or
  2. Resulted in the hiring of even one worker; and
  3. After Pope Francis said:
     a. "Trickle-down economics is a myth;" and
     b. There should be:

1) Redistribution of wealth from "One Percent Devils" to their victims who are poor, working poor, and middle class; and

2) Moral capitalism to prevent more victims...

How or why did Democrats, independents, preachers, and press allow Republicans to get away with "bearing false witness" or "uttering false reports" that Jesuit Priest Pope Francis is a communist because of that? Isn't that one of the most ludicrous Republican oxymoron for morons?

- Aren't Communists atheists who don't believe in a God?
- Isn't the Vatican a democracy?
- Doesn't the Vatican engage in capitalism?
- Isn't the Vatican in the middle of an Italian democracy?
- Isn't helping the poor and needy a Judeo-Christian commandment and soul-saving rule?

During the 2010, 2014, and 2016 campaigns, why didn't Democrat and independent politicians, preachers, and press remind Americans what deregulation under Republican Presidents Reagan and G.W. Bush caused?

**Republicans Don't Want to Leave National Debt
They Caused to Their Grandchildren = BS?**
Republicans fed the U.S. with BS propaganda that they cared so much about their grandchildren that they didn't want to leave them with the huge national debt Republicans caused by eliminating Democrat President Clinton's $400 billion budget surplus and funding two wars, not by raising taxes but by borrowing to pay for the wars from an atheistic Communist Chinese enemy. Ironically they cared so much about their grandchildren that they voted against things that would benefit their grandchildren, such as:

- Clean air, water, land, and food;
- Pre and postnatal care;
- Food stamps and school lunches;
- Medicaid and Affordable Care Act;

- Welfare and public housing for children; and
- Social safety nets for parents who were victims of crimes against humanity by "One Percent Devils and Their Satanic Tools;" and
- Federal funds for grade and high schools, college grants, and loans;

Back to Keynesian Economics, ala Democrat President Obama

After Republican President G.W. Bush's lack of regulation of Wall Street and banks caused the second -greatest stock-market crash and depression, Democratic President Obama employed Keynesian borrowing and economic stimulus to:

- Bail out U.S. auto industry and save millions of jobs even though Republicans wanted U.S. automakers to go bankrupt so Dracula and vulture capitalists like Republican presidential candidate Romney:
  1. Could bleed them dry of liquid assets;
  2. Chop them up into small companies; and
  3. Outsource a million U.S. jobs, production equipment, and technology to:
     a. An atheistic Communist Chinese enemy; and
     b. Third World nations;
     c. So their resources and labor can be exploited
- Bail out Wall Street and banks;
- Fund infrastructure of repairs of roads, bridges, airports, and rail lines;
- To usher in Affordable Care Act health-insurance program and expanded Medicaid to provide another thirty million Americans with health-insurance coverage to prevent bankruptcies and early deaths.
- And he signed legislation or presidential orders:
  1. To give women equal pay;
  2. To reduce student-loan interest and payments; and
  3. To raise minimum wage for federal employees and contractors.

One would think that industrialists, Wall Street, banks, and business-oriented Republicans would be happy with President Obama's achievements.

However, U.S. business is too greedy and wants more ill-gotten gain.

Republicans lambasted President Obama. They were psychotic or schizophrenic because he's a Caucasian Afro-American. Even though Caucasians have enslaved and abused Afro-Americans for four hundred years, they couldn't allow Afro-Americans to have even a half Afro-American president.

Even though Republicans caused the Second Great Depression in 2008, they voted against every Keynesian economic infrastructure proposal by President Obama, even though every one of those Republican congressional representatives and senators had dangerous roads and bridges that were in need of repair or replacement.

My Congressman, Republican Paul Ryan, was duplicitous. He voted against infrastructure spending and secretly wrote President Obama for infrastructure funds to pay off campaign contributors.

There's one simple reason why Republicans vote for Keynesian economic stimulus when a Republican is president and against it when a Democrat is in the White House. They know Keynesian stimulus works and don't want Democratic presidents to improve the economy so the next election they can falsely blame Democrats for a poor economy. Why?

Republicans aren't Judeo-Christian patriots. They don't comply with:

- Goals of Preamble, Enabling Clause, and Bill of Rights of Constitution;
- Commandments, Golden Rule and soul-saving rules; or
- Principles of legal equity, justice and human decency. Why?
- Republicans want to get rich by violating Commandments:
  1. "Thou shall not steal" via insider-trading information; and
  2. "Thou shall not take a bribe...;"
- Because for "One Percent Devils and Their Satanic Tools"...immoral ends always justify immoral means to immoral ends.

Why Do Victims of Republicans Vote Republican?

Why do victims of "One Percent Devils and Their Satanic Tools" vote Republican and against their own economic interests? When I drive around Walworth, Waukesha, Racine, and Rock counties, I'm amazed how many signs for Republican Governor Walker are on lawns of homes and farms that needed paint and other repairs. So did their cars and pickup trucks.

I asked farmers, why do you vote Republican when they vote against:

- Subsidies for biofuel made from grains but vote for subsidies to oil and gas companies?
- School breakfast and lunch as well as Meals on Wheels, which purchase food from local farmers? and
- Raising the minimum price farmers are paid for grains, milk, beef, pork, lamb, chicken, eggs, and produce?

Why not do those things for family farmers? Aren't they the most skilled and hardest workers in America?

- Don't farmers have education and training in:
  1. Horticulture to grow grains and vegetables;
  2. Animal science for cows, cattle, pigs, lambs, and chickens;
  3. Mechanics so they can fix tractors, combines, bailers, and trucks;
  4. Business administration and management?
- Don't farmers:
  1. Milk cows from 6 A.M. to 10 A.M. and 6 P.M. to 10 P.M.; and
  2. In between milking, don't they tend to crops, fixing machines, and business accounting, administration, and management, etc.?

Do you know family farmers who own two hundred acres of land and 150 milk cows only have a net income of twelve thousand dollars per year? Yet except for an hour for breakfast, lunch, and dinner, they work thirteen hours a day from 6 A.M. to 10 P.M. They work seven days a week and 365 days — or 3,650 hour per year.

Divide 3,650 into twelve thousand dollars. Thus family farmers earn $2.52 per hour.

Why won't Republicans allow farmers to earn a minimum wage of $7.50 per hour (or $15 per hour if Republicans had allowed minimum wage to rise with inflation during the last forty years)? Why are family farmers forced to live on less than half of what's considered poverty level?

When there's a drought (as in 2013), grain production was down and farmers got $7.50 per bushel for corn, but many farmers had little or no net income. In 2014 unusually high rainfall caused bumper crops, and farmers got $3.25 per bushel and were financially worse off.

In both years, they had to borrow money to buy seed and fuel. They paid $4 per gallon for gas to run pickup trucks, trackers, and combines. Since fertilizer is made from oil, it costs more when gas prices are high.

The prices of grain, milk, and eggs rose fast during the 2013 drought. Why didn't prices fall as fast and far with the 2014 bumper crops?

When I drove through a trailer park, some owners had Republican Scott Walker signs. I asked those who were outside what they did for a living. Their only source of income was Social Security retirement or disability, and they were on Medicare. Yet don't Republicans like Wisconsin Gov. Walker want to eliminate all social safety nets?

Walker signs were in front of homes with for-sale signs. One home was owned by a couple who were teachers and laid off due to Gov. Walker's cuts of state funds for schools. Other similar homes were owned by state troopers and sheriff and police officers who were laid off after Walker's cuts.

Those farmers, teachers, and law officers had two thing in common:
- They fall for racial, religious, cultural, and gender bias, prejudice, and intolerance Wedge-Issue Tactics; and
- Believe "Satanic Tools:" Republicans, Rush Limbaugh, and Fox News.

CHAPTER V

First Amendment Freedom of Religion Is for Suppression of Sex, Females, Gay/Lesbian, Racial, and Religious Minorities?

Freedom of religion isn't only a Roman Catholic or evangelical right. England's King George and archbishop of the Protestant Church of England reciprocally supported each other in war and suppression of Irish, Scottish, and English Roman Catholics, as well as sex. Puritan Founding Fathers and Mothers risked their lives crossing the Atlantic Ocean to escape church sex patrols looking to arrest couples who sounded like they were having fun during sex in violation of St. Augustine's "Rules against Sex." Eventually those rules would become known as Victorian morality. An English lord and author wrote in 1903, "It's still illegal to write about people having fun during sex."

The First Amendment says "Congress shall make no law respecting an establishment of religion, or prohibiting the free exercise thereof." The Fourteenth Amendment says, "No state shall make or enforce any law which shall abridge the privileges or immunities of citizens of the United States..."

The First and Fourteenth amendments create "separation of church and state." Federal, state, and municipal governments aren't permitted to advocate one religion over another. Thus the U.S. Supreme Court has found the following activities are unconstitutional, especially in a multireligious faith nation:

- Teachers having students recite of a Judeo-Christian "Lord's Prayer" and Christmas nativity-scene plays; and

- County courthouse yards displaying the Ten Commandments or Christmas nativity scenes; or
- If Jewish teachers explain Jewish holidays but the class contains Hindu, Sikh, Buddhist, and/or Christian students, those teachers are obligated to have people from those faiths explain their religious holidays.

It's axiomatic if federal and state governments can't advocate Protestant or Evangelical Judeo-Christianity, then they can't force on people of other religions Roman Catholic and Evangelical:

- Mores, such as St. Augustine's "Rules against Sex";
- Mores against contraceptives and abortion;
- Mores against alcohol and marijuana;
- Mores against gambling and prostitution.

In the 1600s and 1700s, every port from Boston to New Orleans had taverns for alcohol, smoking, and gambling, as well as houses of pleasure. Many wives who were captured by American Indians didn't want to go back to their husbands because Indians were natural-law, human-instinctive lovers. American Indians in the Southwest smoked locoweed for enlightenment.

From 1830 to the 1950s, major cities and villages of a few thousand throughout the Midwest had whorehouses and gambling saloons. In the last half of the 1800s, in every gold and silver mining city were whorehouses and gambling saloons. St. Louis and San Francisco had many opium dens, whorehouses and gambling saloons.

Sigmund Freud used heroin and treated psychiatric patients with it to discover many theories of human behavior that haven't been refuted. Heroin was also the drug of choice of high society.

Judeo-Christian preachers and priests began to preach against God-given natural law human instincts and inclination to gamble, buy sex, sell sex, and self medicate with alcohol, heroin, and marijuana. They preached against it because preachers and priests didn't want people to achieve happiness. They wanted people to be miserable and go to church to pray for relief, happiness, and to put 10 percent of what they earned in offering baskets.

In 1919 they succeeded in passing the Eighteenth Amendment banning manufacture, sale, transportation, importation, and exportation of intoxicating liquors. However, as with every market-driven product, when demand exceeds supply, people will find a way to get it.

The "Roaring 20s" saw development of underground speakeasies where people could drink alcohol, dance, and gamble. That fostered development of organized crime groups controlled by Italians, Irish, and Jews who had been discriminated against and abused by Protestants.

In hard-core Republican Walworth County (the Southern Lakes region of Wisconsin, an hour from Chicago):

- Machine Gun Kelly was killed in Fontana Bay of Lake Geneva;
- Baby Face Nelson was killed in Buttons Bay of Lake Geneva;
- Al Capone and his gang had cottages in Williams Bay, LG; and
- On the other side of Geneva Ridge, Bugs Moran and his crew had cottages or stayed at the French Country Inn on Lake Como.

Legend of the Flying Fish of Lake Como
Before WWI Mother's mother and grandparents immigrated to Chicago from Pilsen, Czechoslovakia, where the Modrey family owned a brewery, tavern, inn, and hotel. When I was five years old, Grandpa Modrey told a story about "The Jumping Fish of Lake Como." I had seen trout and salmon jumping out west, but there were no such fish in Lake Como, and I never saw any jump.

In August 2012, I knew Jim Kirsh, who ran Kirsh's, a five-star French-American restaurant on Lake Como next to the French Country Inn. He said Bugs Moran's daughter married the owner of the restaurant, which operated as a speakeasy (gambling, alcohol, and prostitution) during Prohibition. The rich and famous industrialists and financiers of Chicago bribed officials to build a railroad line from Chicago to the door step of the inn and restaurant.

The first time federal revenuers tried to bust the speakeasy, the owner received a warning from local police or the sheriff's office. So as federal agents approached in Model Ts from three directions, there was time to throw gambling equipment and booze into Lake Como.

From that day on, there was no need for informants in law enforcement. Every time Model Ts came down the three roads at the same time, the fish of Lake Como began jumping out of the water because the first time booze was thrown into the five-foot-deep lake, fish got drunk and wanted to get drunk again. To this day you can walk into the lake and find gambling chips, equipment, and alcohol bottles.

How Marijuana Became Illegal and More Mafia

When I studied film at the University of Wisconsin, the class saw some of the most disgusting propaganda films of the Great Depression. As with the Second Great Depression (starting in 2008), Caucasians in Arizona wanted a means to send Mexicans back to Mexico because they were willing to work for less money. So religious leaders and the federal government created disgusting, false-scare tactic movies showing Mexicans getting high on marijuana and then raping Caucasian women or committing arson, robberies, and murders of Caucasians, even though those are crimes committed when people are drunk and not when they experience the four H's of marijuana (happiness, hilarity, horniness, and hunger). That's why 75 percent of senior citizens want marijuana to be legal again. The movies were pure racism.

Religious leaders and Republicans didn't learn the lesson of Prohibition. Now instead of Prohibition fostering Italian mafia (aka La Cosa Nostra) with illegalization of marijuana, heroin, and cocaine, the U.S. now has Russian, Ukrainian, Korean, Chinese, Japanese, and Columbian mafias and more corruption by law enforcement, prosecutors and judges. Why?

Republicans Encourage and Benefit from
Religious Leaders Who Violate Separation of Church and State

The U.S. Supreme Court has only enforced separation of church and state on governmental entities. It has not stopped Judeo-Christian preachers and press from crossing that line to get governments to legislate religious, narrow-minded mores for Prohibition of victimless crimes such as:

- Alcohol;
- Heroin, cocaine, and marijuana;
- Gambling; and
- Prostitution.

Even though laws banning those activities violate:

- Natural-law rights based on God-given human instincts and inclinations;
- Natural law unalienable rights set forth in the Declaration of Independence of life, liberty, and the pursuit of happiness.

Those activities were legal from the dawn of humanity and for 150 years after the U.S. Constitution and First Amendment were adopted by the Founding Fathers. In the final analysis, instead of discouraging or ending those activities, those laws have created fertile territory for organized crime to exploit natural law human instincts and inclinations. That has caused:

- Massive bribes and other corruptions of criminal justice systems;
- Extensive, violent turf wars between competing mafias;
- Extensive thefts and prostitution to pay for illegal drugs;
- Law abiding, taxpaying citizens to be turned into criminals; and
- Creation of criminal subcultures to protect supplier and consumers.

Far more crime and harm to society has resulted from banning those activities. It would be better to legalize all those activities again, regulate them for public safety, make them taxable events that could balance government budgets, and allow American farmers to earn a decent living farming and selling marijuana.

St. Augustine's "Rules against Sex"
"One can't be sexual and spiritual, so priests and nuns can no longer marry. Sex is only for procreation, so masturbation, premarital sex, contraception, and sex for fun are sins that lead to a sinful life and hell."

However, not long after the Roman Catholic Church adopted those rules, public outcry was so great that in order to prevent revolution, popes, cardinals, bishops and priests set up whorehouses for pedophiles, heterosexuals, and homosexuals (as indicated in a History Channel series).

Research shows God-given DNA that predisposes some to become gay or lesbian. Thus, contrary to Republican dogma, they have no choice as to who they are and how they act as homosexuals.

In violation of the Fourteenth Amendment provision that "No state shall make or enforce any law which shall abridge their privileges and immunities...

nor deny to any person within its jurisdiction the equal protection of the laws," Republicans have extended St. Augustine's "Rules against Sex" to ban rights of a minority group of homosexual or homosexual class by federal and state statues preventing homosexual couples from:

- Engaging in homosexual sex;
- Having same-sex marriages;
- Adopting children;
- Equal rights for gay and lesbian couples to:
    + Inherit from each other;
    + Make medical treatment decisions for each other; and
    + Share one another's medical insurance coverage.

How Can "Rules against Sex" and Laws against homosexuals Be Considered Moral and Constitutional?

How can St. Augustine's "Rules against Sex" and laws against homosexuals be moral or constitutional when:

- One believes God created everyone, including homosexuals, who are predetermined to be gay or lesbian by God-given DNA;
- God-given natural law based upon God-given human instincts and inclinations cannot be controlled by laws;
- Those rules and laws create identity crises and dozens of psychiatric and physical sexual disorders;
- Those laws and rules violate goals of Preamble of Constitution:
    + "In order to form a more perfect Union" (of hetero and homosexuals);
    + "Establish Justice" (for homosexuals and heterosexuals);
    + "Insure Domestic Tranquility" (of hetero and homosexuals);
    + "Promote the General Welfare" (of homo and heterosexuals);
    + "And Secure Blessings of Liberty" for gays and lesbians.

Won't Population Control via contraceptives and Abortion Achieve Goals of Constitution and Reduce Crimes of Theft

Knowing contraception and abortion were constitutional rights, Republicans tried to pass an amendment to eliminate those rights. During the forty years since, antiabortion and anticontraception Republican campaign platforms have continued. It appeared or I thought Republicans really were not against contraception or abortion and never expected to obtain amendments banning them. I thought they were on platforms just to sucker evangelicals and Roman Catholics to vote Republican and against their own economic and social interest.

However, from 2010 to present, Republicans in Washington, D.C., and state houses have either been intellectually dishonest or didn't know that state law can't supersede constitutional law. Yet they passed more federal and state statutes to restrict access to abortion and contraceptives.

Yes, those allegedly budget-conscious Republicans passed laws knowing they were unconstitutional and that attorney generals would waste millions of dollars in court defending and ultimately losing by being told by a federal court that state and federal statutes cannot override the U.S. Constitution and constitutional case law.

In the early 1970s, population experts said, on average American couples should only have 2.5 children to prevent overpopulation that would exhaust food and natural resources and lead to rebellions and wars. Again therefore from the early 1970s to elections in 2010, I believed Republicans didn't want to end contraception or abortion but were merely against those constitutional rights to con votes from evangelicals and Roman Catholics.

During the 2012 presidential campaign, Rick Santorum and Michele Bachmann repeated St. Augustine's "Rule against Sex." I wondered if they had any knowledge about the fact that those rules have caused dozens of psychiatric and physiological abnormalities. Bachmann's husband has a "Pray Away the Gay" treatment program the American Medical Association and American Psychiatric Association found causes psychiatric damage.

After I listened to the soft voice of Michelle Bachmann's husband and saw how he danced, I wondered: Is he a closet homosexual; is she a closet lesbian; and do they adopt children because they don't want to have sex with each other to procreate? What about Rick Santorum and my Congressman, Paul Ryan, who supported unconstitutional bills to ban contraceptives and abortion?

Yet Ryan and Santorum only have a few children. I reviewed "The History of Whately, Mass 1661 – 1899" and Grandma Lydia Little Smith Woods's "Daughter of the American Revolution Diary" shows that of thirteen pre-American Revolution Puritan colonial ancestral grandparents

(Waite, Smith, Dickerson, Little, Kellogg, Hurd, Russell, Clinton, Morison, Johnson, Hamilton, Putman, and Pullman), for two centuries almost every generation of ancestral parents had ten to fifteen children.

However, I have yet to see any Republican president, Supreme Court justice, U.S. senator, representative, state governor, and/or legislator who votes, would vote, or would sign legislation to ban contraception and abortion, who has ten to fifteen children. Therefore, I must ask questions.

How can Republicans be morally against:

- Contraception or abortion; and
- Welfare, Medicaid, food stamps, school lunches, and public housing for unwed, uneducated, unemployed moms or children?

Are Republicans homosexuals, impotent, or use contraceptives and abortion? Have they gotten abortions after rape, incest, when tests revealed fetuses were defective, or their illicit lovers got pregnant? Don't they enjoy frequent sex? Maybe they don't know how to achieve orgasm and are frustrated by unsatisfying sex?

What if Republicans reply, "I don't have many children because my wife and I use rhythm, and I don't mean music during sex?" *Taber's Cyclopedic Medical Dictionary* says rhythm is a means of contraception.

How about my congressman, Paul Ryan, who has drafted legislation to ban contraceptives and abortion. He only has two children. Maybe that's because he doesn't take his wife and kids to live in Washington, D.C.

Now that's interesting. Every time I saw him give a speech with his children and wife present, she looked very unhappy. Is that because she isn't getting enough or any sex?

Then we see photographs of Ryan jogging and pumping iron in the congressional gym. Running and lifting weights causes body to produce testosterone, which increases libido. So who is he working out for and having sex with? A blonde secretary who can't type, like Senator Wilbur Mills's secretary? Does Ryan use brothels on K Street or have a homosexual lover?

No, I am not going too far. Ryan opened the can of worms when he stuck his big nose between women's legs. As President Truman would say to Ryan, "If you can't stand the heat, get out of the kitchen."

If Republicans are so budget conscious, why would they waste many millions of taxpayer dollars legislating state and federal bills to ban abortion and contraceptives, knowing federal courts will strike them? Is that because Republican plans to control the White House, Senate, House, Supreme Court, state legislatures, governors and state supreme courts will eventually succeed?

Since Republicans also want to end social safety nets, other questions need to be answered. What would happen to millions of unwed, uneducated American girls and women who would be forced to get pregnant and bear children if contraceptives and abortion is outlawed and social safety nets are eliminated?

President Obama's and Jimmy Fallon's Skit on Anti-Contraceptives
In summer 2012, I wrote President Obama and said, "Sometimes the best ways to address illogical, immoral, and ludicrous political propaganda is to make fun of its purveyors. Why don't you go on Jimmy Fallon's show with the following skit.

"Mr. President, what is your position on Republican men and women who vote to ban contraceptives?" asks Jimmy Fallon.

"My position is evolving," says President Obama.

"Has your position on same-sex marriage evolved? Didn't Robin Williams, when he ran for president in the movie *Man of the Year* say, 'Everyone who's been married knows sex is always the same.'"

"Michelle would disagree. We 'know' all thirty-two Kama Sutra positions."

"Is your opinion about Republican men and women who are against contraceptives evolving?" asks Jimmy Fallon.

President Obama says, "Some staffers believe Republicans espouse St. Augustine's 'Rules against Sex,' especially contraceptives, for several psychsocio reasons:

- Limp-Dick Republican men have low T (low testosterone);
- Republican guys are physically and/or psychologically impotent and Republican gals are frigid due to Augustine's 'Rules against Sex';
- Republican men are premature ejaculators who leave wives and lovers hanging and unsatisfied; or
- Republican men don't know the seven signs and eleven indications of Kama Sutra, so they can't bring a wife or lover to orgasm;

- Republican men have teeny weenies and don't know how to use them, so wives and illicit lovers don't want to do it;
- Republican guys are too rough and hurt and turn off Republican gals;
- Sour grapes because Republican guys and gals can't find someone with whom they can have sex, so they want to punish others who can have sex by eliminating contraceptives and abortion;
- Republicans are mean-spirited, have no personality or sense of humor and so unattractive no one wants to have sex with them."

"Do others on your staff have non-psycho-socio reasons for opposing contraceptives and abortions?" asks Fallon.

President Obama says, "Other staffers with economic reasons say:

- Republican gals want to ban contraceptives and abortion to get girls and women out of the workforce because Republican women are jealous about the social status and financial independence of single and married career gals who don't have to beg a husband for spending money;
- Republican men want to ban contraceptive and abortion and end all social safety nets:
  1. So all married women in the workforce get pregnant, lose jobs, and are forced to become housewife/mothers;
  2. So all unmarried girls and women in the workforce get pregnant, lose jobs, are forced into marriage, and are home barefoot, pregnant, and under financial control of husbands who beats them with impunity;
  3. So men in the workforce don't have to compete with women for jobs, pay increases, bonuses, and promotions.
- That's why Republican wife-beater men oppose spousal-abuse laws and equal pay for women doing the same jobs as men."

"Housewives/moms work from 6 A.M. to 10 P.M. without help from husbands who come home from work, demand a beer, and watch television. Housewives/moms are jacks-of-all-trades: horticulturists, gardeners and canners of vegetables, fruits, and jams; butchers, bakers, and candlestick makers; nutritionists and gourmet cooks; seamstresses who make and repair cloths; interior decorators; and nurses and therapists" says Jimmy Fallon.

Obama says, "Yes! Shouldn't husbands be required to pay housewives /moms fair market value for those services, such as twenty dollars per hour for fourteen-hour days?"

"What about Congressman Assi, I mean Issa or Issi? Is he frigid? He didn't invite one girl or woman to testify at hearings on contraceptives."

"Over 50 percent of the population is female. It was gender discrimination not to call even one women as a witness. It was immoral to hold hearings on eliminating contraception and social safety nets for pregnant women."

"Did your female staffers comment about the five religious leaders who Assi called to testify?" asked Fallon.

President Obama laughs. "One said, 'Those religious leaders were so unattractive, goofy looking, unappealing, and physically weak, who on earth would want to have sex with them.' Another staffer said, 'They're natural contraceptives.' Everyone agreed that it was immoral for Assi not to call Sandra Fluke, a Georgetown law student who wanted to testify about the life-saving benefits of contraceptives, such as the prevention of cancer or control of other diseases."

"Any comments about Rush Limbaugh accusing Sandra Fluke of being a whore who wanted free contraceptives from the Affordable Care Act?"

"One staffer said, 'Fluke should sue Limbaugh for slander.' Another said, 'That drug-addicted, sexually abusive, four-time marital loser was probably married to wives who didn't want to have sex with him and used contraceptives so as not to procreate idiot sons who would take after him.' Everyone agrees St. Augustine's 'Rules against Sex' can't be found in the Old or New Testaments of Bible."

Fallon asks, "Did anyone on your staff comment about Congressman Pat Robertson's statement, 'If women can't control their libido, the Affordable Care Act shouldn't pay for contraceptives?'"

"One staffer said, 'Is it morally right that guys can buy inexpensive condoms but gals shouldn't get financial assistance to pay for expensive contraceptives?' Another staffer asked, 'Is it moral for "One Percent Devils" to get rich turning people onto products with sexual advertising and then bribing "their Satanic Tools" to ban contraceptives and abortion?'

"However, the most convincing argument against such laws was that the 'libido is based upon God-given natural law human instincts to mate. It's stronger in men because their bodies produce more testosterone. Maybe Assi, Limbaugh, Robertson, or other Republicans are abnormal and never had a wet dream or awoke with an erection. St. Augustine's 'Rules against Sex' are the cause of pedophilia, incest, forcible rape, and rape by false pretence of love to get sex. Women have a right to protect themselves from pregnancy, venereal disease, HIV, and AIDs. The cost for insurance companies is much less for contraceptive preventions than for treatment of those diseases. If those diseases cause death, life insurance companies must pay out. If women leave children behind, then welfare and Medicaid must support them. Of course Republicans want to end Medicare and welfare. If they succeed, what happens to those children?" says Obama.

"What about the Roberts's court holding that corporations are persons who have First Amendment freedom-of-religion rights not to have health insurance pay for contraception?" asks Fallon.

"Since when is freedom of speech more important than physical freedom and pursuit of happiness? The First Amendment bars Congress from establishing a religion or prohibiting free exercise of it. If government can't establish a religion, it's axiomatic that government can't establish mores of a religion. Congress or the court can't impose Roman Catholic/evangelical mores banning contraception on Lutherans, Methodists, Baptists, Muslims, Jews, Hindus, Buddhists, or atheists.

"Corporations as 'persons' is a legal fiction created by the Supreme Court to allow income taxation of corporations. Corporations can say anything they want. However, they can't constitutionally or morally impose their Roman Catholic or evangelical mores on their own employees.

"Roberts's Court was doing what Republicans falsely accused the Warren Court of doing. Roberts's Court wasn't interpreting the Constitution and its case law. It was violating separation of powers by legislating religious mores.

"Warren Court decisions on contraceptives and abortions were unanimous and included Republican, Democrat, and independent justices. In 1968 and 1972, the Warren Court held that contraceptives and abortion are constitutional. A home is every couple's castle and under 'The Penumbra' of the Constitution and Bill of Rights, there's a right of privacy in the bedroom.

"If Republicans don't agree that contraceptives and abortion are constitutional rights, why have Republicans tried to get constitutional amendments to ban abortion and contraceptives? Under the Fourteenth

Amendment, how could they fathom passing such state laws would be constitutional?

"The fact that the Roberts's Court decisions on contraceptives and abortion were 5-4 decisions means four justices disagreed with Roberts's decisions and four agreed with the Warren Court."

How Does Exodus 22 Apply to Women's Rights?

Moses said that God gave him the Commandments. Thus God said, "If a man seduces a virgin who is not married, he must marry her."

How about Rape by False Pretense?

Why does society believe it's moral for "boys to sew their wild oats" and girls to get stuck with baby seeds? What if a Judeo-Christian Republican boy or man says to a virgin, "I love you and want to make love, but my religion bans condoms." Girl or women is overwhelmed, and they have sex. However, after girl or woman gets pregnant, boy or man says, "I won't marry you or help rear, raise, or support the baby?"

Isn't that rape by false pretense? A Golden Rule says, "Do unto others as you would have others do unto you."

Shouldn't Republican males treat females the way they'd want to be treated if they were females? Shouldn't Republicans who claim to represent "the Moral Majority" and "Family Values" honor the Golden Rule by making it the law of the land to require that boys or men marry their victims?

They say, "An ounce of prevention, is worth more than a pound of cure." If there's no law requiring males to marry their victims of rape by false pretense, shouldn't females be allowed to protect themselves and prevent pregnancy before marriage?

Shouldn't females be allowed to use contraceptives to prevent pregnancy due to forcible rape and incest? Hasn't "civilization" banned incest because Egyptian pharaohs and European kings married sisters and first cousins who procreated defective babies?

Yet could you believe that idiotic Indiana Republican senatorial candidate who said, "It is God's plan that women get pregnant from rape or incest"?

Where in the Old Testament Torah and New Testament is there anything about God having a specific plan of life for seven billion citizens of earth? A plan as to when everyone is conceived, gets sick, hurt, violently raped, raped by incest, rape by false pretense, killed, or dies?

In "Theory of Law," St. Thomas Aquinas said that God's plan for mankind was a utopia or heaven on earth free of war and crime. God gave humans the existential choice of doing good or evil and gave criminal justice systems to punish wrongdoers.

Shouldn't contraceptives be allowed to prevent overpopulation that leads to starvation, disease, death, and war to get land to produce food? Aren't contraceptives more moral than the Chinese solution to overpopulation? Couples are only permitted one child, and if another is born, it is drowned in a river or bathtub or suffocated to death.

Shouldn't females who get pregnant due to incest, rape, or rape by false pretense be permitted to have an abortion, especially when females are unwed, uneducated, and cannot financially support a baby and raise it alone?

Isn't it unconscionable and immoral for Republicans to try to eliminate:

- Contraceptives, abortions; and
- Social safety nets (welfare, Medicaid, public housing, food stamps and school lunches) for unwed uneducated mothers and children?

When pregnant girls are not emotionally equipped to raise a baby, shouldn't abortion be permitted? If a pregnant women doesn't know how to raise and discipline or isn't inclined to discipline and raise a child to be a law abiding and productive member of society, should they be allowed to use contraceptives and have abortions?

Don't criminology studies reveal a primary cause of crime by teenagers is single parents who aren't emotionally equipped or inclined to raise and discipline children? Isn't it unconscionable for Republicans to eliminate contraception and abortion under those circumstances and claim to be the "Law and Order" Party that wants to prevent crime?

Aren't execution-for-murder laws immorally unconscionable when each murder represents a societal socialization breakdown and failure by parents, peers, preachers, teachers, and government? How can Republicans be against contraceptives, abortions, and social safety nets for mothers, children, and teenagers but are for killing them in war and by executions?

After Premarital Sex Causes Pregnancy,
Why Should Females Bear Total Responsibility for Raising Baby?
How do we apply principles of legal equity and gender equality? If parents aren't married, wouldn't it be in the best interest of children for:

- Sons to be raised by a man, his father; and
- Daughters to be raised by a woman, her mother;
- Unless one parent is unfit to be a parent.

Wouldn't the risk of a mother losing a baby boy to his father prompt her to be married before giving birth or to use contraception? Wouldn't that prompt boys and men who don't want to risk being stuck raising a boy or identical twin boys to wear condoms or get their tubes tied?

Yet Republicans don't call for a ban on the sale of Trojans. Is it fair or moral then for Republicans only to want to ban contraceptives for women?

Why Should Republican Women be against
Making Roman Catholic Sexual Mores the Law of the Land?
By 2030 Caucasians will no longer be in the majority. They will be a minority. Caucasian Republican men could form a coalition with Mormon, Muslim, Hindu, Sikh, Buddhist, and Jewish men to vote for legislators who will make polygamy the law of the land so they can have more than one wife. They could pass laws allowing stoning of a wife for adultery.

Under the "Satanic Tool" Supreme Court's rationale, laws could be passed to castrate and amputate the family jewels of homosexuals. As to lesbians, their clitoris could be amputated and vagina sewn shut (as some Muslims in Africa do to girls).

So that brings us back to a Golden Rule, which I shall massage: "Do unto others what you would have others to do unto you" if you were in their shoes and vice versa. Bottom line, plain and simple: The First Amendment bans the establishment of a religion and/or mores of a religion.

Why Should Unwed Mothers Bear the Whole Burden?
If a boy or man can't use a condom due to religious beliefs or doesn't want to because sex feels better without one, shouldn't the law have options?

- If a daughter is conceived, mother gets custody; and
- If a son is procreated, the father gets custody; or
- If father declines to marry the woman, shouldn't there be the equivalent of one-bite laws for dogs? If a boy or man knocks up and doesn't marry the girl or woman, the next time he does the same, give him an option:
  1. Life in prison or until he becomes impotent; or
  2. Castrate testicles and amputate penis.

However, if executions don't deter murders better than imprisonment, would amputations deter others from committing rape by false pretense?

Constitutional Amendment to End Antiabortion Debate

"If you vote to ban abortions, put your Social Security number next to your vote. If you vote to ban abortions, you will be required to adopt the next available baby, regardless of its race, religion, gender, or disability."

In other words, Republicans, "put your money where your mouth is." I suspect racial, religious, and gender intolerant Republicans who are against social safety nets for the disabled would vote against that amendment.

Amendment for Corporate Contraception Exclusions

"Corporations that exclude contraception from health insurance coverage shall be required to:

- "Continue paying pregnant worker's income during maternity leave:
  1. During the last three to six months of pregnancy; and
  2. For six months following delivery;
- "Pay for cost of childcare facilities for babies of female workers so they can continue working; or
- "For women who need to stay home to care for and raise babies because of birth defects, the corporation shall pay:
  1. Child support to cover cost of raising child with defects; and
  2. Continue paying the former worker's income; and
  3. If mother doesn't want to rear and raise babies and children, the CEO and Board of Directors shall either:
     a. Adopt those babies; or

b. Pay child support to surrogate, adopting, and/or foster parents."

In other words, for both proposed amendments, if corporate leaders want to impose St. Augustine's "Rules against Sex" on women who don't believe in those rules, again, "put your money where your mouth is."

Whether married or single, racial, religious, and gender prejudiced Republicans who oppose welfare, Medicaid, food stamps, school lunches, and education assistance would not vote for such amendment. Debate over!

After the Warren Court ruled that contraceptives and abortions are constitutional, didn't Republican White House cabinet member Milt Freedman say about the pope's opposition, "He no playa da game? He no maka da rules."

In spring 2012, I wrote to President Obama, "The U.S. has over eleven million illegal Roman Catholic, Latin-American immigrants because popes banned contraceptives. Why not ask the pope the following questions:

'Would you rather permit contraceptives or cause overpopulation worldwide and application of the Chinese solution in every nation? (Couples can only have one child. Subsequent babies are suffocated or drowned by the billions.)'

'Would you rather have billions of people die from starvation, disease, and war due to overpopulation or endorse contraceptives to prevent overpopulation? Is it better to allow abortions to prevent unwanted babies whom unwed, uneducated mothers are not equipped or inclined to raise to be law abiding citizens and cause them to become thieves, murderers, and drug dealers? Would you rather have millions die from illegal abortions?'"

Perhaps President Obama sent such a message to Jesuit Pope Francis and that's why he advised priests to ease off on preaching sexual mores and to preach about moral capitalism and redistribution of wealth.

Motives for St. Augustine's "Rules against Sex" and Why and How Moses Set the Stage for Those Rules.

Doesn't the commandment "honor thy father and thy mother" require us to honor religious beliefs of ancestors? Pagans such as Indian Vedas, European Celts, and Hebrews believed there were two paths to heaven: death in battle for the War God and sex brought couples closer to God, godliness and heaven. Perhaps that's why couples shout "Oh God, Oh God"?

Pagans believed the Creator God was a female God who had more power than her husband God. Every pagan woman was La Sacre Femme (The Sacred Feminine) because the female Creator cloned Adam and Eve and women bear girls and boys in God's image.

In pagan Celtic Europe, women could be priestesses, high priestesses, herbal doctors, surgeons, mediators, judges, and warrior queens. Celtic women had equal rights with men. They went to school with boys, could vote, inherit, buy and sell property, and were free to engage in premarital sex and pick their mates. In *The Ancient World of the Celts*, Peter Ellis wrote, "The Romans seemed preoccupied with the 'liberated' attitude of the early Celts. Dio Cassius commented on the fact that Empress Julia Augusta criticized what she saw as a lack of morals in the way Celtic women were free to chose their husbands and lovers but did so openly without subterfuge.

"The object of her criticism was the wife of a north British chieftain named Argentocoxos. The encounter took place early in the third century A.D. According to Dio Cassius, the wife of Argentocoxos turned to the empress and replied with dignity, 'We Celtic women obey the demands of nature in a more moral way than the women of Rome. We consort openly with the best men, but you of Rome allow yourselves to be debauched in secret by the vilest.'"

That's consistent with God-given natural law human instincts and inclinations. Celtic women were also fiercer warriors than men. Ellis quoted Ammianus Marcellinus, who wrote, "A whole troop of foreigners would not be able to withstand a single Celt if he called his wife to his assistance. The wife is even more formidable. She is usually very tall, strong, and has blue eyes. In a rage, her neck veins swell. She gnashes her teeth and brandishes her snow-white, robust arms. She begins to strike blows mingled with kicks, as if they were so many missiles sent from the strings of a catapult."

The Ancient World of the Celts relates examples about combat skills and triumphs of warrior queens. Women were fiercer warriors and warrior queens than men and kings because their natural law human instincts to protect husband, children, family, and community had evolved to a higher level than in men. However, Celtic women weren't inclined to vote for war to loot, rape, and/or conquer land.

Pagan Roman Emperor Constantine feared that if he went to war against pagan Celts, the War God may favor the Celts. Constantine didn't order pagan Romans to convert to Judaism because their God allowed pagan Babylonians to drive the Twelve Tribes of Israel from Israel. Constantine wanted his warriors to follow another God.

At the time there were two philosophies about Jesus Christ. Agnostic Christians believed Jesus was a mortal man, faith healer, prophet of love and peace, and savior of souls. Other Christians wanted Christ to be a warrior king who warriors would follow into wars to loot and conquer land.

Constantine wanted his troops to follow a warrior king to defeat the Celts. He ordered religious leaders from around the Mediterranean to travel to Nicaea to put together the New Testament. The Nicene Counsel of A.D. 325 was heavily weighted in favor of male-chauvinistic, warrior-king advocates.

As indicated in Dan Brown's book and movie *The Da Vinci Code*, they didn't include in the New Testament the books of Philip, Thomas, and Mary Magdalene because those books talked about Christ's marriage to Mary Magdalene, their daughter, Sarah, and that Jesus wanted Mary Magdalene to lead his followers after his death. Decades after the Nicene Council, St. Augustine "uttered a false report" that Mary Magdalene was a prostitute.

After Constantine ordered pagan Romans to convert to Christianity, he had the same problem as Moses when he descended Mt. Sinai with commandments and found pagan Hebrews engaged in ritual La Sacre Femme sex in front of a golden calf of fertility. Moses ordered two thousand of the men to be slain.

Under legal philosophers, whether Fuller or Hart, that violated morality of law. A law cannot be morally enforced until after it is published so everyone knows about it. Those who violate that law before it is published cannot morally be punished.

So after Emperor Constantine found Romans worshiping pagan gods, he took a page out of Exodus and had two thousand Roman men put to the sword.

Dan Brown's *The Da Vinci Code* book and movie says Mary Magdalene fled to southern France, where Christ's daughter, Sarah, was delivered. Sarah Christ married into the Merovingian family. Her descendants married into royal families and turned the Merovingian family into a dynasty.

European royalty married Sarah's descendants because Jesus and Mary Magdalene were descendants of King David. Since God gave King David sovereign or divine power, Jesus and Mary inherited that power. So any descendant king had God's permission to go to war and violate half the 10 Commandments via killing, looting, raping, conquering, and enslaving.

That's why King John said to the English barons, "I didn't make myself king, God did." (See the movie *Robin Hood* staring Russell Crowe.)

Four hundred years after Sarah Christ, her descendant, pagan Celt Clovis, king of the Franks (of northern France), promised his Christian wife, Chothilde, that if he defeated the Germanic tribes, he would convert to Christianity. After King Clovis defeated the Germanic tribes, German officers promised to convert to Christianity. However, Clovis caught them worshiping Celtic gods and chopped off the heads of two thousand. (See *Atlas of World Military History* by Richard Brooks.)

Pagan Viking King Olaf had the same problem as Emperor Constantine. Would the War God favor him or the Viking clans he wanted to conquer. He saw Christianity as a means to unite Viking clans.

He ordered his subjects to convert to Christianity but found his subjects worshipping pagan Celtic gods. So like Moses, Constantine, and Clovis, Olaf also had two thousand put to the sword.

Evil Triads of War
King/President/Dictator

Military Industrial Complex

Priests, preachers, and clerics who preach war or don't preach against it

The reason Moses, Constantine, and kings converted pagans to Judaism or Judeo-Christianity was to dethrone La Sacre Femme so women couldn't:

- Vote against wars to loot, rape, and conquer;
- Inherit, buy, or sell property;
- Learn to become priests, doctors, mediators, or warrior queens; or
- Warriors who fought side-by-side with husbands; and

- So fathers could sell daughters into legalized marital prostitution slavery to procreate warrior sons and daughters to be sold at age thirteen before fully grown and able to defend themselves against husbands.

St. Augustine aided and abetted by writing "Rules against Sex" to psychologically and physically turn off girls and women to sex. After all, prostitutes don't have to be turned on to have sex and procreate. Slavery, male polygamy, and that only the eldest son could inherit an estate or kingdom was endorsed by commandments in Exodus.

Other sons who wanted to be rich and powerful became priests, bishops, cardinals, popes, and Templar knights. When it came to war, Roman Catholic priests, bishops, cardinals, and popes got rich in two ways:

1. For conning parishioners into believing God or Christ wanted them to go to war against a heathen savage enemy, they got a share of loot;
2. And while men were away fighting the war, their offering baskets would be filled by wives, fiancés, sisters, and friends who prayed for safe return or a speedy flight to heaven if killed in battle.

Moses set the scene for dethroning La Sacre Femme and male-chauvinistic dominance in several ways. The Five Books of Moses do not indicate that God had a wife but said a male God was the creator. In the Adam and Eve story, Moses "bore false witness" that Eve was the first to eat the forbidden fruit and talked Adam into eating it. From that Moses said Eve was the originator of sin, and since she was a women, females were too immoral to pick mates and only a man, their father, or the eldest son (if father was dead) could sell girls into marital prostitution slavery.

Why Eve wouldn't have been the first to pick and eat the forbidden fruit evolves from natural law human instincts that are consistent with Chinese philosophy and religion where:

- Men are or have Yang and are positive, bright, and masculine; and
- Women are or have Yin and are negative, dark, and feminine.

Positive men were risk takers who hunted, went to war for loot, and explored dangerous new lands for gold, etc. Negative women were more conservative than men. They had to stay home to care for and protect kids.

Thus it's more likely that positive, risk taker Adam picked and ate forbidden fruit before conservative Eve. That theory is supported by FBI NCIS crime data that shows 90 percent of thefts are perpetrated by men or women doing it for men, and I don't mean sex.

However, just as they say, "you can't keep a good man down," the same goes for women. Natural law human instincts and inclinations of women to be gatherers meant they didn't just gather vegetables, fruits, nuts, and berries but also herbs to prevent infections, relax, calm, elevate moods, and aphrodisiacs to sexually stimulate. That allowed wives to control husbands. Those instincts and inclinations led women to learn to read so they could study alchemy to produce chemical drugs with the same effects.

However, after women read the Bible, they started to question and rebel against Roman Catholic doctrine that was immorally biased against women. Roman Catholic witch hunt inquisitions had fifty thousand to one million women burned at the stake as a sorceress to discourage other women from studying, learning, and demanding equal rights with men.

Exodus 22:18 says, "You shall not permit a sorceress to live."

However, there's no similar commandment applicable to warlocks (aka male sorcerers). So doesn't that commandment represent immoral male chauvinism? (Again, see Dan Brown's book and movie *The Da Vinci Code*.)

Now here we are 1,500 years after St. Augustine wrote "Rules against Sex," and men are still trying to control women's bodies. Their laws against contraceptives and abortion are aimed at forcing women out of the workplace and back home to procreate warriors and care for children.

Natural Law Human Instincts for Sex Can't
Be Consciously Controlled or Controlled by Laws
The means to their ends is St. Augustine's "Rules against Sex."

However, they're based upon a false assumption that powerful, hormone-fueled human instincts for sex can be consciously controlled. The evidence that one can't consciously control sexual instincts comes in two forms:

- While we're conscious, we daydream about sex. Those fantasies are stimulated by God-given natural law human instincts that respond to sexual smells, smiles, sounds, words, body movements, and physical contact that causes swelling and lubrication of sexual organs and stimulates sexual drives that lead to sex or masturbation; and
- While sleeping surplus testosterone causes humans to have sexual dreams characterized by visual images that stimulate imaginary foreplay, masturbation, and culminates in an orgasm (wet dream).

What did Puritan Founding Fathers Believe about Sex?

When presidential candidates like Santorum and Bachmann talked about the intensions of Founding Fathers and espoused Augustine's "Rules against Sex," they apparently forgot or never learned that our Puritan Founding Fathers and Mothers risked their lives crossing the Atlantic Ocean to get away from Church of England sex patrols that roamed neighborhoods and arrested people who were having fun during sex.

Fact is, at least seven branches of my family were Puritans who risked their lives sailing across the Atlantic Ocean to colonize America in order to escape English sex patrols because they believed God intended sex to be fun so they'd "be fruitful and multiply." The "History of Whately, Mass 1661-1899" shows that most of my Puritan ancestors had ten to fifteen children.

Unfortunately, because St. Augustine's "Rules against Sex" violate God-given natural law human instincts and inclinations, "DSM-IV" (Diagnostic and Statistical Manual of Mental Disorders of the American Psychiatric Association) and "The Merck Manual" lists dozens of psychiatric sexual disorders resulting from St. Augustine's "Rules against Sex." Most psychologically damaging of sexual disorders are pedophilia (especially when the pedophile's a priest), incest, and rape of 25 percent of women.

Furthermore, decades ago surveys of women by *Cosmo* and *Glamour* revealed much more damage to women from "Rules against Sex." One survey found "Sixty percent of women never or rarely had orgasms." That's because:

- "Sex is wasted on the young and inexperienced";
- Parents don't teach children how to make love or Kama Sutra; and
- Premature ejaculating boys or men can't bring a woman to orgasm.

Another survey found that 60 percent of women, when seeking a mate, placed a higher priority on income, assets, and social status than on romance, love, good relationship, and sex. Those predispositions are a product of 1,500 years of women being sold to the highest bidder into marital prostitution.

Why U.S. Students Rank Low in
Math, Science, and Reading Comprehension

Above surveys show reasons why "Men Are on Mars and Women Are on Venus" and why the divorce rate is over 50 percent with many having two or three marriages. Now I'll explain why the high divorce rate has caused U.S. students to drop from first to seventeenth in math, twenty-first in science, and twenty-fifth in reading comprehension.

It starts with a misconception that mothers are always better parents. Therefore, in 99 percent of the divorces, mothers are given custody of daughters and sons, even when wives are the primary cause of divorce and husbands are better parents. Before the Baby Boomer Generation, husbands were head of household and allowed to rape their wives if they didn't want to have sex.

However, Baby Boomer husbands who embraced the new marital contract of joint decision making, could not be the head of the household. Baby Boomer wives became head of household and forced husbands to do what wives wanted or allowed wives to do what they wanted via:

- Withholding sex; and
- Threats of divorce and paying child support for children they lost.

However, many fathers who agreed to "The New Marital Contract," were or are far better parents than mothers. Feminists in the 1960s said, "If husbands share household and childcare responsibilities, wives will become 'happy, whole persons' with a career, husband, and children. The husband's quid pro quo will be wives who love, respect, and give all the sex they can handle."

Some New Marital Contract husbands got all the sex they could handle. Most after five years were lucky to get sex once a month or once a year. Excuses for not having sex included headaches, neck, back, or belly aches, or stress or depression, night after night. Baby Boomer men who learned science, the art of Kama Sutra, and acupressure reflexology could eliminate such excuses and sexually stimulate their wives at the same time.

New Marital Contract husbands have been better parents because their wives are disciplinary cowards and don't ask children to contribute to the family by doing household and yard work because of natural law human instincts that make wives feel guilty for having a career. Their husbands, on the other hand, have no guilt about having a career and "killed four birds with one stone" by sharing childcare responsibilities. They:

- Spent quality time with children; and
- At the same time, prepared kids to take care of themselves by teaching them how to cook, do dishes and laundry, clean house, do yard work, repair and maintain house, cars, and boats, and how to play sports; and
- During those activities, taught relevant commandments, Golden Rules and family adages, traditions, and how to succeed in life; and
- Children felt like contributing members of the family.

After divorce, career moms made daughters "crack the books" so they could support themselves and didn't have to be financially dependent upon a man. However, girl moms didn't know how to train and discipline boys to become men, especially when they didn't have a father at home.

Therefore, boys were left to run free and wild and didn't study. In school they became class cut ups. After school they were pied pipers who drew other boys and girls down a path of skipping school, smoking, alcohol, drugs, crime, and a life of failure.

Baby Boomer Generation boys outperformed girls in science and math in high school, college, and post-graduate schools because daily activities between fathers and sons (sports and making and repairing things) involved reading and rudimentary math and science.

In the next June, look at newspaper stories of students who graduated at top of high school, college, and professional school classes. You'll see Caucasian girls, Jews, and Asians of either sex are at the top of almost all classes.

You can see the results of girl moms getting custody of sons by watching young couples on dates. Usually the girlfriend drives and pays for dinner and/or drinks because the boyfriend got drunk and lost his driver's license and job. Then when September rolls around, girls go back to college and boys stay at home playing with themselves.

U.S. scores on math, science, and reading comprehension can be significantly increased and divorce rates decreased if divorce court judges:

- Apply equal gender rights and principles of legal equity to give custody of:
  1. Sons to fathers; and
  2. Daughters to mothers;
  3. Except when one parent is unfit to be a parent.
- Then wives can't extort control of families and oppress husbands via:
  1. Withholding sex; and
  2. Threats of divorce and taking children away from fathers if they:
     a. Won't agree to take children to wife's family for holidays;
     b. Won't agree to give wife "A Girl's Night Out" or a vacation with "girlfriends," which is often a pretense for wife:
        1) To have an affair with her boss or coworker; or
        2) To meet other men to have an affair; and
  3. Making ex-husbands pay one third of their income in child support for what they lost in divorce.

When I was a law clerk for the leading family court judge in New Jersey, the Honorable Theodore T. Tams, he asked me to survey husbands and wives about whether there'd be divorce if husbands got sons and wives got daughters after divorce. Ninety percent said no, and they'd find a way to work out differences.

Every Religion Is a Socialization and Civilizing Force
Because It Preaches Essentially the Same Eternal Law
Preachers, priests, rabbi, and clerics can facilitate good marriages and moral governments. Let me explain how by relating what happened the last time I went to church a few years ago. During the sermon, the preacher said, "You can't be a good Christian unless you go to church on Sunday."

After the service, I shook the minister's hand and said, "My family and I were not hurt by people who didn't go to church but people who went to church on Sunday and sinned on Monday. The converse of what you're say-ing is that people can sin all they want during the week as long as they go to church on Sunday, ask God's forgiveness, and oh by the way, put 10 percent of what they stole in the offering basket. But for those who don't buy into the weekly redemption plan, they can buy their way into heaven by giving away all or most of what they stole before they die.

"Your sermon ignored the fact that when we get to St. Peter at the pearly gates, he will do a cost-benefit analysis to make sure we did good and not evil. You'd help your congregation more if you'd discuss at least one com-mandment, Golden Rule and soul-saving rule each Sunday."

Unfortunately many preachers and priests are unwilling to preach:

- "Thou shall not commit adultery"; and
- "Thou shall not steal" via white-collar crime.

Just as the press censors itself, so do ministers of religions. Why would adul-terers or white-collar criminals (of medicine, law, business, government, etc.) go to church and listen to preachers chastise them for sins and thank them by putting 10 percent of what they stole in the offering basket?

More Ironies of "One Percent Devils and Satanic Tools"
As a result of the power of sex and sexuality, "One Percent Devils" get rich selling products via commercials with sexy men and women:

- So men think, "If I buy that car, I can get a beautiful and sexy woman";
- So women think, "If I buy that perfume and shampoo/conditioner, I'll get a handsome, sexy, and/or rich man."

While "One Percent Devils" get rich selling sex, they bribe "Their Satanic Tools" (Republican politicians, preachers, and press) to employ repetitive lies and Hitler-Nixon-type, Machiavellian, Divide-and-Conquer, Wedge-Issue Tactics to stimulate gender bias, prejudice, and intolerance and to force all Americans to comply with St. Augustine's "Rules against Sex." So gen-der-intolerant citizens vote Republican and against their own economic and social interests as well as interests of friends and family.

Republicans Representing
"The Silent Moral Majority" is a Crock of Cow Manure

Another irony is that Republicans "bear false witness" and "utter false reports" when they claim to represent "The Silent Moral Majority."

In 1972 there was a survey of prostitutes in NYC, Philadelphia (The City of Brotherly Love), Chicago, and L.A. The survey revealed that prostitutes preferred Republican National Conventions over Democratic Conventions because Republicans are hornier and have more money.

President Nixon, who ran on a Law and Order platform and was the first to "utter false reports" that Republicans represent the "Silent Moral Majority," skipped town to avoid impeachment for Watergate burglary of Democratic National Headquarters and his attempt to cover it up and violation of rights in the Bill of Rights of 50,000 antiwar, feminist, and civil rights activists and news reporters, as well as 150,000 of their friends and family.

Without warrants supported by probable cause, Nixon ordered illegal wiretaps, mail openings, IRS audits, and/or denied federal benefits without due process of law for 200,000 law-abiding Americans. President Nixon also transferred a large chunk of money from Democratic President Johnson's "War on Poverty" to the Law Enforcement Assistance Administration to beef up state, county, and municipal law enforcement, some say because Republicans would rather imprison and execute Afro and Latin Americans than to help them rise out of poverty and crime.

In the mid-1990s, Republicans in Congress took the "moral high road" when they investigated President Clinton's BJs in the Oval Office. Larry Flint of *Hustler* magazine offered one million dollars for info about senators and congressmen who were having illicit affairs. Shortly thereafter twenty-four male and female Republican legislators resigned.

In 2016 news indicated that the Washington Madam's clientele book contains the names of over eight hundred senators, congressmen, their staffers, and lobbyists who bought sex, including Republican Senator Ted Cruz, who's cited five times. However, a Republican court order prevents the Washington Madam's attorney from making the client names public. Some pay one thousand to two thousand dollars for high-class call girls. Remember the Mayflower Madam in NYC decades ago? She was a descendent of the Puritans who landed in America in 1620. I wonder how many call girls Republican Presidential Candidate Donald the Duck Trump has bought?

Other "One Percent Devils" travel to Thailand to buy sex with under-aged girl and/or boy sex slaves. Some "One Percent Devils" get rich in the illegal sex slave trade that kidnaps teenage girls and sell them to Muslims.

Don't Preachers Have a Moral Duty to Preach Eternal Law, Immorality of Political Lies and Machiavellian Wedge Ploys, and Mistakes by Misguided Preachers and Priests

As indicated, my father wrote to his Lutheran minister father, "If people fail to interest themselves in political matters, which is their duty to investigate, then someone must make it their task to stimulate such an interest as a patriotic citizen. Who can better bring it to their attention than the minister? Is it not a part of a minister's calling to try to ascertain whether political institutions and daily practices are in conformity with Christian standards?

"Is not our democratic system based upon Christian principles? Did it not originate under Christian tutelage and in a Christian era? Then if capitalism and democracy are stepchildren of Christianity, is it not Christianity's duty to give parental advice to its offspring? Or should Christianity allow its brainchild to become a savage robot with no interference?

"If you haven't been using this analytical approach, it probably will be hard to change, but remember, we are moving into a propaganda world, which necessitates a keen observation and study of what is the truth."

I've discussed how misguided ministers advocate racial, religious, cultural, and gender intolerance. The following is more fundamental.

According to a History Channel series, a god, gods or aliens thought to be gods enlightened (most of the following) founders of religion about science and mathematics and gave eternal laws for civilized society:

- Rama, Revji, Moses, Buddha, Christ, and Muhammad;
- They founded, based upon eternal law, the Hindu, Sikh, Jewish, Buddhist, Christian, and Islamic faiths.

However, subsequent misguided money- and power-hungry leaders of each of those religions abused their religions by:

- Telling followers that God wanted them to violate eternal laws against people of other god-inspired religions by "bearing false witness" and "uttering false reports" that those people were savage, heathen, godless devils;
- Degrading and demoting women from being La Sacre Femmes and a path to spirituality, godliness, and heaven to slaves and second-class citizens without any rights, even though many women were and are superior to most or all men; and
- Again, St. Augustine's "Rules against Sex" enabled subsequent priests to drive an unnatural law wedge between not just women and men but sexuality and spirituality.

Pope Francis Has a Solution

Pope Francis advised priests to stop preaching St. Augustine's "Rules against Sex" and rules against gays and lesbians. He also recommended that priests preach about moral capitalism and redistribution of wealth.

The next approach Pope Francis could advise priests is that every Sunday:

- They read at least one commandment, soul-saving rule of Christ, and Golden Rule and apply them to everyday activities of parishioners, politicians, business, government, trades, professions, and press;
- Explain what St. Thomas Aquinas said in "Theory of Law":
  1. That God's plan for mankind is a utopia or heaven on earth free of war and crime;
  2. How Aquinas proposed that plan can become a reality; and
  3. That priests must expose obstacles to achievement of the plan:
     a. Repetitive lies with truth; and
     b. Hitler-Nixon-type, Machiavellian, Divide-and-Conquer, Wedge-Issue Ploy Tactics.

However, Preachers Don't Preach Eternal Law
or How to Achieve Mankind's Goal — Happiness

Preachers and priests apparently don't seem to want happy congregation members. They don't want people to consume alcohol and social drugs or have sex and gamble to relieve sorrow, disappointment, pain, suffering, and attain enlightenment and money to pay debts. Some even preach that people shouldn't seek medical treatment. Some parents have been convicted of child abuse for not seeking medical treatment that include drugs or surgery.

In other words, preachers and priests don't want people to use God-given means to relieve suffering and to achieve happiness. They want people miserable so they go to church, pray for help, and put 10 percent of their income or what they stole in an offering basket.

I don't know if there's a heaven, but I know there's a hell because I have been living in hell. Preachers and priests don't preach that:

- God's plan for mankind is a utopia or heaven on earth;
- Mankind's goal is happiness;
- "Theory of Law" by St. Thomas Aquinas identifies the means for God's plan to come about and for mankind to achieve its goal: and
- Preachers no longer give hellfire and brimstone sermons about "thou shall not steal" via white-collar crime while looking at guilty doctors, attorneys, business people, tradesmen, and government employees for economic reasons:
  1. Who among those professions or trades would want to go to church and be publicly chastised for their sins; and
  2. Then want to put 10 percent of what they stole in an offering basket.

I used to pray for help, relief, and even for a girlfriend. That ended a few years ago, give or take, for three reasons.

I realized God must laugh at us. I imagined God saying to Jesus, "Christ! Do people think a Supreme Being God has a low self-concept or ego and needs humans to pray thanks for what they have and achieved? Why do they think I want them to pray for help? I gave humans everything they need to solve their own problems: resources, brains, hands, voice boxes, science, and math."

One Sunday a preacher talked about Moses warning Pharaoh that if he didn't let his people go, God would visit seven wraths on Egypt. Then I saw a History show indicating Moses was Pharaoh's chief scientific advisor. As such he knew signs of an eminent volcano explosion and adjacent earthquakes were eminent, and they would cause seven wraths.

For the first time in my life, I read the Five Books of Moses and other books until I got to the Book of Kings. I was too disgusted to go on.

One question I asked myself was, "Why would God give Moses commandments like 'thou shall not kill, steal, wrong a stranger, afflict any widow and orphan' and then tell Moses and Joshua to have Hebrews kill every Semite cousin, man, woman, and child in over thirty cities of Jordan, Syria, Lebanon, and Canaan? Didn't Moses say God cloned Adam and Eve in his own image and that everyone is God's child and he loves his children?"

Did God really give Moses a post-combat commandment that warriors pray and bathe for seven days to wash away sins of war? Or did Moses fabricate that commandment in order to get Hebrews to go to war?

Then I read about God visiting natural disasters (lightning, fire from heaven [volcanic balls], etc.) to wipe out cities to punish sinners. I thought, "Why would God indiscriminately kill innocent men, women, and children to make a point sinners would remember? Why not use lightning bolts just to kill sinners?"

Perhaps the saddest story I have ever heard was about a Colombian women who brought her daughter to the U.S. to get away from drug murderers. After her daughter was killed by a drive-by shooter, she cried, "Why would God take away my good daughter?"

I thought, "That mother and other God-has-a-plan-for-our-lives thinkers miss the point. God gave us commandments, Golden Rules, and an existential choice to do good or evil. God then gave us criminal and civil justice systems to punish wrongdoers and provide compensation for their victims."

There's Truth behind Biblical History Stories
Pastor Payton said stories in the Old Testament were told and retold for thousands of years before Moses wrote Genesis. Each time the stories were retold, they changed. In some ways, it was like a fish story where the fish got bigger each time the story was told. In the case of Noah, therefore, Genesis says he was five hundred years old when his oldest son was born.

You can imagine the jokes that flew when we returned from a church outing and someone said, "Ah...we have 'Returned to Payton Place.'"

In order to show how stories change when passed on from one to another, psychology and criminology professors have entered lecture halls and whispered a story to the first student, told the student to pass the story on to next student, and told each student to write down the story they just re-lated, etc., etc., etc.

When written versions were compared, the last version was significantly different from the first version told by the professor. That's because each person remembered and forgot different elements of the story. That left gaps in the story. The human brains then logically deducted from other facts missing facts.

Noah's Flood

If it rained enough to submerge all land, after the water receded and the ark came to rest on fourteen-thousand-foot-high Mt. Ararat, where'd the water necessary to cover earth (a twenty-five-thousand-mile circumference) come from? Where'd all that water go as the flood receded? Did most water appear and disappear like magic?

History and Discovery Channels have aired shows about the nature of Noah's flood. However, it appears those shows have missed the real cause.

Ancient American Indians, Indian Vedas, and European Celts have legends of a Great Flood. Ten thousand years ago, the last Glacial Age started to melt. Glacial dams contained a mile of ice on a mile of water so compressed it couldn't freeze. Glaciers began to melt ten thousand years ago.

By 5000 B.C., the southern face of glacial dams of the Columbia, Colorado and Wisconsin rivers had melted until all three dams exploded. Hundreds of billions of gallons of highly compressed water shot out of dams at thousands of miles per hour. The force of water was so great, the Grand Coulee in Washington state, the Grand Canyon in Arizona, and the Wisconsin Dells were gouged out.

However, in southern Europe, the Mideast, and northern Africa, there was no such gouging. Northern and southern hemisphere glacial dams opposed each other. Five southern running European rivers were blocked by glacial dams at the Black Sea. Those dams were five hundred miles north of Mt. Ararat.

Five hundred miles south of Mr. Ararat was a glacial dam of the northern running Nile River. It had more water beneath and behind the Nile glacial dam than beneath and behind all five European glacial dams.

In 5000 B.C. as the sun moved east to west over Mt. Ararat, the face of European and Nile glacial dams simultaneously exploded. Hundreds of millions of square miles of water shot out at thousands of miles per hour.

When the walls of southern and northern water slammed into each other, the basin between the mountains of southern Europe and northern Africa filled like a bath tub. Noah's ark rose fourteen thousand feet above Mt. Ararat. As water receded to the Atlantic and Indian oceans, the ark landed on Ararat.

Before the glacial dams exploded, sea level was two hundred feet lower because much of the earth's water was trapped by two-mile-high glacial dams. No one knows how many cities became buried under the higher sea level, but one of those cities was The Lost City of Atlantis.

Seven-Day Creation Story Is Not a Myth
but a Result of Misinterpretation of One Word in Genesis

The creation story in Genesis was passed on for thousands of years before written in Genesis. Pastor Payton said the creation story was first written in Hebrew, translated into Greek and then English. The Hebrew word that was translated into "day" didn't mean a 24-hour day. Fact is, a supreme being god wouldn't tell Moses a creation myth and give humans carbon-dating science indicating the earth was created in seven billion years of days.

CHAPTER VI

First Amendment Freedom of Speech and Press, Right to Peaceably Assemble and Petition Government for Redress of Grievances

Republicans don't believe in First Amendment rights for those who oppose Republican campaign platforms and legislation. For seventy years they "uttered false reports" or "bore false witness" that opponents, press, and protestors were communists or aiders and abettors of communism. Yet don't Republican false accusations and foreign policy acts and omissions treasonously give "Aid and Comfort" to communist and Muslim enemies?

When political issues involve academic disciplines such as biology, microbiology, biochemistry, engineering, cloning, mining, and oil and gas drilling, news reporters and commentators must use systemic analysis that requires workable knowledge of a dozen or so academic disciplines that impact or are impacted by proposed solutions. Often issues can most effectively be resolved with knowledge of U.S., world and military history; political science and economics; psychology, sociology, law, and criminology; medicine; religion; business; and environmental science.

Workable knowledge in those disciplines enabled me to win over one hundred straight personal-injury defense jury verdicts and write thirteen publications on criminal and civil justice, including:

- "Police Community Relations 1975" for International Association of Chiefs of Police;

- Standards and Goals for Crime Prevention, Law Enforcement, Prosecution, Defense, Courts, Corrections and Victim Assistance for a New Jersey Governor's Advisory Committee;
- "Portier Case Note" on Negligent Infliction of Emotional Distress published in *Seton Hall Law Review*;
- "Discrimination against Women in the Criminal Justice System," published in *Boston Law Review* by Prof. Lawrence Bershad; and
- Seven articles cited on using Subpoena, Medical Research and Investigation to Defeat Fraudulent Injury Claims.

What Impact Can News Reporters and Commentators Make?

The best example is Great Uncle Rufus Woods, owner/editor of *Wenatchee Daily World*, circulation 200,000. In the early 1900s, his editorials led to the closing of whorehouses, opium dens, and crooked gambling saloons. Then Rufus published editorials and used political connections for twenty-three years to get hydroelectric and irrigation dams on the Columbia River, Grand Coulee Dam, and Chief Joseph Dam (behind which is Rufus Woods Lake). Those dams helped turn desert into farms, orchards, and gardens. Dams brought electricity to modernize the Northwest and Boeing to Seattle, where tens of thousands of B-17, B-25 and B-29 Bombers were built for WWII.

That story is memorialized in *Rufus Woods, The Columbia River, and the Building of Modern Washington* by Robert E. Ficken, Washington State University Press; a PBS show on Rufus Woods; and a book by Rufus Woods, *The 23 Year Battle for the Grand Coulee Dam*.

How the Woodses Met the Roosevelts

In Grandpa Lebbeus Bigelow Woods's book *My Christian Experience: Is It an Illusion?* is the following from the *Atchison Daily Globe*, February 1904.

"It is such a long call back to the days of Demosthenes that the people have grown careless and forgetful of the powers of oratory...At St. Mark's English Lutheran Church last night five orators appeared...

"The occasion was the annual contest to determine what modern Demosthenes will represent Midland College at the coming state oratorical affair, to be held this year in Topeka...

"This place was given to Lebbeus Woods of Surprise, Nebraska, who flung an oration on 'The First American Triumvirate' to the audience in a manner indicating that he wouldn't be afraid to try it before twice as many. He did so well that some in the back seats forgot their surroundings and bet he would carry off the honors.

"… Herman Rhode of Oakland, Neb., handed a bunch of bouquets to President Roosevelt in a speech on 'The Strenuous Life.'"

In 1911 Grandpa Lebbeus was practicing law in Seattle with Great Uncle Ralph (Rufus's identical twin). Uncle Ralph represented interests of railroad, mining, and timber companies. He also won the first medical malpractice trial in Washington. His client was a girl born with jaundice. She was left under a sun lamp so long, a large part of her skull never converted from cartilage to bone. Uncle Rufus, an environmentalist like President Teddy Roosevelt, wrote editorials about responsible mining and lumbering that doesn't pollute the environment and ravage pristine, scenic lands.

After President Teddy Roosevelt and cousin Franklin Delano Roosevelt arrived, they traveled by train with Gramps and Uncle Ralph to Wenatchee. They went there not only to fish and savor the world's best cherries, apples, and salmon but for Uncle Rufus to show where a dam should be built on the Grand Coulee.

As indicated in *The Express Messenger* (October 1934), Great Uncle Hiram Howard Smith, as superintendent of the Alaska-Yukon Railroad, accompanied and expedited problem solutions for President Franklin Delano Roosevelt. They took a train to see progress on construction of the Grand Coulee Dam. Uncle Hi retired as vice president of Union Pacific Railroad.

He survived five wives. I barely survived two.

Editorial about Those Who Let Opportunities Pass Them By
The following July 8, 1908, editorial in *Wenatchee Daily World* by Uncle Rufus is quoted at the beginning of chapter two of *Rufus Woods, The Columbia River*…. It is important for news people and others to read.

> "The ranks of mediocrity — of the half-successful — are crowded with people with fine natural abilities, who never rise above inferior stations because they never act independently. They are afraid to take the initiative in anything — to depend upon their own judgment and resources — and so let opportunity after opportunity pass them by."

Communist Nations Progress toward Democracy and
Rights as U.S. Regresses toward Plutocratic, Autocratic Tyranny

For decades communist Nations have progressed toward democracy and freedom of speech and press, and "unalienable Rights to Life, Liberty and Pursuit of Happiness." Meanwhile, "One Percent Devils and Their Satanic Tools" are regressively driving 99 percent toward plutocratic tyranny.

An autocratic tyranny that would mirror and parrot George Orwell's books *1984* and *Animal Farm*. A tyranny where a one-percent ruling class of an Anglo-Saxon New World Order would own all land, resources, factories, stores, homes, and businesses. The other 99 percent would be mindless, robotic slaves. They would be spied on by Big Brother (domestic spy agencies) and constantly brainwashed by Ministry of Truth espousing:

1. Repetitive lies until truth becomes a lie and lies become truth; and
2. Hitler-Nixon-type, Machiavellian, Divide-and-Conquer, Wedge-Issue Tactics to stimulate racial, religious, cultural, and gender intolerance: to divert anger, resentment, and hostility away from totalitarian government by blaming plight of the masses on:
    a. A fictitious enemy; and
    b. Those who are not male, Caucasian Christians.

Hitler blamed communists and Jews for Germany's economic woes.

Nixon Republicans and now "One Percent Devils and Their Satanic Tools" (Republican politicians, preachers, and press) blame economic woes on their victims: Latin, Afro, Asian and Native Americans; working women; non-Christians; and social safety net beneficiaries. Woes result from "One Percent Devils," who caused 2008 stock-market crash/depression.

That second-greatest depression was caused by Republican:

*   Violations of commandments in Exodus 20-23:
    1. "You shall not join hands with a wicked man" (One Percent Devils);
    2. "You shall take not bribe" (via insider trading and campaign bribes);
    3. "You shall not pervert justice due to the poor";
    4. "You shall not wrong a stranger or oppress him";

5. "You shall not afflict any widow or orphan";
6. "Thou shall not steal";
*   Violation of goals of Preamble of U.S. Constitution:
    1. "... in Order to form a more perfect Union (for 99 percent of Americans)";
    2. "Establish Justice (for 99 percent of Americans)";
    3. "Insure Domestic Tranquility (for 99 percent of Americans)"; and
    4. "Promote the General Welfare" (for 99 percent of Americans)";
*   Failure to enforce of Wall Street and banking regulations so "One Percent Devils" could steal billions of dollars from the other 99 percent;
*   Tax cuts, deductions, and subsidies for outsourcing millions of jobs to:
    1. An atheistic Communist Chinese enemy; and
    2. Third World nations;
    3. So their laborers and resources can be immorally exploited by means that are illegal in the U.S.

Fifty years of "Satanic Tool" repetitive lies and Hitler-Nixon-type, Machiavellian, Wedge-Issue Tactics, saying opponents in press were pinko communists, elitist (Republican code word for Jewish), and aiders and abettors of communist enemies, put a chill on freedom of press.

Is there any real difference between Communist Chinese or Russian Communists and U.S. "One-Percent Devil and their Satanic Tools"'s use of:

1. Domestic spy agencies?
2. Censorship of news or schoolbooks and use of news media for undemocratic and immoral capitalistic propaganda purposes?

Free Speech Right Induced by American Revolution

During the American Revolution, British troops censored news and freedom of press by destroying printing presses, shops, and jailing and shooting journalists. Founding Fathers wanted press to be a fourth branch of government to report when Congress, the president, the Supreme Court, and state houses violate U.S. Constitution, Bill of Rights, and other laws of the land.

Nothing I've read indicates Founding Fathers considered that "One Percent Devils" of industry, finance, "and their Satanic Tools" would use news media to destroy democracy and moral capitalism. Have you ever heard evening news anchors or editorialists for NBC, CBS, or ABC say, "Republican President and Vice President Candidates Romney and Ryan lied seven times and employed seven Machiavellian Wedge Issues to get voters to vote Republican and against their own social and economic interests"?

Or "Speaker of House Boehner 'bore false witness' seven times by psychologically projecting his failures onto President Obama?"

Wasn't one of the most incredible psychological projections of sins by Congressman Boehner. He said, "President Obama is trying to create class warfare." Didn't class warfare start forty years ago when bribes from "One Percent Devils" to "their Satanic Tools" led to:

1. No increases of minimum wage to keep pace with inflation;
2. No equal pay for women, and they earn 87 percent of what men earn;
3. Tax subsidies for outsourcing U.S. jobs to destroy labor unions;
4. Overburden on social safety nets for victims of:
   a. Outsourcing; and
   b. Racial, religious, cultural, and gender bias and prejudice.
5. Lack of regulation of Wall Street and banks whose cons, scams, and schemes stole billions from working poor and middle class:
   a. Caused twenty million to lose jobs (and become unemployable or underemployed), pensions, savings, homes, and health insurance;
   b. But criminal bankers and brokers were financially bailed out and not charged, convicted, or sentenced to prison for crimes.

Ripley's Believe it or Not: One Percent Devils and Their Satanic Tools Commenced Class Warfare Sixty Years Ago

How many times have Republicans such as Congressmen Boehner "uttered false reports" and "bore false witness" that President Obama has been trying to instigate class warfare. However, there's statistical evidence that "One Percent Devils and Their Satanic Tools" started it. According to the vulture capitalist chart of Ed Schultz of MSNBC, during the last forty years:

1. Income of "One Percent Devils" sky rocketed by 272 percent;
2. Income of the other 99 percent has flatlined and not increased 1 percent even though cost of living has increased 9 percent to 2 percent per year;
3. "One Percent Devils"'s share of national wealth has increased from 40 percent to 72 percent; and
4. Share of national wealth by 99 percent dropped from 60 percent to 28 percent.

A disparity is because "One Percent Devils" bribed "Satanic Tools":

1. To not increase minimum wage to keep pace with inflation;
2. For tax cuts, deductions, and subsidies to:
   a. Outsource tens of millions of middle-class industrial and service jobs; and/or
   b. Buy other companies and make those companies pay for their acquisition by laying off a high percentage of employees; and
3. "One Percent Devils" of service and manufacturing can also keep income of the other 99 percent flatlined by:
   a. Early retirement of seniors who made One Percent Devils rich;
   b. Replacing them with inexperienced cheap labor; and
   c. Hiring cheap labor after stock-market crashes.

So when Republicans repetitively lied that President Obama created class warfare, why don't all newspapers, magazines, radio, and television news repetitively tell the truth as per the above facts? Hasn't President Obama tried to reverse class warfare by "One Percent Devils and Their Satanic Tools?" Why don't the news media repetitively repeat Pope Francis's call for a return to moral capitalism and redistribution of wealth from "One Percent Devils" to their victims, 99 percent of Americans?

When "One Percent Devils and Their Satanic Tools" call for deregulation of banks and Wall Street, why don't evening news anchors or editorialists explain how lack of regulation and deregulation caused stock-market crashes, depressions, or recessions every twenty years since the Civil War? When Republican "Satanic Tools" want to reduce and eliminate social safety nets, why don't news anchors or editorialists explain that the U.S. has social safety nets for victims of "One-Percent Devil" greed and propaganda tactics of "their Satanic Tools" that suppress minority groups?

Why doesn't news media remind Americans of warnings by President Eisenhower about the dangers of U.S. Military-Industrial Complex getting the U.S. into unnecessary wars to protect industrial and financial interests of "One Percent Devils" who are ruthlessly exploiting foreign workers and resources? Why doesn't the news media repetitively point out that President G.W. Bush and Vice President Cheney owned huge amounts of stock in Military-Industrial Complex businesses (U.S. oil and gas for Bush and Halliburton mercenary army and weapons factories for Cheney)?

Why didn't anyone in the news media say, "There's no difference between Hitler lying that Poland was a threat so he could conquer Poland and G.W. Bush-Cheney lies about weapons of mass destruction in Iraq; that Saddam Hussein would sell nuclear bombs so terrorists could attack the U.S;. and that Bush and Cheney's real motives were based upon the root of all evil: money from their immoral war profiteering?"

They say, "When there's a character debate, the news media is a willing participant." Why doesn't the news media talk about a lack of moral character by G.W. Bush, Cheney, and "One Percent Devils and Their Satanic Tools?"

Republicans since Civil War Have Put a Chill on
First Amendment Freedoms of Speech, Press, and Right to Protest

The Civil War and the Thirteenth, Fourteenth, and Fifteenth Amendments, freed Afro-American slaves and extended the right to vote and protection of the Bill of Rights. However, for one hundred years since the Civil War, an evil alliance prevented them from enjoying their rights: "unalienable Rights to Life, Liberty and Pursuit of Happiness," as well as the right to vote and hold public office.

Evil Anti Afro-American Alliance
Northern Republicans and FBI

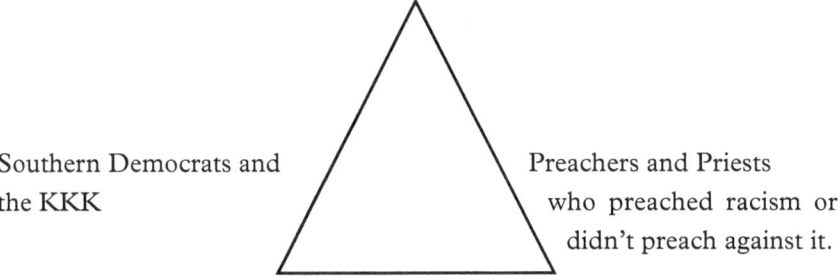

Southern Democrats and the KKK

Preachers and Priests who preached racism or didn't preach against it.

President Lincoln freed slaves and gave them equal rights. Racist Southern, Republican Caucasians had a knee-jerk reaction and became Southern Democrats because Lincoln was Republican. Former slaves ran, won office, and voted Republican.

That was too much for Caucasian Southern Democrats. They passed Jim Crow laws to disenfranchise Afro Americans and eliminate their rights under the Bill of Rights. They had two tools: racist criminal and civil justice systems. The Klu Klux Klan controlled law enforcement and Afro Americans by arson or blowing up homes, churches, newspapers, and communities; torture, castration, shooting, and hanging Afro-American men and boys; and raping Afro-American women and girls. (See movies *To Kill a Mocking Bird*; *Mississippi Burning*; *Catch a Fire*"; and *A Time to Kill*.)

From the U.S. Constitution in 1783 until the Nineteenth Amendment in 1920, women didn't have a right to vote. They protested for it and against alcohol.

From the late 1800s into the early 1900s, "One Percent Devils" bribed law enforcement agencies to suppress labor unionists via beatings, shootings, arson and bombing, arrests, torture, beating, and murder while in jail. Criminal and civil justice systems did little or nothing to protect or compensate labor unionists and families of disabled or dead unionists.

After J. Edger Hoover was appointed director of the FBI, he violated the Bill of Rights while trying to show a connection between communists and leaders of civil rights, labor unions, antiwar, feminist, and environmental protection movements, as well as the press. State, county, and local law enforcement suppressed their freedom of speech and right to peacefully assemble to protest government acts and omissions.

In the late 1960s, boys could be drafted into the military at age eighteen but couldn't vote against war until twenty-one. Wasn't that unfair and immoral?

Ironies about Right to Peaceably Assemble and Protest

Labor unions formed to end exploitation by "One Percent Devils." Auto, steel, dockworker, rail, Teamster, and construction labor unionists had no problem shutting down the U.S. economy to extort wage increases and fringe benefits from employers. Police officers had no qualms about endangering public safety by striking for a $1-per-hour pay increase.

However, neither unionists nor law enforcement officers believed civil rights, antiwar, feminists, and environmentalists had a right to protests for rights, freedoms, equality, and clean environment.

Perhaps most incredible of all was the brutality and suppression of the 99 percent Wall Street movement by municipal and university police from coast to coast. Incredible because the 99 percent movement was protesting for things that would benefit police officers, their pensions, families, and friends.

Based on the history of law enforcement repression, if there's a re-emergence of the 99 percent movement, and "One Percent Devils" of finance bribed police chiefs, would they order officers to shoot protestors? Would officers shoot into crowds of family members, neighbors, and friends?

Hasn't Press Been Willing Accomplice to Misinformation from Mayors and Police Chiefs about Real Causes of Civil Disobedience and Riots

On television for fifty years, I've witnessed protests, demonstrations, and marches in the Deep South, on university campuses, and around the globe. They always start out peaceful because the organizers wanted it that way, from Gandhi to Martin Luther King to antiwar demonstrations at Columbia University, the University of Wisconsin, UC-Berkley, and Kent State.

Civil disobedience or riots didn't start until police/soldiers attacked.

Two interesting phenomenon resulted:

1. Protesters threw back tear gas, rocks, and bricks.
    a. But why would otherwise law-abiding people do that?
    b. God-given natural law human instincts and inclinations of people who truly believe they're in the right and don't like being pushed around and having their rights violated; and
2. News media not only arrived too late to witness police attacking and causing riots but unwittingly became accomplices to police blue-code lies that antiwar student protestors caused violence;

   a.   So the press automatically believed lies by police chiefs who
        "bore false witness" that civil rights or antiwar protestors started
        violence; and

   b.   Press interviewed radical, anarchistic, revolutionary activists
        whose views didn't represent 99 percent of antiwar protestors,
        but without interviewing them, readers and viewers were misled
        into believing all protestors were anarchistic revolutionaries;

3.   See editorial comment "July 4th, 1967 Assault, Batteries and Riot
     by Police" at end of this chapter before "Crooked Man Poems."

As indicated in that editorial comment, the fact was no reasonably prudent
student would want to risk getting convicted of a felony. That would prevent
them from getting licenses to teach, be a nurse, doctor, or lawyer. If a male
college student was convicted of a felony, he would be expelled from school,
lose college military deferment, and be drafted and sent to Vietnam to be
killed or disabled, physically and/or psychologically.

As a result of news media being willing accomplices to lies by police
chiefs and sheriffs, parents and children still at home acquired false, unjust,
and unfair opinions that ungrateful, spoiled students started the riots. That
didn't just produce anti-democratic results at poll booths.

The generation of teenagers living at home turned against protesting for
anything. They became the Feel Good-Designer Jeans Generation.

"If it feels good, do it, but if not, don't." Ten-dollar Levi jeans were not
good enough. They had to have ninety-dollar Jordache jeans, fifty-dollar Izod
shirts, and one-hundred-dollar designer gym shoes.

The Feel Good Generation also had a different view about the purpose
of college educations. Most of the Baby Boomer Generation of Morality went
to college to get a multidisciplinary, liberal arts education to enable them to
systemically analyze problems, alternatives, and solutions. However, "The
Feel Good Generation" saw education as a means to get a job and career.

They were more interested in training than education. They also believed laws and rules should be stretched and broken as long as there was a
reasonable chance they could get away with it.

Baby Boomers learned "to do what is in the best interest of children."

Feel Good Generation parents did "what's best for parents." If marriage
did not feel good, divorce and why not turn kids against a disappointing spouse?

Has there Been Freedom of the Press for the Past Fifty Years?

There hasn't been freedom of press during Baby Boomers's lives. In the late 1940s and early 1950s, Republicans "bore false witness" and "uttered false reports" that Democrats and press opponents were communists. That's how Nixon defeated his first Congressional opponent, a female incumbent.

Wisconsin Sen. Joseph McCarty's communist witch-hunt terrorism via Un-American Activity Hearings abused his office, the goals of the Preamble of the Constitution, and the First, Fourth, and Fifth Amendment rights, while aided and abetted by FBI Director J. Edger Hoover. He violated amendments against warrantless wiretaps and mail openings of movie stars, senators, congressmen, presidents, and Democratic and Republican candidates. (See movie *J. Edgar.*)

Those illegal investigations were often based upon false accusations made by business or political opponents, jealous wives or husbands, and spurned lovers. They were similar to false accusations made against girls and women during the witch hunts of the 1600s based on the commandment "You shall not permit a sorceress to live" (Exodus 22:18). That's a male-chauvinistic commandment. There's no similar commandment against warlocks.

After Great-Grandfather Philip Smith died in 1685 at age fifty-two, Rev. Cotton Mather said he was "murdered with an hideous witchcraft." In the 1950s, a relative accused my father of being a communist because he stopped her from borrowing money from his father.

Arthur Miller couldn't write a play about McCarthy's witch hunt. He would've been labeled a communist and blacklisted like many Hollywood screenwriters. So Miller wrote about the Salem witch hunt and left the audience to draw the correlation or analogy to McCarthy's witch hunt.

Newspaper, television, and radio news people and commentators were afraid to attack McCarthy's tactics, except Edward R. Murrow of CBS. William Palely, the CEO of CBS, didn't interfere with editorial content. (See movie about Murrow, *Good Night and Good Luck.*)

President Nixon upped the ante in a Republican war against the press when he "bore false witness" and "uttered false reports" that "the press are leftist, liberal, pinko communist, elitists (a code word for Jewish)." After the disastrous Vietnam War Tet Offensive, Paley continued editorial freedom. Anchorman Walter Cronkite and his editorialist, Eric Severide, and Vietnam War correspondent Dan Rather became antiwar doves.

After Nixon's black-bag CIA operatives broke into Democratic National Headquarters in the Watergate Hotel, CBS News and Woodward and Bernstein of *The Washington Post* generated public opinion pressure. Sen. Sam Nunn began hearings to impeach President Nixon. (Read book and see movie about Woodward and Bernstein, *All the President's Men.*)

Republicans are called elephants because, like elephants, they don't forget who hurt them. Dan Rather wouldn't let President Nixon "pull a Nixon" (avoid answering questions by changing the subject). It took Republicans thirty years to plant a false story with Dan Rather. He was fired as anchor of CBS News after it was broadcast. Nixon's German mafia had planted false stories about Democratic presidential candidates during Nixon's campaigns in 1968 and 1972. (Read *Selling the President* and *All the President's Men.*)

In retaliation for Watergate hearings by Democrats, elephant Republicans have also tried to setup and impeach Democratic Presidents Carter, Clinton, and Obama. Ever since Nixon, they also have continued to "beat the drums" that Democratic opponents and press are communists.

After Pope Francis urged priests to follow Judeo-Christian principles and preach against immoral capitalism by "One Percent Devils," their Satanic Tools" (Republican politicians, preachers, and press) "bore false witness" and "uttered false reports" that Pope Francis is a communist.

Why didn't news media counter by asking:

1. Isn't that an oxymoron for morons?
2. Aren't communists atheists?
3. Aren't the pope and cardinals Judeo-Christians?
4. Isn't the Vatican a democracy and capitalistic?

Bottom lines: Agree with Republicans, and you're a Judeo-Christian patriot. Oppose them, and you're an un-American communist traitor.

One Percent Devils Are Destroying Freedom of the Press

Satanic Republicans now have what Nixon wished he had. "One Percent Devils" are in control of a sizeable percentage of major newspapers, radio, television stations, and networks. Koch Brother Devils own dozens of major newspapers, television, and radio stations. The Rupert Murdock Devil owns over 250 newspapers, television, and radio stations around the globe, especially in industrial nations and Third World victim nations.

Foreigners are not supposed to own U.S. newspapers, radio, and TV stations. So how did Australian Rupert Murdock, who lives in England, get U.S. citizenship so he could purchase Fox, *Newsweek* and the *Wall Street Journal*? Wasn't the *Journal* as guilty as Standards and Poor's for not preventing the stock market and bank collapse of 2008?

There's Also No Freedom of the Press in a Resort City and County for Chicago's Rich, Famous, and Infamous

This book began as a commentary submitted to the Walworth Sunday newspaper. Why in a Republican county couldn't I get a commentary published with a title "One Percent Devils and Their Satanic Tools"?

A commentary about their anti-democracy and immoral-capitalism agenda, as evidenced by violations of commandments, Golden Rule, U.S. Constitution, and Bill of Rights. Could it be that Chicago's rich and famous industrialists, financiers, and mafia still control and rule Walworth County and Lake Geneva as they did during the "Roaring 20s" and Prohibition?

Could it be fear of retaliation from those same forces that prevented the *Walworth County Sunday* from publishing a commentary about groundwater pollution due to illegal toxic-waste dumping on farmland in Lyons Township. The story started with a twenty-year memory about flying to O'Hare, driving north on I- 94 and west on Route 50 until I spotted and followed an eighteen-wheel tank truck leaking a fowl-smelling toxic chemical to a farm in Lyons.

I sent an anonymous notice to the mayor and police chief of Lyons but nothing ever came of it. In the heart of Lyons is Ye Olde Hotel. To the left of the restaurant entrance, a sign says, "Streetwalkers who bring in sailors must pay for room in advance."

That commentary also explained how Chicago and Lake Geneva land developers were trying to drive homeowners out of country estates because it is highly prime real estate. Schemes perpetrated so those "One -Percent Devils" can purchase homes and land for ten cents on the dollar.

Two Kinds of Selective Incorporation Controls Press

Narrow-minded readers or viewers don't want to read or hear news that differs with their biases, prejudices, and intolerances. So news media caters to those with selective incorporation deficits by not printing facts and opinions that would disturb their environment, ease, or peace of mind.

Other Tactics That Are Destroying Freedom of the Press

"One Percent Devils" suppress freedom of the press in several ways:

- "One Percent Devils" cancel newspaper, television, and radio advertisements when news reporters and editorial commentators issue stories that are against their interests;
- They purchase newspapers, radio, and television stations so they can prevent news that could damage interests of "One Percent Devils":
  1. *Milwaukee Sentinel* was a progressive, liberal newspaper;
  2. Until conservative Republican-oriented *Milwaukee Journal* bought *Sentinel* and merged papers into a conservative newspaper; and
  3. Now there's no longer a progressive, liberal newspaper in Milwaukee, a Democratic stronghold city;
- "One Percent Devils and Their Satanic Tools" Karl Rove and Norquist spin, twist, and distort news for Republicans who are bribed by "One Percent Devils" to get voters to vote against their own economic and social interests and interest of family and friends via:
  1. Orwellian *1984*-style repetitive lies; and
  2. Hitler and Nixon-type, Machiavellian, Divide-and-Conquer, Wedge-Issue Tactics to stimulate racial, religious, and gender prejudice to bully people to vote against their economic and social interests;
  3. Aided and abetted by Republican politicians, preachers, and press.

Anglo-Saxon New World Order Plan to Control All News Media

George Orwell warned about Anglo-Saxon New World Order plans in *1984* and *Animal Farm*. In *1984* the nation's only source of news was Big Brother in the "Ministry of Truth." The nation's masses were brainwashed, controlled, and turned into impoverished, mindless, robotic slaves by repetitive lies and Machiavellian, Divide-and-Conquer, Wedge-Issue Tactics.

To prevent discontent, anger, and rebellion by mentally and physically impoverished masses, Big Brother diverted anger and resentment away from government toward a foreign enemy that didn't exist. At the beginning of *1984*, the enemy was China and Russia an ally. However, there wasn't an actual war. The government fired its own missiles into its cities. Later propaganda flip-flopped, and China was an ally but Russia was the enemy.

The same tactics were and are used in the Mideast to divert anger away from Muslim clerics and national leaders toward Israel and its leading ally, the U.S., which has six million Jewish citizens. Sunni and Shiite leaders were happy to divert anger of the masses away from themselves by shouting jihad against Israel, Jews, the U.S., and Americans. Anger was generated because Shiite and Sunni leaders didn't share oil and gas wealth with the masses but used it to buy secret police, guns, tanks, and jets to suppress the masses they ruled.

Clerics ordered jihads to divert anger by Muslim women and men because they told Muslim men they only needed to read Koran. Thus clerics made Muslim men education and career inferior to highly educated Israeli male or female scientists, architects doctors, attorneys, and industrialists.

Jihads were declared to divert anger of Muslim women who must be covered head to toe when in public, can't pick a mate, are sold into marital prostitution slavery, and can't go to school. Muslim women are jealous, resentful, and hate Israeli women who were doctors, lawyers, scientists, and soldiers in shorts and shirts or bikinis with hair blowing in the wind.

Americans Can Easily Be Conned into Voting to Eliminate Bill of Rights
Oh! You don't think that's probable or even possible? In the late 1960s or early 1970s when "One Percent Devils" didn't own chains of newspapers, television, and radio stations, an NBC white-paper report paraphrased the Bill of Rights into questions such as:

1. Should poor criminal defendants be given free legal counsel?
2. Should college students be allowed to protest the Vietnam War?
3. Should people be allowed to protest against the U.S. government?
4. Should police have to get a warrant to search a suspect?
5. Should children say the Lord's Prayer in school?
6. Should criminals be forced, by any means, to admit their guilt?

7. Should the press be allowed to print stories against the U.S. government?

Survey results indicated that a majority of Americans opposed eight of the ten amendments in the Bill of Rights. NBC concluded that a majority of Americans would vote to repeal the Bill of Rights.

The most influential cause was President Nixon and VP Agnew's repetitive lies and Machiavellian, Divide-and-Conquer, Wedge-Issue Tactics aimed at destroying credibility of the Warren Court and American Civil Liberties Union (ACLU) for defending the Bill of Rights. Chapters VIII, IX, and X have more about Nixon/Agnew attacks on the Warren Court.

Solutions to Restore Freedom of Press and Honest Reporting?
The Founding Fathers foresaw First Amendment freedom of press as a fourth branch of government watchdog to ensure the legislative, administrative, and judicial branches of government operate within the four corners of the United States Constitution and amendments and to warn the public when special-interest groups want to gain special advantage at the expense of taxpayers.

The Founding Fathers couldn't possibly have foreseen an Industrial Revolution that would replace King George and U.S. government with kings of industry and finance that had more money than either form of government and bribed for more to everyone else's disadvantage.

Similarly the Founding Fathers likely couldn't envision radio or television and newspapers with millions of listeners and subscribers but owned by "One Percent Devils" who slant news to reflect their immoral agenda, aided and abetted by "Satanic Republican Tools" (politicians, preachers, and press) who spread Orwellian *1984*-style repetitive lies and Hitler-Nixon-type Machiavellian, Divide-and-Conquer, Wedge-Issue Tactics to stimulate citizens to vote Republican and against their own interests.

News Reporter and Editorialist Licensing
Medical doctors, nurses, attorneys, engineers, and accountants must be licensed to practice, and continued licensing is contingent upon practicing within a code of ethics. Each of those professions has a sword. As has been said, "The pen is mightier than the sword."

155

However, "the pen" is only as mighty as it is allowed to be. It can be a positive or negative force. The Preamble of U.S. Constitution states, "We the People of the United States, in Order to form a more perfect Union, establish Justice, insure domestic Tranquility, provide for the common defense, promote the general Welfare and secure the Blessings of Liberty to ourselves and our Posterity, do ordain and establish this Constitution for the United States of America."

Yet has any reporter or editorialist tested even one Republican campaign platform item and concluded, "Platform is inconsistent with goals of Preamble and Enabling Clause of Constitution, Commandments, Golden Rule, soul-saving rules of Christ, and principles of legal equity?

News media "is only as strong as its weakest link." Licensing should be based upon earning a BA in journalism/broadcast news media; a journalistic version of ABA or AMA examinations for licensing based upon a systemic base of knowledge from at least seven academic disciplines; and testing via a personality profile and MMPI-II to weed out or rule out those with psychiatric disabilities and tendencies toward racial, religious, cultural, and gender bias, prejudice, and intolerance.

News Code of Ethics and Enforcement Mechanisms

A code of ethics should stress the importance of factual accuracy, intellectual honesty, and objectivity without racial, religious, cultural, or gender bias, prejudice, and intolerances.

Each profession is best regulated by its members. Enforcement of a code of ethics should be done by state-level boards of news: anchors, casters, hosts, and commentators. Board members should be retired members of those professional categories and voted into office by those active in those categories. Boards should have the power to fine, suspend, and revoke licenses. For nationwide networks, there should be a federal board.

Divestment of "One-Percent Devil" Ownership of News

America cannot afford to allow those who benefit from inaccurate news to own news outlets. That's like giving a bank robber a key to the bank and combination for the safe. The Federal Communications Commission should be given power to purchase newspapers, television, and radio stations from "One Percent Devils" and corporations whose main function is not news products. The FCC should then set up corporations for each news media and sell stock, but no one should be allowed to own more than 5 percent of any newspaper, television, or radio network, station, or outlet.

First targets should be "One Percent Devils" and corporations that contract with U.S. and/or state governments; are part of U.S. Military Industrial Complex; hide taxable income from IRS in offshore accounts; and lobby in Washington, D.C., and statehouses for immoral results.

Need for a Murdock Solution

Special interest should be given by U.S. Immigration and the FCC to Australian-born and raised Rupert Murdock, who lives in England. How'd he get citizenship without living in the U.S. for seven years. Given Murdock's ownership of over 250 newspapers, televisions, and radio stations around the globe, how could anyone in U.S. government have given him citizenship knowing he intended to purchases Fox Television, *Wall Street Journal*, and *Newsweek* and turn them into "One-Percent Devil" propaganda tools.

Didn't he take them down the sewer where he lives? *Wall Street Journal* once had a legendary reputation for accuracy and thoroughness. Yet the *Journal* is as much responsible for not warning investors about dangers of mortgage bundling and other derivatives as Standard and Poor's.

In the late 1960s at the University of Wisconsin, I wrote a comparative analysis of news magazines. I found *Time* was liberal progressive; *Newsweek* was centrist or objective; and *U.S. News and World Reports* was conservative. Murdock's *Newsweek* is now ultra-conservative.

If you can stand it without regurgitating, watch repetitive lies and Machiavellian, Wedge-Issue Tactics on Fox News. Otherwise watch MSNBC's clips of Fox News Puke and subsequent rebuttals.

Models of News Reporting and Commentators

Periodically documentaries should show the models or icons of objective and moral news reporting. Models documented should be:

1. Edward R. Murrow, Walter Cronkite, Eric Severide, and Dan Rather of CBS News;
2. Woodward and Bernstein of *Washington Post*; and
3. Huntley and Brinkley of NBC or ABC News.

Role of State Universities

Let's start with my home state Wisconsin. Journalism and media departments at the University of Wisconsin can rank major newspaper, television, and radio reporters, editorialists, and commentators on the basis of factual accuracy, intellectual honesty, and bias. State universities from UW-Whitewater to UW-Eau Claire could do the same for media in communities surrounding those schools.

Their reports should be forwarded to the state Board of News Anchors, Casters, and Editorialists and state and local news media professors, preachers, and teachers for dissemination to their audiences.

At top left of newspapers and at the top of the hour of radio and TV news should be names of politicians who issued repetitive lies and wedge issues.

If preachers, teachers, and press don't keep politicians honest and moral, who will? Can America and Americans afford for them not to do so?

Educated Citizens Must Tell the Press When They're Wrong

Loren Johnson is a fellow classmate and band member at Delavan Darien High School and the University of Wisconsin, where he earned a BS in agriculture and a masters in business administration. He's a farmer in Congressman Ryan's district. We're ashamed and embarrassed that Gov. Walker graduated from DDHS, where he must have failed poli-sci, econ, and U.S. and Wisconsin history. Walker must be so proud about rejecting:

1. Federal education aid to DDHS so eleven teachers had to be laid off;
2. Medicaid expansion and setting up an Affordable Care Health Insurance Exchange so that thousands of Wisconsinites will die from lack of medical treatment; and
3. Advice of environmentalist that allowing fracking in Wisconsin will poison water supply and cause sinkhole collapses and earthquakes that will kill our children and descendants.

Loren wrote the following editorial comments for *Walworth County News Sunday Edition.*

Voter Suppression

Last week Gov. Scott Walker quietly signed into law legislation that further restricts the hours polls are open for absentee voting and eliminated it altogether on weekends — all under the guise that voting hours must be uniform across the state.

While Republicans try hard to explain the importance of uniform voting hours, this legislation is nothing more than an attempt to address their paranoid perception that people who wait in long voting lines are casting their ballots for the other guys. How much more damage will be done to our democratic process before the general electorate catches on?

When Tommy Thompson was governor, there was a bipartisan consensus that government should encourage voting.

This is no longer the Republican party of Tommy Thompson. Unable to center themselves, yet intoxicated with power, Republicans busy themselves by passing needless legislation not because they should but because they can.

Voters are the "customers" who must be accommodated in a democratic process.

If you live in Walworth County, know that all of your elected representatives voted for these measures. It is obvious that we have not sent our best and brightest to Madison to serve us in the state legislature.

Loren Johnson, Elkhorn

Global Warming — It's All Science

Kudos to our fellow concerned citizens for having the courage, foresight and sense of global stewardship to go to D.C. and protest the Keystone pipeline.

Global climate change is real, not a hoax. It is potentially catastrophic and difficult to reverse.

It's a cumulative problem in that if we stop putting CO_2 into the atmosphere today, it will take years to see any difference, as evidenced by how long it has taken to restore the ozone layer.

On the other hand, if we stay the course, it becomes much harder to stop this process, as it tends to feed on itself.

It would be akin to trying to stop a gigantic ship as it approaches a huge waterfall. We barely have begun to slow it down.

I am perplexed by the insistence of some that climate science is pseudoscience or "not yet settled science," and yet they enthusiastically embrace the Internet, GPS for their cars, satellite imagery, space travel, or complicated medical procedures that prolong their lives. It's all science.

We can't be selective and accept only that which does not require change or cause discomfort. It is time we heed the warnings of the overwhelming majority of climatologists. We never will have unanimous agreement when some "scientists" are paid to deny global warming, and there are still folks who believe that the earth is flat. (You can join them if you like...flatearthsociety.org) Some even believe gravity does not exist.

(Mind boggling.)

Moreover, there is no biblical justification or mandate for mining carbon and putting it into the atmosphere.

The Alberta tar sands contain a "dirty" or energy-intensive form of fossil fuel. The externalities or side effect of this oil are just too costly to society.

It is for that reason that the Keystone pipeline should not be built.

The Stone Age did not end for lack of rocks. Fossil fuels must be phased out in favor of renewables.

Loren Johnson, Elkhorn

Koch Brothers Bribe Republicans to
Vote against Alternatives to Fossil Fuels

Exodus 23:1,8-9 and 20:15-16 commandments say,

1. "You shall not join hands with a wicked man...";
2. "You shall take no bribe, for a bribe blinds the officials and subverts the cause of those who are in the right";
3. "You shall not steal";
4. "You shall not bear false witness..."; and
5. "You shall not utter a false report."

Next to Exxon-Mobile commercials, the most nauseating and deceiving commercials are by Koch Industries. They tout how much Koch does for Americans. Conspicuously absent is mention that the Koch Brothers bribes cause polluted land, water, air, and politics via massive corruption.

Republicans "bear false witness" and "utter false reports" that they're for free enterprise, competition, oil and gas self-sufficiency, so the U.S. doesn't have to purchase it from the Mideast. Yet the Koch

Brothers Keystone Pipeline across an underground reservoir of drinking and irrigation water:

1. Won't contribute even 1 percent to self sufficiency;
2. Presents a significant danger to public health from tar-sand fracking to pipeline ruptures from Canada to Texas and huge piles polluted sands after refining.

The Koch Brothers and Canadian oil and gas company purchased with bribes:

1. No legal obligation to cleanup oil tar sand pollution or compensate for damages, not even via a performance bond;
2. Eminent domain rights of U.S. and state governments to "steal" treaty lands of American Indians and farmers; and
3. Elimination of subsidies to corn farmers and biofuel plants;
4. Elimination of free enterprise, competition and self-sufficiency.

So why do most of those farmers vote Republican and against economic interests of themselves, family, and neighbors? How can Republicans get away with cowardly chickening out or dummying up to "bear false witness" and "utter false reports" about not understanding the science on global warming despite the fact that the Arctic and Antarctica are melting and raising the sea level, which makes storms more destructive.

The Koch Brothers own a conglomerate of the largest newspapers from coast to coast. "Satanic Tools" (Republican politicians, preachers, and press [Rush Limbaugh and Fox News]) repeat over and over such disclaimers.

Wasn't it amazing during campaign years 2010-2014 that Southern evangelical ministers (who preach about God exacting punishment on sinners via tornados, hurricanes, flood, droughts, and forest fires) didn't shout during sermons that God was punishing Republicans from Georgia to Southern California for violating Commandments, Golden Rule and soul-saving rules? Why don't they preach that 100 percent of credible climatologists are clear that fossil fuels are polluting air, land, and water that God gave humans and causing global warming and severe weather?

MSNBC reported that Republicans "Join Hands with Wicked Men" the Koch Brothers. They purchase (in violation of "thou shall not steal") $7 billion in "income" for every $1 billion invested in bribes to Republican secrete Super PACs.

If it sounds like, looks like, and smells like a bribe, a campaign contribution is a bribe. When newspapers in Republican districts do not print the truth, it is up to intelligent readers to send editorial comments, such as the following by Loren Johnson, Nick Haviland, and me.

Stop the Keystone Madness

In recent letters to this paper, a proponent of the Keystone pipeline inferred that President Obama is irresponsible for not approving the pipeline and touted the many jobs that would ensue. I beg to differ.

In the last two weeks, several reports have emerged, all reinforcing the concept that climate change is caused by burning fossil fuels, that it is happening faster than previously thought, and that we have little time to act.

The bitumen that would flow through the proposed pipeline is particularly carbon intensive and would only exacerbate the climate problem. Keystone XL is more about climate change than it is about jobs and oil. There would be many more jobs in the emerging alternative and renewable energy field.

Most Americans are blissfully unaware of the consequences of carbon-cause climate change, unaware of the uncomfortable changes in lifestyle needed to accommodate climate change, and unaware that global warming is irreversible in any kind of human time frame. And yet too many of our political leaders are willfully blind to the evidence and are content to pretend that human activity has no effect on climate change.

Albert Einstein once observed, "We cannot solve our problems with the same kind of thinking that created them."

And that is the problem with the Keystone XL. It is an example of the kind of thinking, "drill baby drill," that got us into our predicament in the first place. Nix the Keystone XL. It would be the most responsible choice.

Loren Johnson, Elkhorn

Certainly no one is more concerned about weather change than farmers who produce our food. Consumers should be concerned about national and worldwide food supplies that can diminish during droughts and too much rain. They should also be concerned about Keystone XL pipeline ruptures that would poison water we drink and farmers use to irrigate crops.

As an attorney, I defended cases with underground erosion from deteriorated waterlines. It causes ground surface collapse (sinkholes). Will that occur from fracking? Will fracking for oil or gas cause earthquakes, sinkholes, and gas to come out of water faucets. I said to and asked Loren, "Farmers like you must be knowledgeable about animal science, horticulture, engineering, mechanics (to repair farm machinery), and business administration and work from 6 A.M. to 9 P.M. Why do Walworth County farmers vote Republican when Republican representatives vote against:

1. A decent minimum income for family farmers?
2. Food stamps, school lunches, and Meals on Wheels?
3. Subsidies for biofuels, such as alcohol/gas alternatives?
4. But for $400 million in subsidies for the top five U.S. oil and gas companies, who charge four dollars per gallon when it only costs eighteen cents per gallon to extract, refine, and sell (2012, give or take a few years).

"How can Walworth County farmers vote Republican under those circumstances and after Republicans in Washington, D.C., who own huge, corporate farms, voted for subsidies that will add to their wealth but reduced funds for food stamps and school lunches for children and Meals on Wheels for elderly, which financially hurts local farmers?"

After *The Lutheran* published Loren's piece on global warming, I thought about writing a commentary for *The Lutheran* based upon my father's December 24, 1945, letter to his Lutheran minister father about the power of the ruling class and propaganda to cause citizens to vote against their own interests. At the end of the letter, Dad said,

"If people fail to interest themselves in political matters, which is their duty to investigate, then someone must make it their task to stimulate such an interest as a patriotic citizen. Who can better bring it to their attention than the minister? Is it not a part of a minister's calling to try to ascertain whether political instructions and daily practices are in conformity with Christian standards?

"Is not our democratic system based upon Christian principles? Did it not originate under Christian tutelage and in a Christian era? Then if capitalism and democracy are stepchildren of Christianity, is it not Christianity's duty to give parental advice to its offspring? Or should Christianity allow its brainchild to become a savage robot with no interference?

"If you haven't been using this analytical approach, it probably will be hard to change, but remember, we are moving into a propaganda world which necessitates a keen observation and study of what is the truth."

Along those lines, I have contemplated sending the following commentary for publication in *The Lutheran*:

I remember a story Lutheran minister Grandfather Lebbeus Bigelow Woods heard from his nephew Col. John Oscar Woods, who counseled and prayed with Nazi war criminals during the Nuremburg Trials. Col. Woods said, "There was a German Lutheran minister who said, 'First they came for Jews, and I said nothing. Next they came for Roman Catholics, and I said nothing. After they came for Gypsies and I said nothing, they came for me.'"

Given how Hitler used Machiavellian, Divide-and-Conquer, Wedge-Issue Tactics to lure our Lutheran German cousins into racism and WWII, shouldn't *The Lutheran* publish editorials against Hitler-Nixon-type, Machiavellian, Divide-and-Conquer Tactics that stimulate racial, religious, and gender bias, prejudice, and intolerance so citizens vote Republican and against democracy and moral capitalism?

If Preachers Don't Say It, News Reporters Must

When I was at the University of Wisconsin, Republicans wanted to put cameras on State Street in Madison to intimidate students and make them think twice about engaging in protests to chill their First Amendment rights. In 1967 and '68, I was still a pro-Vietnam war hawk. I was caught up in three Madison police attacks on student protestors and students during the Stuart Block Party. Police had turned peaceful demonstrations and a block party into chaos and riot on Stuart Street by a biker gang vs. police.

On July 4, 2013, the *Lake Geneva Regional News* published a front-page story, "A look back at '67 Riot" and a commentary called "An Independence Day Trip Down Memory Lane." I was angered by a quote from a former Lake Geneva police officer who said, "Police did everything they could to prevent a riot by students." On August 1, 2013, the *Lake Geneva Regional News* published my response as the following two commentaries.

July 4, 1967 Assault, Batteries and Riot By Police

Thousands of college students who supported the Vietnam War were viciously assaulted, battered, and bloodied, and five hundred were falsely imprisoned July 4.

At the time, I was a pro-war hawk sophomore at the University of Wisconsin. I was hanging out in front of The Black Knight (now Hogs and Kisses) with two friends who were about to fly off to the Vietnam War and my brother, who had just been drafted after his sophomore year at UW Eau Claire. Two years later Warren returned as a staff sergeant with a Silver Star, Bronze Star and Purple Heart.

Several months after July 4, 1967, I was assaulted and injured by Madison police during the Dow Chemical Sit-Down Strike in front of the Commerce Building on the University of Wisconsin campus. When I arrived for accounting class, I walked through fewer than 100 antiwar protestors dressed like hippies or love children. Most were from New York, New Jersey, and Connecticut. They had to be in the upper 10 percent of their class to be admitted to UW.

They were engaged in a peaceful sit-down strike because Dow Chemical, a manufacturer of napalm, was interviewing students. I do not know whether it was planned or negligence, but Madison police attacked protestors with batons as hundreds of business students exited the Commerce Building. Business students were conservative and supported the Vietnam War.

We carried seventy-six battered UW students with concussions, broken arms, legs, and ribs to UW Hospital ER. My roommate, George Bogdanich, made the cover of *Newsweek*. His hand was out as he shouted "stop" to police.

As a result of those and other police riots, I decided to try and reform law enforcement. I studied police science and earned as master of science in administration of justice. I became a special police officer to determine whether laws could be enforced without political and racial bias.

For the International Association of Chiefs of Police, I wrote "Police Community Relations – 1975." For a Governor's Criminal Justice Advisory Commission, I wrote Standards and Goals for Crime Prevention, Law Enforcement, Prosecution and Courts. Lake Geneva and Madison Police riots are featured in my book *Tortious Lies: Wedge Issues and Morality*.

On July 4, 1967, the vast majority of college students in Lake Geneva were pro-war hawks from small, conservative, Midwestern colleges. The last thing any reasonably prudent college student wanted was a felony conviction, a conviction that could prevent them from becoming a teacher, nurse, attorney, or doctor. A conviction would cause expulsion from college, loss of college military deferent, and boys would be drafted.

Before Lake Geneva police rioted, thousands of college-age kids were peacefully talking and joking between the Main and Broad Street traffic lights and the Riviera. We were there for one purpose: to find a cool girl or boyfriend. However, the scene was different from previous years. On July 4, 1967, Lake Geneva Police had helmets, shields, shotguns, semiautomatic rifles, and German shepherds. A dozen officers with dogs stood from traffic light to traffic light across Broad Street.

The only problems Lake Geneva police faced were from motorcycle gang bikers who shouted "Nazi Gestapo Storm Troopers" and threw firecrackers at Lake Geneva police. Suddenly police threw tear gas, unleashed German shepherds and marched down Broad Street, bashing the heads of anyone in the way, even petite, frail girls half their size.

We jumped on cars to get out of the way of the teeth of dogs and ran South to the Riviera, Wrigley Drive, and our car. However, in a well-orchestrated pincer movement, National Guard troops with fixed bayonets marched toward the Riviera from both ends of Wrigley. We swam to safety.

My investigation was easy. Father Wendell Woods was president of the Walworth County Bar Association. Uncle Burnise Olsen was a legendary investigator and sheriff of Walworth County.

I learned that bad blood had been brewing between Lake Geneva Police and biker gangs who didn't fit their image of moral Americans. Bikers accused police of unlawful stops, searches, seizures, and brutality. As a matter of fact, most small-town police forces warned bikers to move on.

Police officers were military veterans who strongly supported the Vietnam War. The police culture thought college antiwar protestors were communist traitors or aiders and abettors of communist enemies.

I also learned what the Kerner Commission and Katzenback Commission Reports found about causes of racial and civil disobedience. Police applicants were not given personality profiles and background checks to weed out those with racial, religious, gender, and political bias. There was no college education requirement for police applicants. Police academy training didn't include police community relations, cultural diversities, sociology, psychology, conflict resolution, and Bill of Rights.

Many had become police officers to serve and protect the public. However, there was, and still is, an us (police) vs. them (civilians) mentality in law enforcement. They still ride around in glass-steel bubbles shielded from the public. They rarely walk the streets to talk with and get to know the people they police.

There's an irony in the way law enforcement handled the Wall Street 99 percent movement, a movement that wanted changes that would benefit police, their families, and friends. Yet police treated Wall Street protestors the way police treated antiwar and civil rights protestors in the 1960s.

Let me also address comments by a judge and prosecutor after July 4, 1967. A judge was quoted as saying to arrestees, "You do not meet our moral standards. You have shaggy manes and dirty clothes, and I wish you would not come here again."

That judge's job was not to illegally impose moral and personal grooming standards but to apply the strict letter of the law. Before the Lake Geneva police assaults and batteries, everyone was well-groomed because they were there to meet girls or guys. Dirty clothes and shaggy manes were caused by police chasing, assaulting, and beating and then incarceration in cow pens at the Walworth County Fairgrounds.

How about District Attorney Robert Reed's comment, "Those arrested were a 'mob of overage brats?'" Yet Mr. Reed didn't convict any of the "brats," did he?

I knew at least one hundred of the July 4, 1967, victims. Every one of those teenagers grew up in a church, Cub and Boy Scouts or Brownies and Girl Scouts, and in sports. Our Baby Boomer Generation of Morality believed in Commandments, Golden Rules, the United States Constitution, Bill of Rights, and The American Way of Fair Play.

I don't recall what happened the previous year on July 4, 1966. The *Regional News* had sketchy details about "street lights and bottles broken, shrubs and signs ripped out and cars pushed."

Did youths start that or did police cause it? Did July 4, 1966, justify Lake Geneva police to set a trap and attack in a preemptive strike by 125 police officers and 600 National Guard against 3,000 to 5,000 defenseless college and high school students with bayonets, tear gas, batons, dogs, shotguns, rifles, and a National Guard machine gunner who had "shoot to kill orders"?

The judge, prosecutor, police, National Guard, and governor who planned and executed the July 4, 1967, attack, assaults, and batteries were negligent, grossly negligent, or had criminal intent. Did any of them ask, "What if an officer mistakenly thinks a firecracker, M-80, or cherry bomb explosion was a gunshot from the students? What if an officer accidentally or purposely fires a gun? Other officers may think the shot came from students and open fire. If National Guard troops thought students were shooting at police, would they fire rifles and machine gun?"

Another irony of July 4, 1967, is that National Guard troops who supported Lake Geneva police were primarily college or high school graduates who joined the Guard to avoid being drafted and sent to Vietnam.

After July 4, 1967, where was the governor's brain? He allowed college-student hating Madison police supported by the National Guard to enter a great institution of learning to suppress student First Amendment freedom of speech and protest rights. At the time, there was only a few hundred students who were hard-core, antiwar protestors out of forty-two thousand students, two-thirds of whom graduated from high schools in conservative, small towns of Wisconsin.

Starting in the 1950s nationwide in grade and high school, we read in civics classes *Current Events*, a CIA publication that told stories about atheistic communist countries not allowing freedom of speech, press, religion, and protests against government actions.

The CIA turned parents of UW students against them by sending a letter to parents. It was allegedly written by a UW professor who didn't exist. The CIA falsely alleged communism was being taught in every UW classroom and communists were behind civil rights, antiwar, and feminist movements.

Fact was, the communist witch hunt terrorism of Wis. Sen. Joe McCarthy, put a chill on freedom of speech. UW professors didn't talk about communism, even in political science courses I took.

During the past fifty years of watching television, I have witnessed protests, marches, and demonstrations in the Deep South and dozens of cities around the globe. They all had two things in common. Protestors were peaceful until attacked by police or soldiers. Then protestors threw back tear gas, stones, and bricks. Why? Because of natural law human instincts and inclinations of people who think they're in the right and don't like being pushed around.

Those involved in decision-making in Lake Geneva and Madison were either seriously deficient in knowledge of U.S. history or disregarded it. On July 4, 1776, when the Declaration of Independence was signed, half the colonies and their citizens didn't want to break ties with Great Britain. Seven years later our Founding Fathers gave us ten amendments to the U.S. Constitution. We call those amendments the Bill of Rights. Why?

To prevent majorities in government from violating innate, human rights of freedom of speech, press, religion, and to protest government action or inaction. To prevent the U.S. government from doing what British troops did to American colonists who supported the American Revolution. The post-Civil War Fourteenth Amendment prohibited state governments from violating the Bill of Rights.

As for me? My Republican, pro-war, hawkish dogma was no match for my roommate's antiwar, dovish answers. Finally out of frustration about losing every debate or argument, I asked George Bogdanich to give me something to read about Vietnam. He gave me *The Pentagon Papers* and *Roots of Conflict*. The disastrous Tet Offensive of 1968, *Pentagon Papers*, and Walter Cronkite of CBS News (the most trusted man and news caster in America) turned public opinion against the Vietnam War.

My brother, like all soldiers, was put through the pro-Vietnam War army indoctrination program in boot camp and advanced infantry training. He was furious when I became antiwar. To this day, I don't think he believes me when I say, "99 percent of antiwar protestors were not against soldiers but against an immoral and wrong war that could kill their friends and relatives."

As a result of the false CIA letter about communism being taught in UW classrooms, my father was furious. I said, "I have never heard any UW professor talk about communism. Trick Dicky is probably behind the letter." Dad pointed to the door and shouted, "get out" even though I had just graduated from UW and had no job but did have a wife and baby.

My father and I didn't talk for almost five years until Law Day after President Nixon skipped town to avoid impeachment. Dad called and said, "You were right. An OWI/OSS colleague who is now in the CIA confirmed your suspicion that the CIA authored the UW professor letter."

We never talked about politics for the rest of his life. My brother still won't talk about politics.

Perhaps the most incredible thing about the 1960s was that police had no problem going on strike and endangering public safety for a dollar- per-hour pay increase. Yet they didn't believe civil rights, antiwar, and feminist activists had a right to protest for equal rights and justice and against a war.

They ignored the Bill of Rights and forgot a Golden Rule, "Do unto others as you would have others do unto you" — a lesson Caucasians should remember because in eighteen years, Caucasians will be a minority.

Curtis A. Woods JD, MS, BA, has thirteen criminal and civil justice publications

As indicated, the July 4, 2013, *Lake Geneva Regional News* lead story quoted an officer who said police did everything they could to prevent what happened. The only other person who witnessed and wrote about events submitted the following editorial commentary that blames police volunteers.

"Volunteers" Cause of Skirmishes
To the Editor:

Your telling of that story was good. I was there tending bar at the Geneva Hotel.

I said then, and I'll say it again, that some of those "volunteers" (police volunteers from neighboring cities) were the root cause of several skirmishes during the whole episode. They were on the prod for several hours at the intersection of Main and Broad Streets, pushing and shoving with their sticks or big flashlights, telling kids who were there to move on.

Respectfully submitted…

Nick Haviland, Lake Geneva

How About "Crooked Man" Poems in the Press

Wisconsin Governor Walker Is a Crooked Talker

Gov. has a crooked smile,
As he walks a crooked mile.
He has crooked Yin and Yang,
As he talks like a crooked man.
Gov. takes Koch Bro Bribes,
That he most certainly hides.
So Koch Bros can frack and mine,
Til poisoned water and earthquake
Makes us realize he was a mistake.
So Wisconsinites will pine,
For the Good Old Days,
When Wisc. govs had spine
And kept One Percent Devils in line.
After he flunked economics,
He went through histrionics,
And fed Wiscs a crooked line,
About jobs for Wisconsinites,
But he is almost out of time.

Congressman Paul Ryan has been Lying

Ryan speaks with forked tongue,
About wanting to help the young,
But he believes in Ayn Rand Dung
And wants poor kids to die young.

Lying Ryan is against infrastructure aid?
But wants One-Percent Devil contributors paid,
Secretly via infrastructure Welfare Aid
But votes against Social Safety Net Aid,
Irish Ryan ignores a Golden Rule norm
And so he opposes Immigration Reform.
By avoiding duties Reps should perform,
Ryan's showing the other 99 percent no concern.

I forwarded "Wisconsin Governor Walker is a Crooked Talker" to his Democratic gubernatorial challenger Mary Burk, along with suggestions about how to exploit Walker's violations of the U.S. Constitution, Golden Rule, Commandments and soul-saving rules. I sent a similar letter to Wisconsin and national Democratic leaders. No one had the guts to exploit his weakness.

The following commentary was sent to the *Capital Times* in Madison.

The University of Wisconsin Is a Rare Jewel

We live in a world of global technology. Yet high school students in the United States rank seventeenth in math, twenty-first in science, and twenty-fifth in reading comprehension. How do Republicans want to get the U.S. back into a number-one ranking? Republicans in Washington, D.C., cut federal education assistance funding for schools. Wisconsin Governor Walker cut state funding for grade schools and high schools and proposes to cut $300 million of state funding for the University of Wisconsin System.

The University of Wisconsin–Madison is one of the leading social science and hard science universities in the United States and world. As a result, surrounding UW are dozens of high-tech research and development companies. When my father and aunt attended in the 1930s, they were taught by professors who wrote textbooks. That remained true during the Baby Boomer Generation when UW had Nobel Prize-winning biologists and chemists. UW experimental psychology ranked number three. My U.S. military history professor was among the top three. My criminology professor was on loan for a one-year sabbatical as the most popular professor at Ohio State.

My ex-wife and I were hired not based upon our graduate degrees but based on our BS and BA from UW. So too for a niece and nephew.

Economic times are difficult for state universities, especially during economic depression. Instead of cutting UW System budget, Wisconsin should invest in the future by bringing to UW the best researchers and writers. Many top flight professors left UW for greener pastures.

CHAPTER VII

Second Amendment Insanity

The Second Amendment gives us a right to bear arms. When adopted in 1791, Americans only had single-shot pistols, smooth-bore muskets, and rifles for hunting, self defense, defense of family, and defense against British, Indians, highway robbers, government, and other burglars.

Our Founding Fathers couldn't possibly have foreseen that 140 years later Bonnie and Clyde would bear Browning automatic rifles and Machine Gun Kelly would carry a Thompson submachine gun. They outgunned every law enforcement agency in America.

In the 1930s, a Republican U.S. Supreme Court had no problem ruling that the Second Amendment didn't include a right to purchase, own, or sell a Thompson or Browning. However, an argument can be made justifying sane, noncriminal and nonpsychopathic Americans to carry military assault rifles.

Democratic President Lyndon Baines Johnson funded a War on Poverty to prevent racial war and provide minorities with opportunities to rise out of poverty and illiteracy. Sane, moral Republicans, like my father, respected and applauded Rev. Martin Luther King's peaceful protests for preventing a racial civil war and preaching against violence.

However, insane and immoral Hitler-Nixon-Hoover-McCarthy-type Republicans didn't honor or believe in Commandments, Golden Rules, or the U.S. Constitution and Bill of Rights. Nixon Republicans were psychopathically crippled by racial, religious, cultural, and gender bias, prejudice, and intolerance. They didn't want to help minority groups that had been victims of their racism. Some Nixon Republicans wanted racial and religious wars of genocide against Afro, Latin, Asian, Jewish and Native Americans.

In accordance with Anglo-Saxon New World Order plans to suppress any and all dissent against government, "One Percent Devils and Their Satanic Tools" Nixon Republicans transferred War on Poverty funds to the Law Enforcement Assistance Administration (LEAA) under President Nixon's pretext of maintaining "Law and Order."

LEAA issued grants to state, county, and municipal governments to computerize; hire more law enforcement officers and investigators; create regional communication systems and SWAT teams; and to buy more patrol cars, helicopters, and tanks and arm all officers with M-15s, shotguns, sidearms and ankle arms, Tazers, batons, and tear and pepper gas.

However, as indicated in my editorial comment in Chapter VI ("July 4, 1967, Assault, Batteries and Riot by Lake Geneva Police," which also discussed Madison police riots against University of Wisconsin students) there is an us (police) vs. them (civilians) mentality.

This is in part because most officers were in the military and almost all contact between police and civilians is during negative situations: traffic stops, response to crimes, domestic violence, prostitution, and drugs. Also police officers and their families only socialize and party with police and families of police officers. Their former high school and churchgoing friends who smoke marijuana stop inviting them to social events.

In addition while on patrol, officers are shielded from the public in steel and glass cars. They rarely get out to walk streets with a smile and greetings or talk to and get to know teens, business people, laborers, and the poor.

Perhaps worst of all, municipalities use state troopers and sheriff and police officers as a cash cow to balance budgets. Officers are promoted based on numbers of arrests or traffic tickets issued. Thus either officially or unofficially, their ability to exercise discretion to not arrest or issue a ticket is eliminated. Instead of giving normally good kids and adults a break and a warning, their lives, careers, and families are ruined or damaged to balance municipal budgets so cowardly inept Republicans don't have to raise taxes.

Bill Cosby once said, "Where I grew up in Philadelphia, you either became a cop, priest, or criminal." Those who become police carry into their jobs racial, religious, cultural, and gender bias, prejudice, and intolerance they learned from families and in neighborhoods where they grew up.

National Criminal Justice Standards and Goals Commission wrote standards and goals to eliminate law enforcement applicants with racial, religious, cultural, and gender bias and provide Police Community Relations Training:

1. Law enforcement agencies should reflect the racial, religious, cultural, and gender composition of the citizens they police;
2. Screen out law enforcement applicants who have biases and prejudices via:
   a. Personality profiles; and
   b. Background checks;
3. Training in cultural and religious diversities, dispute resolution (for domestic, gang, and neighborhood disputes), police community relations, Bill of Rights, and related case law.

However, after billions of LEAA dollars to modernize and professionalize law enforcement, too many "Judeo-Christian," Caucasian "law enforcement" officers are neo-Nazis with racial, religious, cultural, political, and gender biases. As minority members and women became law enforcement officers, they faced peer-group pressure that made them as disrespectful and brutal to minorities and women. Police protect each other with a blue code of silence to hide their crimes to enforce the law.

In other words, Caucasian neo-Nazi officers employed Machiavellian, Divide-and-Conquer Tactics to turn Afro- and Latin-American officers against Afro- and Latin-American brothers and sisters. Caucasian officers killing innocent Afro-American teens, as recently occurred in Ferguson, Missouri and in other cities, tends to generate two things: peaceful protests and marches, but police officers pushed, assaulted, and battered marchers and protestors and caused chaos, riots, and looting.

Those illegal, knee-jerk reactions by law enforcement officers are spun against protestors by police chiefs, prosecutors, and mayors to hide truth and protect criminal law enforcement officers. Somehow jury after jury lets them get away with murder and other brutalities.

When two police officers were shot outside the Ferguson Police Department, I thought, "It's amazing that hasn't happened before. I wonder if police will see those shootings as a warning of things to come if they don't stop racial profiling and abusing their law enforcement powers to suppress Afro and Latin Americans."

"Given the number of disgruntled employees who have taken a gun to their former place of employment and killed several coworkers, isn't it also amazing that 'One Percent Devils' and their boards of directors who outsourced jobs of former veterans haven't been gunned down or blown up."

Police assaults and batteries of 99 percent Wall Street protestors is most troubling for two reasons. Billions of LEAA dollars were spent to screen, train, and professionalize law enforcement. However, they still cannot respect the First Amendment "right of the people peaceably to assemble and to petition government for a redress of grievances."

Historically Chiefs and Kings Promised to Protect or Punish and Give Restitution to Citizens Who Promised to Give Up Natural Law Rights to Private Vengeance and Compensation

Under "Theory of Law" by St. Thomas Aquinas, the Declaration of Independence and other writings by Thomas Jefferson, if government breaks its covenant to protect citizens, punish criminals, and compensate their victims, shouldn't they be entitled under natural law to exact private vengeance and compensation from criminals. Similarly if "One Percent Devils and their Satanic Tools" use police to protect their interests (as they did during peaceful, First Amendment, 99 percent Wall Street protests), shouldn't protestors be allowed to defend themselves with equal firepower?

One can understand why police officers in the 1960s assaulted and battered civil rights, antiwar, and feminist protestors. They were allowed to illegally enforce their racial, political, and gender bias against protestors.

Would Mutually Assured Destruction Stop Police from Shooting Unarmed Afro and Latin Americans?

As indicated in Chapter II, long ago citizens relinquished their natural law human instincts and inclinations to seeks vengeance or retribution in exchange for a promise from the village chief or king that he would:

1. Protect everyone from crimes;
2. But if the king or chief failed to do so:

a. He promised to catch the criminal, punish him, and exact restitution from the criminal for the victim;

b. But if the chief or king failed to punish and exact restitution:

   1) If a goat was stolen and eaten, the owner would get four goats from the king or chief;

   2) If a child was killed, the king or chief would give the parents an orphan of the same age and abilities as the killed child;

   3) If a wife was seduced away from husband, the chief or king would give husband a widow who resembled wife.

Instead of King John vs. John Doe, in a democracy, cases are labeled State vs. John Doe. When the state fails to protect citizens from crimes, punish criminals, and exact restitution for victims, the state is in breach of its historical covenant or promise. Yet the state's breach is more significant when law enforcement agencies and criminal justice systems don't:

1. Reflect racial, religious, culture, or gender makeup of community;
2. Screen out undesirable police applicants who have racial, religious, cultural, and gender bias, prejudice, and intolerance;
3. Train police recruits to treat all citizens with respect for their rights under the Bill of rights;
4. Discipline and punish law enforcement officers for crimes and abuse of criminal and civil rights; and
5. Have honest and fair trials of law enforcement officers because other officers honor the blue code of silence and won't testify against a fellow officer; and
6. Prosecutors:

   a. As in Ferguson case, purposely confused and gave grand jurors contradictory evidence so they can't indict officers;

   b. Or when police officers are on trial, prosecutors are so incompetent that even when jurors see on film five police officers kicking a defenseless Afro American lying on the ground in a fetal position, jurors don't convict police officers.

Rev. Martin Luther King prevented racial war by leading peaceful protest marches, but marchers were brutalized for asserting their First Amendment rights. However, in the 1960s, heavily armed Blank Panther, Symbionese Liberation Army, and Students for a Democratic Society Anarchists advocated armed rebellion, revolution, and killing police officers.

This year alone, police have killed unarmed Afro Americans in Ferguson, Baltimore, New York City, etc., etc., etc. Protest marches followed each death, and police officers attacked many of those protestors.

If police officers don't want loved ones and friends of their Latin- and Afro-American victims to extract good-old-fashioned Old Testament "an eye for an eye" revenge and won't tolerate peaceful First Amendment protests, what are Afro and Latin Americans supposed to do? Should Latin and Afro Americans be allowed to be armed to the gills like police officers?

The United States, Russia, and China produced enough nuclear bombs and missiles to destroy each nation many times over under a theory that mutually assured destruction would prevent normal and sane leaders from ordering a preemptive nuclear attack. That, of course, presumes that leaders of those nations will always be rational and sane.

Would mutually assured destruction by allowing Afro and Latin Americans to be as armed as law enforcement officers prevent them from racial profiling, abusing rights, and shooting Latin and Afro Americans?

However, one cannot understand why police did the same to 99 percent Wall Street protestors. They were protesting for reforms of Wall Street that would benefit police officers, their families, and friends. Shouldn't laws under Second Amendment allow 99 percent Wall Street protestors to protect themselves with sidearms, Tazers, pepper gas, tear gas, and M-15s?

If neo-Nazi law enforcement officers armed with military assault rifles want wars to kill Afro, Latin, Jewish, and Muslim Americans, shouldn't they carry military assault rifles under Second Amendment? Since juries will not convict police officers for murder even when murders are on videotape and police won't testify against each other due to the blue code, shouldn't all Americans be allowed carry a military assault rifle?

In accordance with Anglo-Saxon New World Order plans by "One Percent Devils and Their Satanic Tools," Nixon-McCarthy-G.W. Bush Republicans enacted the Patriot Act. It added five new domestic spy agencies and eliminated the Bill of Rights for any American who is Muslim or associates with Muslims.

So now Republican presidents can "legally" do what President Nixon did illegally. What's to stop a Republican president from secretly declaring that Methodists are terrorists because they disagreed with the president?

Historically "One Percent Devils and Satanic Tools" ordered law enforcement officers to assault, batter, jail, and kill labor unionists. Shouldn't they be allowed to defend themselves with military assault rifles if necessary?

So governments have two choices. They can recruit law enforcement officers who want to legally and morally enforce the law and provide proper training and discipline. Or citizens should have the right to defend themselves against police who violate rights of citizens and criminal laws.

John Wayne Stand-Your-Ground Laws when Juries Acquit Caucasians Who Murder Afro and Latin Americans but Convict and Execute Them for Murdering Caucasians

Caucasian prosecutors and judges intentionally or negligently caused acquittal of Caucasian murderers in State vs. Zimmerman and State vs. Dunn by failing to apply knowledge from spouse-murder cases. In the 1970s when I wrote Standards and Goal for Prosecution, Courts and Corrections, I attended a conference of prison wardens. They reported a sequence of escalating hostilities that led to men killing wives or girlfriends.

Hostilities at home started with disagreements. Disagreements evolved into arguments. Arguments evolved into threats. Threats evolved into slaps. Slapping evolved into pushing against the wall and hitting with fists, bats, and frying pans. That evolved into beatings until the man or women thought, "The next time she (or he) does (or says) that, I'll kill her (or him)."

Didn't the evidence in the Zimmerman and Dunn trials reveal a sequence of escalating racial hatred that led to them gunning down law-abiding Afro-American teenagers? However, after a physically abused Afro American woman merely fired a warning shot, she was sentenced to sixty years in prison. Laws that allow inconsistency or inequity are, for all practical purposes, saying to the public, "Caucasians can be acquitted for killing Afro Americans, but if they fire a warning shot or murder a Caucasian, they're imprisoned or executed."

Before Trayvon Martin was murdered, Zimmerman's 911 police calls about Afro-American teens revealed increasing frustration about Afro Americans getting away before police arrived. Those calls also revealed a racial profiler who hated Afro Americans. So why didn't Caucasian prosecutors insist there's clear and convincing evidence of a racist intent to kill? Why did a Caucasian judge order "race wasn't an issue?" Wasn't Zimmerman's and Dunn's lack of remorse for killing an innocent teenager further evidence of a racial murder or psychosocial pathology?

Neighborhood Watch and Stand-Your-Ground Laws

In the early 1970s, the National Criminal Justice Standards and Goals Commission said, "Neighborhood Watch volunteers should not be armed. They should report criminal suspects and not make citizen arrests."

In order to receive Law Enforcement Assistance Administration funds to create Neighborhood Watch programs, states were required to adopt those rules of thumb. After I parroted those rules for the New Jersey Governor's Criminal Justice Standards and Goals Committee, they adopted those rules and the legislature turned them into law.

Didn't Florida do the same? If so, shouldn't Zimmerman have been charged with violation of such laws and false arrest? If Florida law made it a felony for Neighborhood Watch volunteers to carry a gun and make an arrest, wouldn't that be a reason for the jury to convict Zimmerman of second-degree murder or killing someone while committing a felony?

In the Dunn case, evidence showed a similar escalation of resentment, hostility, and anger toward Afro-American teens who played rap music and talked back to Caucasians. If I was the prosecutor in the Dunn and Zimmerman cases, I would have told the above story about escalation of hostility in spouses who kill spouses. Then I would have said to each jury, "Wasn't there enough evidence to conclude that Zimmerman had reached a point and thought, 'The next time a n.... tries to get away before police arrive, I'll kill him.'" Why didn't the prosecutor's closing arguments say, "Facts, statements, evidence, and timing reveal that Zimmerman shot Trayvon Martin not because he feared for his life but because he couldn't tolerate an Afro American getting better of him, a weak, racist Caucasian."

If I was the prosecutor in the Dunn case, I would have insisted that racism was a motive for murder and said in closing arguments, "All generations hate the music of the next generation. My parents listened to classic and big band music but didn't like rock and roll. There were many statements by Dunn from which you can infer and conclude that he's a racist. Just like spouses can engage in escalating hostilities that end in murder, you can infer that Mr. Dunn eventually said to himself or thought, 'The next time a n.... talks back to me, I will kill him.'"

Stand-Your-Ground laws are based upon a John Wayne complex that Means, "You can kill anyone as long as you think you're in the right." The fact is that the script always showed that John Wayne had a right to kill.

No aggressor should be able to claim a Stand-Your-Ground defense when an aggressee turns the tables. When I was in high school and college, I never witnessed a fight during a party. It seemed like my sons and step-kids never went to a party where there wasn't a fight over a girl or sports. I said, "Any girl who wants you to fight for her doesn't love or respect you. What if your punch kills or disables? Before you can claim self-defense after a fight or killing someone, you must retreat until you can no longer safely retreat. Then you can only use reasonable force to defend yourself. You can only kill and claim self-defense when trapped and faced with serious bodily harm or death."

TV Violence and Killers of Fellow Students

In the 1960s, the school of psychology at University of Wisconsin did a study to determine effects on children of television violence from cartoons to the most graphic and grotesque killing. Results showed that:

1. Cartoon violence was the least real and thus least harmful;
2. Killings that didn't reveal graphic and grotesque results were most harmful because children didn't witness actual horrors;
3. Killings that showed graphic and grotesque results such as:
   a. Bloody heads, arms, and legs being blown apart by bullets;
   b. Blood spurting from neck after shotgun blew off a head; or
   c. Guts lying open and on ground from a high-powered rifle;
4. Had two results:
   a. Some kids were sickened and turned off by blood and guts;
   b. Others experienced a cathartic release of anger and desires to kill a parent, neighborhood or school bully.

As a result of that study and studies at other universities, TV violence ratings allow parents to prevent children from watching violence that leads to violent children. The rating system may have had the opposite effect on many children.

Cleaned-up killing and John Wayne complex themes (you can kill if you're in the right) have the worst effect on children.

Bully Political Tactics Turn Children into Bullies
and Causes Their Victims to Take Guns to School to Kill Bullies

When Baby Boomers of Republican Walworth County, Wisconsin, were in school:

1. There were not fights over girls or sports and no murders; and
2. Blessed kids didn't pick on children who were fat or unattractive;
3. Unintelligent students didn't call intelligent students or those with glasses "geeks."

Almost every Baby Boomer in Walworth County went to church to learn Commandments and Golden Rules. Such eternal law was reinforced by parents who also told family adages about how to treat other people with respect. Most Walworth Boomers also learned morality in Cub Scouts or Brownies and Boy or Girl Scouts. Some of the adages parents related to children are listed in the Introduction. Others included:

1. "But for the grace of God and your genes, you're tall, handsome or beautiful, thin, intelligent, athletic, and don't wear glasses";
2. "It's immoral to pick on others who are smaller and weaker";
3. "Don't kick a man when he is down";
4. "It's cowardly to pick on those with physical or mental defects";
5. "Don't allow others to control you with teasing";
6. "Best way to stop someone from teasing is to learn to laugh at yourself and do teasers one better by smiling as you say something that makes them feel guilty or laughed at by bully friends, such as":
   a. "It's a pity your manners don't match your looks";
   b. "I may be a geek, but I'll be rich, famous, and marry for love, but the only way you'll become rich is to be a:
   c. "Gold digger whose husband will trade you in for a newer model"; or
   d. "A prostitute and then a madam";
7. "Your self-esteem is so low you must put others down to elevate your pathetic ego";

8. "Why do unto me what you wouldn't want others to do to you";
9. "If you knew what others said about you, you'd be humble";
10. "When people see they can't upset you, they'll stop teasing";
11. "Do not build your self-esteem at the expense of others. Build your ego by doing well in school, sports, music, or art."

Racial, Religious, Cultural, and Gender Bias Starts at Home

Children learn to become bullies from parents and Satanic Tools (Republican politicians, preachers, and press) who employ Hitler-Nixon-type Machiavellian, Divide-and-Conquer, Wedge-Issue, Tactics to stimulate racial, religious, gender, and cultural bias, prejudice, hatred, and intolerance.

Most amazing, Republican candidates do it in front of their own children and spouses. Perhaps they're trying to teach their children how to run for office like a Republican.

Solutions to end bullying and massacres in schools:

1. Parents must not express racial, religious, cultural, and gender bias;
2. Parents and children should watch news on television but only news shows such as MSNBC, which is factually accurate, objective, and intellectually honest because for most issues hosts bring in Republicans, independents, Democrats, university professors and authors who expose:
   a. Orwellian *1984*-type repetitive lies; and
   b. Hitler-Nixon-style, Machiavellian, Divide-and-Conquer, Wedge- Issue Tactics to stimulate, racial, religious, cultural, and gender bias so people vote Republican and against their own interests;
   c. Preachers and press (such as four-time gender-abusive husband, drug addict Rush Limbaugh and commentators on Fox News);
3. Parents must not let children watch or listen to Satanic Republican politicians, preachers, and press;
4. Parents shouldn't let kids watch John Wayne complex movies;
5. Parents should teach Commandments, Golden Rules, and adages;
6. Satanic Tools (Republican politicians, preachers, and press) of One

Percent Devils must end preaching racial, religious, cultural, and gender bias, prejudice, and intolerance;

7. Criminal history and domestic violence record checks and personality profiles to prevent criminals, those with a propensity to be criminals, and neo-Nazis from legally buying guns; and

8. Learn how Australia has prevented mass killings in schools.

CHAPTER VIII

Fourth, Fifth, Sixth, Eighth, and Fourteenth Amendment Rights Violated by State Troopers, Sheriffs, Police, County, and Municipal Judges

Two or Three Wrongs Don't Make a Right

Justice William O. Douglas said rights of individuals or a minority group shouldn't be the subject of a majority vote. He was a member of the Warren Court of four Republicans, an independent, and four Democrat justices. They have been criticized by Republicans for sixty years for unanimous decisions on criminal, civil, racial, gender, privacy, bedroom, and elderly rights.

Since 1975 Supreme Courts with five Republicans and four Democrats have chipped away at those rights. So they've violated the key constitutional principle of Justice Douglas and made rights of minorities and individuals the subject of majority votes.

Until 1975 Supreme Court decisions were based upon extending precedents that made future constitutional law predictable. Republican majorities have made constitutional law unpredictable. According to legal theorists (Fuller and Hart), that violates morality of law.

Founding Fathers gave us the Bill of Rights to prevent a majority in government from doing what British troops did to colonists and their supporters during the American Revolution. They wanted to prevent a majority government from violating innate human rights of political opponents and minorities.

Warren Court saw that state, county, and municipal law enforcement agencies violated constitutional rights of criminal suspects, especially Afro-American civil rights protestors, Latin Americans, and long-haired hippie guys and gals wearing lovechild clothes and beads. State troopers, sheriff officers, and police officers engaged in:

- Racial and political profiling and without probable causes conducted illegal searches and seizures. If they found a gun or marijuana, they lied about seeing a gun or smelling marijuana before the search.

That's called a pretext arrest;

- Planting evidence — In the 1990s, I sat on a jury (in Mercer County, NJ) where:
  1. A Trenton police lieutenant testified as an illicit drug sale "expert" that within a reasonable degree of probability possession of more than ten marijuana joints in a school zone was prima facie evidence of intent to sell to children but based upon the Frye test for admission of only scientific expert opinions as set forth in Chapter XII, I was surprised that:
     a. Prosecutor didn't have the witness support his opinion by citing published peer-reviewed research;
     b. Defense attorney failed to demand such evidence;
     c. trial judge also didn't do his job as gatekeeper who is supposed to allow only scientific expert opinions; and
     d. As a knowledgeable juror, I didn't asked about the Frye test;
- Defendant admitted possessing six marijuana cigarettes and testified that the arresting officer reached into the wheel well of his patrol car for a pill canister containing six more joints. During deliberations the jury concluded:
  1. The six joints defendant admitted possessing meant that he was guilty of possession;
  2. Those six joints were the same length, width, and color;
  3. But the other six joints were different lengths, color, and width; and
  4. Although the police officer who testified was not the arresting officer, he said he marked both ziplock evidence bags and pill canister;

5. However, the jury concluded:
   a. Handwriting on the ziplock with six uniform joints was significantly different from handwriting on pill canister and ziplock that held an odd assortment of joints;
   b. Both types of handwriting were contained on police report;
   c. That meant:
      1) Police officer lied under oath; and
      2) The other officer had planted evidence;
      3) Defendant couldn't be found guilty of intent to sell in a school zone; and
      4) Defendant's public advocate defense attorney was incompetent in not recognizing differences in handwriting;

- Rather than learning to be thorough and scientific police investigators, law enforcement officers were lazy. They employed torture (beatings, water hosing and boarding, deprivation of water, food, cigarettes, and sleep, blinding lights and loud noises) for as many days as needed to force confessions:
  1. Many who were innocent confessed to end torture;
  2. Many of them were executed for murders they didn't commit; and
  3. Some who were deprived of sleep developed psychotic symptoms before confessing;
  4. Others were convicted and executed based upon faulty witness identification (by Caucasians who couldn't tell one Afro American from another); and
  5. Research by governor of New York and Northwestern University showed 1, 2, and 3 led NY and Illinois governors to end executions.

Warren Court picked cases (Mapp, Escobedo, and Miranda) to assert that even the most heinous criminals have rights under the Bill of Rights. Founding Fathers and Warren Court also tried to prevent use of criminal and civil justice systems to suppress rights of minorities and individuals. In other words, the rights of individuals and minorities were more important than rights of the majority and government.

Fourth, Fifth, and Sixth Amendments

In 1961 the Warren Court held in Mapp v. Ohio that the federal exclusionary rule barred use of illegally obtained evidence at trial. That included under Fourth Amendment, evidence obtained by warrantless and thus illegal wire taps, searches and seizures of mail at home or business, and under Fifth Amendment confessions induced by beatings and other tortures.

In 1966 the Warren Court held in Miranda v. Arizona that suspects must be informed of their rights in the Bill of Rights before being questioned about a crime. That led to the Miranda warning, a warning that had been standard operating procedure in the FBI since 1948.

That is, except when FBI Director J. Edgar Hoover violated those SOPs by ordering FBI agents to do warrantless searches and wiretaps of suspected communists in U.S. government, movie stars (like Marilyn Monroe when she had an affair with President Kennedy), singers (like Elvis Presley, who was considered a bad influence on teenagers), news reporters, presidents, vice presidents, senators, representatives, and candidates running for office, and civil rights, antiwar, feminist, and environmentalist activists. Hoover's source of power as director of FBI was dirty and crooked secrets.

That's how he survived eight presidents. Hoover also followed orders from President Nixon to do warrantless searches and wiretaps of civil rights, antiwar, and feminine activists, reporters, their friends, and family.

My First and Fourth Amendment Rights Violated in 1971 and 2012

I complained about the illegality of Lake Geneva and Madison police assaults, batteries, and riots to Uncle Bernise Olsen, a legendary investigator and sheriff of Walworth County. I wanted to do something about it. He said, "Why don't you get a master of science in administration of justice at American University in Washington, D.C.? Professors at American U are on or advising a federal Criminal Justice Standards and Goals Commission."

While at American U, my mail was illegally opened and telephone illegally tapped because a sister-in-law was writing weird letters to a Soviet Union premier and other world leaders. After I graduated, I wrote "Police Community Relations – 1975" for the International Association of Chiefs of Police to determine whether Law Enforcement Assistance Administration grants to police departments had improved police community relations.

I not only found little improvement but two egregious problems.

Police departments from coast to coast were assigning to police community relations units officers for political patronage reasons and officers with reputations for abusing citizen rights.

I was shocked at the end of a two-week police community relations course at the FBI Academy. The hundred attendees were police community relations officers, sergeants, and lieutenants who had attended college and had two- or four-year degrees. At the end of the course, an officer shouted, "We should line up all the n...., antiwar, and feminist protestors against a wall and mow them down."

I was shocked and dumbfounded. Every police community relations officer jumped to their feet and cheered and clapped. Those were supposed to be the most psychologically, sociologically, and culturally empathetic police officers. What does that say about the rest of the officers on their forces?

Then a few years ago I watched peaceful demonstrations by 99 percenter Wall Street protestors in New York City, Oakland, and Cal Davis being pushed around, beaten, and mercilessly sprayed with pepper gas. I said, "It was one thing for police in the 1960s to abuse protestors because police disagreed with their politics or race, but Wall Street protestors were protesting for things that would benefit police, their families, and friends."

It sent a chill up my spine. I realized that if One-Percent-er Devils of the Anglo-Saxon New World Order told state police generals, sheriffs, and police chiefs to turn their weapons on Wall Street protestors, it is likely they would do so even if their friends and relatives were protestors. Unfortunately Anglo-Saxon New World Order tools have equipped large, medium, and small cities coast to coast with SWAT units and M-15 assault rifles for exactly that purpose.

After Chief Justice Earl Warren retired, it was also unfortunate that Republican presidents replaced him with Brennan, Rehnquist, and Roberts. Gradually they chipped away at Fourth and Fifth Amendment rights and set the stage for elimination of Fourth and Fifth Amendment rights of Muslims in the "Patriot" Act. Republican Roberts's Court, as a tool of an Anglo-Saxon New World Order, "bore false witness" that the "Patriot" Act was constitutional.

I was a victim of domestic spying after I sent letters to President Obama:

1. From a March 2012 letter, twenty-six of my concepts, suggestions, phrases, and words wound up in President Obama's first major economic speech; and

2. Then letters recommending that he turn immoral Republican words, acts, and omissions against them by showing they violate:
    a. Commandments;
    b. Golden Rules;
    c. Preamble of U.S. Constitution; and especially
    d. Bill of Rights.

Then in May, my First and Fourth Amendment rights were violated by an illegal mailing opening; wiretap of my telephone; and my laptop was hacked. All 269 of my incoming email messages were gone and replaced by emails from unknown companies. I called White House Secret Service and the FBI to warn of a Republican mole who was trying to get dirt to discredit me. The FBI gave me a number for ICE (federal computer hackers). Within seconds of dialing, unsolicited emails disappeared, and my 269 emails reappeared.

What is to stop a Republican president like Nixon, who was raised as a nonviolent Quaker, from secretly declaring that evangelical, Lutheran, or Methodist opponents of Republicans and the Anglo-Saxon New World Order were communists or terrorists. Such a Republican president could legally do what Nixon and Hoover did illegally.

Were First and Fourth Amendment rights of my writing coach at the University of Wisconsin violated? Professor Ron Kuka had been helping me write *Tortious Lies: Medical Myths, Legal Fictions and Junk Science.* I sent him email copies of my strategy and tactics letters to President Obama.

However, Prof. Kuka stopped scheduling meetings to review parts of *Tortious Lies* and didn't respond to emails, direct mail, and telephone calls.

Did ICE hack his emails? Did a Republican threaten him with loss of his job if he didn't stop helping me? Did a Republican threaten the University of Wisconsin chancellor with a cutoff of federal and state grants to the university if Prof. Kuka didn't stop helping?

Gandhiism
Principles of Noncooperation and Passive Resistance to Gain Reforms, Due Process, and Equal Protection of Law

The movie *Gandhi* shows that the Hindu led peaceful protest marches in South Africa and India. He and followers suffered beatings, death, and imprisonment by British troops but didn't fight back.

Rev. Martin Luther King employed Gandhiism principles during civil rights marches in the 1950s and 1960s. Male, Caucasian, neo-Nazi, Klu Klux Klan (KKK) dominated Southern law enforcement officers mistreated, abused, killed, and jailed Afro-American protestors, similar to the ways British troops treated Gandhi's protest marchers and colonists who supported the American Revolution.

Over 600,000 died during the Civil War before Republican President Lincoln's "Emancipation Proclamation" after the Battle of Gettysburg. It freed Afro-American Slaves and gave former slaves citizenship. In 1868 the Fourteenth Amendment was adopted. It said in Section 1, "All persons born or naturalized in the United State, and subject to the jurisdiction thereof, are citizens of the United States and of the state wherein they reside. No State shall make or enforce any law which shall abridge the privileges or immunities of citizens of the United States; nor shall any state deprive any person of life, liberty or property, without Due Process of Law; nor deny to any person within its jurisdiction, Equal Protection of the Laws."

In 1870 the Fifteenth Amendment was adopted. It said, "The Right of citizens of the United States to vote shall not be denied or abridged by the United States or by any State on account of race, color or previous condition of servitude."

For a short time thereafter, Afro Americans not only voted but ran for office as Lincoln Republicans and won offices in local governments and legislatures. Southern Republicans became Democrats, and with the support of Northern Republicans, enacted Jim Crowe laws to take away from Afro Americans their Fourteenth and Fifteenth Amendment rights, which included all ten of the Bill of Rights amendments. Unconstitutional literacy tests, poll taxes, and gerrymandering eliminated the rights of Afro Americans to vote, hold office, to become civil servants (state troopers, county sheriffs, municipal police officers, prosecutors, trial judges, and appellate court judges) and to be on criminal juries.

Caucasian men were able to get away with raping Afro-American wives and girls and murder of Afro-American boys and men for talking back or even merely saying hello to a Caucasian girl. Afro-American homes, churches, schools, communities, and farms were blown up and burned (including all livestock). Afro-American men and women were sterilized without their knowledge or consent to prevent them from procreating.

Afro-American boys and men, for merely saying "hello" to or looking at a Caucasian girl or woman, were castrated, shot dead, hung, skinned alive, or burned at the stake. After WWI and WWII, returning Afro-American soldier war heroes had their medals torn off and were hung in uniforms.

While Caucasian, Southern juries convicted every Afro American of any charge involving Caucasians, no Caucasians were convicted of harming or killing Afro Americans (elsewhere I've listed a number of movies about it).

In 1948 Democrat President Harry Truman desegregated the military. In the 1950s, the unanimous Warren Court (four Republicans, four Democrats, and an independent) desegregated schools and businesses and enforced the Bill of Rights, Thirteenth, Fourteenth, and Fifteenth Amendments. Republican President Eisenhower sent U.S. troops to enforce desegregation.

After Texas Democrat President Lyndon Baines Johnson signed the 1965 Voting Rights Act, Southern, Caucasian Democrats became Republicans again. The Kerner Commission Report on Civil Disobedience and Civil Rights ordered by President Johnson resulted in two actions.

He secured funds for a "War on Poverty" to prevent a racial revolution by providing Afro and Latin Americans with means to rise out of a life of poverty and crime and enable them to have the same opportunities as Caucasian Americans. The massive multidisciplinary National Criminal Justice Standards and Goals Commission produced six eight-inch-by-eleven-inch reports on crime prevention, law enforcement, prosecution and defense, courts, corrections, and victim assistance.

National and State Criminal Justice Standards and Goals
In order to receive federal Law Enforcement Assistance Administration (LEAA) funds, each state was required to have a state Criminal Justice Standards and Goals Commission adopt national standards and goals. All applications for LEAA grants to states, counties, and municipal governments had to address state standards and goals. For the purpose of this book, the following were the most pertinent goals:

1. Personnel in police departments, prosecutor and public defender offices, courts, and correctional facilities should reflect the racial, cultural, and gender composition of the community;

2. Personality profiles and background checks should be done on applicants for criminal justice positions to eliminate everyone with racial, religious, cultural, and gender bias, prejudice, and intolerance;

3. Police applicants should have college degrees in sociology, psychology, or criminology;

4. Police academy training should include:

    a. U.S. Constitution, Bill of Rights, and constitutional case law;

    b. Racial, religious, cultural, and gender diversity and police community relations;

    c. Neighborhood dispute, gang, and domestic violence resolution;

    d. Nonlethal methods such as extensive martial-arts training; and

    e. I recommended role-play training in "Police Community Relations 1975" for the International Association of Chiefs of Police and for the New Jersey Governor's Criminal Justice Standards and Goals Committee:

        1) Role-play training based upon the first ninety pages of the book *I'm Okay, You're Okay* to train police officers how to act as an "adult" instead of as a "child" or "parent(al);" and

        2) Role-play training alternatives to acting "parental" or "authoritarian" so that instead of police officers ordering people what to do and not to do, they should say:

            a) "I recommend that you not make things worse";

            b) "It would be in your best interests that you do not resist";

            c) "Please do not make things worse";

            d) "I will help you if you do not make things worse."

I said "I recommended" because for "Police Community Relations 1975," the project director Peter Frievalds (a politically savvy former Capitol Hill staffer) edited out 4.e. as well as recommendations to model American law enforcement officers after the very calm and respectful English bobbies. Law enforcement officers on the New Jersey Criminal Justice Standards and Goals Committee also voted against 4.e.

They also voted against personality profiles because their children who wanted to be state troopers, sheriffs, or police officers had their racial, religious, cultural, and gender bias, prejudice, intolerance, and hatred. However, rumors said that after New Jersey State Police started administering personality profiles of police applicants that the psychologist in California could be bribed to fudge test scores.

Golden Rule, Soul-Saving Rules, and Commandments Apply to Police
"Do unto others as you would have others do unto you";

"Love thy neighbor as you love yourself";

"Judge not lest thee be judged";

"You shall not pervert justice due to the poor";

"You shall not wrong a stranger or oppress him";

"You shall not afflict any widow or orphan";

"You shall not bear false witness against your neighbor";

"You shall not utter a false report";

"You shall take no bribe for a bribe blinds an official and subverts the cause of those who are in the right"; and

"Thou shall not kill."

Profiling and Pretext Arrests Violate
Standards and Goals for Law Enforcement Officers
Racial profiling (traffic stops merely because driver is Afro or Latin American) became a hot New Jersey topic in the 1990s, as if it was a new phenomenon. I recall profiling in the early 1970s from the instant I arrived in New Jersey to write state Criminal Justice Standards and Goals. Back then profiling included traffic stops of anyone with long hair and/or wearing lovechild clothing, especially when driving a VW bus with antiwar messages.

When Afro, Latin, and antiwar Americans were stopped, they were spread-eagled against their car while it was illegally searched (without probable cause). However, if a Caucasian in a business suit was pulled over, they sat in their cars while traffic citations were issued.

Other Factors that Cause Bad Police Community Relations,
Prevent Crime Prevention and Solving of Crimes
Officers Don't Know Citizens of Communities They Police

It is axiomatic that efficient and effective crime prevention and crime solving is facilitated by good Police Community Relations (PCRs). It is also axiomatic that PCRs is facilitated by several means.

Good PCRs evolves when police officers join community social organizations and spend more time out of their patrol cars in neighborhoods and business districts, walking and talking to residents, business owners, and store clerks. Mistakes and legal malpractice can be avoided and wise use of police discretion is effectuated when police officers know who is honest, who are criminals, and who represents threats. Mistake or legal malpractice can be prevented when police have a working knowledge of people in businesses and residential neighborhoods.

Good Police Community Relations results in residents and business people reporting criminals and testifying against them. However, a number of factors in law enforcement prevent good Police Community Relations, crime prevention, and solving crimes:

1. Police officers spend too much time in steel and glass bubbles shielded from the public;
2. Police officers and their families only socialize with themselves:
    a. Many officers smoked marijuana before becoming officers;
    b. But after becoming police officers they lose touch because their pre-law enforcement friends continue smoking marijuana;
3. Municipalities that turn police departments into cash cows to balance budgets damages Police Community Relations by eliminating wise application of police discretion:
    a. Natural law inclinations of teenagers are to stretch and break rules and laws by speeding, shoplifting, and getting drunk;
    b. During the Baby Boomer Generation, police officers didn't destroy careers of teenagers who were children of prominent families, good students, and athletes by filing charges;
    c. Instead they wisely applied police discretion and merely issued warnings to not violate those laws again; and
    d. So many of those teenagers were able to become doctors, attorneys, engineers, accountants, teachers, and nurses;
4. Blue-code peer pressure from police prevents officers from telling the truth when a police officer is accused of a crime, and governors, mayors, police chiefs, and county prosecutors and judges are more interested in preventing tort claims and lawsuits against police than protecting rights of victims of police abuse and murder.

Tag Team Illegality by Police and Municipal Court Judges

The Brown family, for their lawsuit against Officer Miller and the Ferguson Police Department, should learn what national and Missouri Criminal Justice Standards and Goals (set forth above) were implemented in Ferguson, Missouri, and rejected. State vs. Miller begs several questions:

Why did Missouri Governor Nixon only warn antipolice protestors not to be civilly disobedient or riot? In my experiences in being dragged into chaos by police rioting against antiwar demonstrators and viewing demonstrations in the Deep South and around the globe, demonstrations are peaceful until provoked by police. Why didn't Gov. Nixon advise police officers not to turn demonstrations in Ferguson into chaos or riots?

All legal experts on MSNBC who talked about the prosecutor opined that he did everything possible to prevent indictment of Officer Miller. Instead of feeding the grand jury only enough good evidence to indict Officer Miller, he confused the case by presenting contradictory and not credible evidence to overwhelm the effect of credible evidence.

The prosecutor also didn't do his job by helping apply credible evidence and testimony to laws of the case. He merely allowed the grand jury to try and figure out what to do on their own, and they failed to indict. In their civil suit, the Brown family attorney should investigate:

1. Was Officer Miller given a personality profile and was a thorough background check done to make sure he didn't have racial, religious, cultural, and gender bias, prejudice, and intolerance?
2. Did Officer Miller's training include constitutional law, cultural diversity, police community relations, psychology, sociology, criminology, and peaceful dispute resolution?
3. Does Officer Miller's personnel file contain complaints of police abuse and illegality against minority groups?
4. Does Officer Miller's military records show racial intolerance?
5. Was Officer Miller on medication at the time? If so, could the side effects of the medication affect his judgment?
6. Was Officer Miller under stress at home from wife and/or children?
7. Was Officer Miller under stress from trying to get a promotion or upset for being turned down for a promotion?

8. Have there been charges filed against Officer Miller for using excessive force; and

9. Officer Miller and his victim, Brown, an Afro-American Teenager were both six-foot-four, but Miller said he was afraid of the teen because Brown weighed more. However, why did Officer Miller have to fire twelve shots at point-blank range?

    a. Didn't Officer Miller receive hand-to-hand combat training in the military and by the police department?

    b. Why didn't Officer Miller use a baton, Tazer, tear, or pepper gas instead of deadly force with a gun?

Brutal Police Assault on Rodney King and L.A. Riots

How could a jury of sane Americans not convict any of the police officers who brutally beat Rodney King. That jury saw a video of five police officers kicking and hitting King with batons as he defenselessly laid on the ground in a fetal position. Was their failure because:

1. Afro-American Rodney King had a criminal record?

2. Some of the police officer defendants were Afro Americans?

3. Caucasian officer peer pressure caused Afro-American officers to be just as brutal toward Afro Americans as Caucasian officers?

4. Blue code of silence prevented honest, moral police officers from testifying against the five police officer defendants; and/or

5. Did the prosecutor purposely do an incompetent job of presenting opening statement, testimony, and evidence and closing arguments, as appears to have been done by the prosecutor during the grand jury phase in State vs. Miller (regarding his murder of an innocent Afro-American teen in Ferguson, Missouri, in 2014)?

Other Personal Experiences with Illegal Acts,
Omissions, and Cover-Ups by Police and Municipal Court Judges

When I lived in East Windsor, New Jersey, East Windsor police abused my rights several times, in part because they didn't like standards and goals on law enforcement I wrote for the Governor's Criminal Justice Advisory Committee. Perhaps also in part because I had the audacity to question East Windsor police acts and omissions:

1. In 1985 as I was merging onto Route 130 east of East Windsor, an East Windsor patrol car sped by. I pointed to my speedometer and was pulled over. The officer saw a tape recorder and asked,
    a. "Is that a tape recorder?"
    b. I said, "Yes." The officer asked, "What were you pointing at?"
    c. I said, "My speedometer because you were speeding."
    d. Officer said, "License, registration, and insurance card."
    e. I said, "You were speeding, weren't you? But you were not pursuing anyone and your red lights were not on, were they?"
    f. The officer didn't deny that but wrote tickets for failure to have a driver's license, insurance card, and registration before I could withdraw them from the compartment;
2. East Windsor Municipal Judge Tom Doig was the husband and law partner of my attorney Jo Doig. I brought a certified transcript of the tape recording of what took place, as well as my driver's license, insurance card, and registration:
    a. I arrived in court at 7 P.M. but was the last case handled at 2 A.M. when no one except the court clerk, officer, and I were in court;
    b. After Judge Doig couldn't get me to admit the officer had probable cause to stop me, he made that finding but didn't charge the officer with speeding;
3. Later that year the officer was fired for a series of abuses.

In 1984 I turned left from the south end of Robertson Road onto Twin Rivers Drive when an East Windsor patrol car (over a hundred yards away) was at the north end of Robertson turning right. While I had traveled thirty yards, the Patrol Car traveled a hundred yards and put on the siren and light to pull me over. Again I had a tape recorder but also passenger witnesses. I said, "You must've gunned your engine to get here so fast. Were you following that car that turned ahead of you?"

The officer said nothing and left.

However, during the next several days, every time my wife or I left Robertson Road, we were followed until East Windsor police ticketed my now ex-wife and me. Jean was able to defeat the charge of illegal switch of lanes by showing that the statute doesn't give an officer a basis for the ticket because it was her judgment as to when it was safe to switch traffic lanes and other traffic didn't alter their speed to accommodate her lane switch.

I was charged with running a red light. However, I saw the East Windsor police officer on the cross road. He wasn't looking at me when I entered the intersection as the light turned from green to orange. He also didn't see me get cut off by a car turning left across my path and that the reason I didn't make it through the intersection before the light turned red was because I yielded to that car. Yet Judge Doig's replacement judge convicted me of running a red light.

In August 1986 on a rainy night, a drunk driver pulled out of a shopping center across my lane and stopped in front of my car because of northbound traffic on Princeton Hightstown Road. I hit the brakes and slide into the side of that car. The impact was so great that Mary Kay (second wife) went in and out of consciousness.

At the hospital, the officer asked for blood to be drawn from me and asked me to drop by the East Windsor Police Department the next day. I thought he wanted to take my statement. However, he started writing a ticket for DWI. I said, "Before I left the hospital, I asked the doctor for my blood alcohol reading. The doctor said I had .001, which he said was the amount of alcohol that was pulled into the body by a hypodermic needle."

However, the lieutenant continued writing the ticket. I said, "Please wait until I go to the hospital and get the blood test report." He continued writing the ticket, so I said, "I live in East Windsor, have clients here, and I'm the attorney for Christ Lutheran Church. If you issue a ticket, it will be printed in the news and could harm my ability to practice law."

At the time I was an accident defense attorney for Methfessel and Werbel. John Methfessel offered to pay for an alcohol expert and to assign a firm attorney to represent me.

A few days before the hearing, the municipal prosecutor called and said he would dismiss the DWI charge. However, when I showed up in East Windsor Municipal Court, Judge Doig tried to extort or blackmail an admission from me that the officer had probable cause to issue the ticket.

I refused and added, "The other driver's alcohol blood level was .02, but the police report says her breath didn't smell of alcohol. My blood alcohol level was .001, but the police report contains a late edition of information, in a different type of handwriting, that lied about my breath smelling of alcohol. I have no intention of suing the lieutenant and police department, but I will not lie about probable cause. All the officer had to do was let me get the hospital report on my blood alcohol level or wait for the hospital to send a copy. I didn't bring an attorney or alcohol expert because the prosecutor said the DWI charge would be dismissed."

Judge Doig said, "Either admit probable cause, or I will reschedule trial."

So I was forced to "bear false witness" that the officer had probable cause in order to avoid needless waste of John Methfessel's money. In the final analysis, Judge Doig wasn't interested in right and wrong or justice. He saw his job as protecting East Windsor from a tort claims action suit.

Police, Prosecutor, and Judge Illegal Conspiracy
September 2000, Tybee Island, Georgia

My sons (Trent and Grant) had read the book and watched the movie *Midnight in the Garden of Good and Evil*. After they learned that Savannah's tourist industry was focused around that story, they wanted us to vacation in Savannah, Georgia. I rented a home on the beach of Tybee Island.

The first night out we went to a dance club. My sons were excellent dancers. As I stood at the bar, one girl after another approached, bought me a drink, and waited for one of my boys to exit the dance floor.

However, I then saw Grant nose to nose with a guy his size. I signaled Trent and Grant to leave. As we exited into a torrential rainstorm, the guy followed with three other rednecks. The guy pushed Grant. Grant pushed back. The guy then hit Grant's jaw and knocked him down. His face hit the curb. Grant swung but missed and got knocked down again.

I pulled the guy off of Grant, ducked a swing, faked, and gave the guy a hook that sent him reeling. Another redneck came at me. I faked again and kicked him in the testicles. The third redneck wanted no part of me.

It all took about thirty seconds, yet suddenly the only three patrol cars on Tybee Island slowly proceeded up the street, one car in front and two in back. I thought, "Great reaction time. In Standards and Goals, we recommended a three-minute reaction time for police."

Grant (bleeding from nose, lip, and chin) leaned in through the window of the lead police car and asked for help but was put in handcuffs. When Trent and I tried to explain that Grant was attacked, we were put in handcuffs while the rednecks laughed their asses off.

When we arrived at the police lockup, a sergeant's eyes bulged when he saw my lawyer's badge in my wallet. Grant was taken to a hospital to get stitched. Trent wouldn't shut up and asked several times, "Why are they doing this to us?" until he was hauled off to the county prison.

Although we were charged with public intoxication, Breathalyzer or blood tests weren't done to prove it. Our court dates could've been scheduled for later that week. Instead separate hearings were scheduled for the next three weeks after our vacation.

Before we left Georgia, we found out that Tybee residents hate Yankees. Rednecks were hired to caused Yankees to get into fights. Bail for the three of us cost $2,100. The plan was always the same. Make Yankees pay and then forfeit bail.

The Tybee Island prosecutor and judge were in on the scam. From New Jersey, I wrote to them and promised that I did not intend to file a tort claims act case, but I did request that charges be dismissed. The Judge ordered me to return to Tybee Island. However, wisely I didn't go.

Perjury by Police during Accident Litigation

My next book, *Tortious Lies, Medical Myths, Legal Fictions and Junk Science*, is about white-collar crime in accident cases. Police officers aid and abet by handing out business cards from plaintiff lawyers at accident scenes or in hospital ERs. Later during pretrial depositions and/or civil trials, police officers often add information that's not found in their notepads or accident reports to help plaintiffs with liability problems.

My typical cross examination of such officers went as follows:

"The accident at issue was over three years ago?"

"Yes," said the officer.

"How many accident reports do you write per year?"

"Over 350."

"Since the accident at issue, you've written over 900 accident reports?"

"Yes."

"I'm curious, how could you remember three facts that aren't mentioned in your three-page police report or notepad?"

Eighth Amendment Bans "Cruel and Unusual Punishment"

In 1848 Wisconsin was the first moral state to ban executions. When I was thirteen years old, I asked Grandpa Lebbeus, a Lutheran minister/attorney:

"What do you think of the death penalty?"

He said, "As a Lutheran minister in Illinois, I was called to the bed of a dying man. He confessed that someone else was electrocuted for a murder he committed. Two wrongs don't make a right.

"Many people have been proven to be innocent of murder after they were executed. Executions eliminate ability to correct jury mistakes.

"Premeditated murder by execution violates 'thou shall not kill.'

"Murders occur because of a failure of parents, teachers, and preachers to properly civilize and socialize, and peers cause or contribute to murder.

"It is 'cruel and unusual punishment to force a human being to count down the months, weeks, days, hours, minutes, and seconds until execution.'"

. . .

I have bones to pick with Republicans. How can they morally justify supporting and cheering about executions and murder of abortion doctors but against abortion of unwanted fetuses who won't be properly socialized by unwed, uneducated moms and become thieves, murderers, and drug dealers? How can Republicans morally justify execution when they cause children to die by voting against welfare, Medicaid, Affordable Care Health Insurance, food stamps, school lunches, and clean air, water, land, food, and education that can prevent them from becoming murderers?

CHAPTER IX

Natural Law, Eternal Law, and Positive Law
and United States Constitution and Bill of Rights

In Article I, Sec. 9, Cl. 8 of the U.S. Constitution, Founding Fathers intended to prevent anointment of royalty in the United States:

"No Title of Nobility shall be granted by the United States; and no person holding any Office of Profit or Trust under them, shall, without the Consent of Congress, accept any Present, Emolument, Office, or Title, of any kind whatever, from any King, Prince, or foreign State."

Founding Fathers replaced King George and royal family with a Constitution and Bill of Rights to establish democracy to protect rights of the majority, individuals, and minority groups. A constitutional covenant replaced the covenant between King George and his American colonial subjects. Their theory was that voters can better determine "what is in their best interests" and under Preamble of U.S. Constitution, how to:

- Promote the General Welfare;
- Establish Justice;
- Insure domestic Tranquility;
- In order to form a more perfect Union;
- Provide for the common defense; and
- Secure the Blessings of Liberty to ourselves and our Posterity.

My father wrote on December 24, 1945, "Is not our democratic system based upon Christian principles? Did it not originate under Christian tutelage and in a Christian era? Then if capitalism and democracy are stepchildren of Christianity, is it not Christianity's duty to give parental advice to its offspring? Or should Christianity allow its brainchild to become a savage robot with no interference?"

Judeo-Christian Founding Fathers didn't envision an Industrial Revolution that would create "One Percent Devils" (robber-baron kings of industry and finance: Vanderbilt, Carnegie, Rockefeller, and J.P. Morgan) and their "Satanic Tools" (Republican politicians, preachers, and press) who would violate Commandments, Golden Rule, and soul-saving rules:

1. "Thou shall not covet thy neighbor's house, property, wife, or ass:;
2. "Thou shall not join hands with a wicked man:;
3. "You shall take no bribe, for a bribe blinds the official and subverts the cause of those who are in the right";
4. "Thou shall not steal";
5. "Honor thy father and thy mother";
6. "Thou shall not pervert justice due to the poor";
7. "You shall not wrong a stranger or oppress him";
8. "You shall not afflict any widow or orphan";
9. "If you loan money to the poor you shall not charge interest";
10. "Do unto others as you would have others do unto you";
11. "Love thy neighbor as you love yourself";
12. "I am my brother's keeper";
13. "Help those in need" and "those who have more should give more."

Due to immorality of robber-baron kings of industry and finance:
- Republican President Teddy Roosevelt had immoral horizontal and vertical monopoly empires divided into many companies to create competition and lower prices;
- Democrat President Woodrow Wilson endorsed progressive taxation so those who benefit most from U.S. economic system pay more taxes;
- To redistribute a small part of unnecessary income by "One Percent Devils to compensate their victims via social safety nets and programs to give everyone a chance to succeed in life; and

- Democrat President Franklin D. Roosevelt signed legislation:
  1. To regulate Wall Street and banks;
  2. To enforce Fair Labor Standards Act that forbid child laborers, established a minimum wage, maximum hour work week, and unemployment compensation
  3. To implement Social Security and other social safety nets;
  4. National Industrial Recovery Act to set standards for business administration; establish fair trade practices; and ensured unions the right of collective bargaining; and
  5. Massive infrastructure building to employ and modernize the U.S.

However, during the past sixty years, "One Percent Devils and Their Satanic Tools" ignored and repeatedly violated goals of Preamble of U.S. Constitution, Commandments, Golden Rule, and soul-saving rules in order to reverse progress of Presidents Wilson, Franklin D. Roosevelt, and Teddy Roosevelt. When "One Percent Devils" go to Capitol Hill, they're treated like de facto royalty who give "presents" and "emoluments" (i.e. bribes) to buy votes violating Article 1, Sec 9, Cl 8.

"One Percent Devils and Their Satanic Tools" and their Immoral Alliances of War

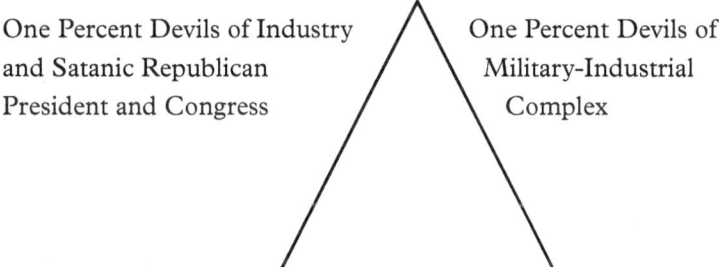

One Percent Devils of Industry and Satanic Republican President and Congress

One Percent Devils of Military-Industrial Complex

"Satanic Tool" Preachers and Press who Preach War or Don't Preach against War

Five-star general, supreme allied commander, and then -Republican President Dwight D. Eisenhower warned, "...the conjuncture of an immense military establishment and a large arms industry is new to the American experience.

Added to this, 3½ million men and women are directly engaged in the defense establishment. The total influence — economic, political, and even spiritual — is felt in every city, statehouse, and office of the federal government...

"We recognize the imperative need for this development. Yet, we must not fail to comprehend its grave implications. Our toil, resources and livelihoods are involved and at stake. So is the very structure of our society.

"In the councils of government, we must guard against the acquisition of unwarranted influence, whether sought or unsought, by the Military-Industrial Complex. The potential for the disastrous rise of misplaced power exists and will persist.

"Therefore, we must never let the weight of this complex endanger our liberties or democratic process. We should take nothing for granted. Only a knowledgeable and alert citizenry can compel the proper meshing of a huge Military-Industrial Complex with our peaceful message and goals so our security and liberty may prosper together."

President Washington warned against alliances and treaties that could obligate the U.S. to go to war. He and other Founding Fathers didn't anticipate an alliance between "One Percent Devils and Their Satanic Tools" that would cause the U.S. to go to war to protect interests of kings of industry and finance who immorally exploit foreign resources, labor, and governments.

President Monroe's Monroe Doctrine told Europe to stay out of the Americas and the U.S. would not intervene in European affairs. Again the Founding Fathers didn't foresee an evil alliance of war composed of "One-Percent Devil" kings of industry, finance, and Military-Industrial Complex "and their Satanic Tools" (Republican politicians, preachers, and press) who'd get the U.S. into wars against European, Asian and Muslim alliances of war.

During the past fifty-five years, independent and Democratic politicians, preachers, and pres haven't used repetitive truth to counter repetitive lies and remind voters about warnings by Presidents Washington, Monroe, and Eisenhower. They have also not used repetitive truth to expose violations of U.S. Constitution, Commandments, Golden Rule, soul-saving rules and principles of legal equity.

Founding Fathers also didn't anticipate "One-Percent Devil" kings of industry and finance would bribe "Satanic Republican Tools" to violate:

- First Amendment freedom of religion separation of church and state;
- First Amendment freedom of press role as the fourth branch of government;
- Principals of democracy; and
- That One-Percent Devil bribes to their Satanic Tools (Republican politicians, preachers, and press) would fund dissemination of:
  1. Orwellian *1984*-style repetitive lies; and
  2. Hitler-Nixon-type, Machiavellian, Divide-and-Conquer Tactics;
     a. So citizens vote Republican and thus against their own constitutional social and economic interests and interests of family and friends; and
     b. So "One Percent Devils and Their Satanic Tools" can violate: eternal law and Preamble of Constitution with impunity; repetitive lies and Wedge-Issue Tactics by Satanic Tools (Republican politicians, preachers, and press) and good-old-fashioned bribes have caused what Pope Francis called immoral capitalism. That's inconsistent with:
- Six goals of the Preamble;
- Declaration of Independence rights to Life, Liberty and Pursuit of Happiness, based upon:
  1. Majority rule that protects rights of minorities and individuals;
  2. A proper balance between natural, eternal and positive law to produce zero-sum outcomes so that:
     a. "One should not benefit from one's wrongs"; and
     b. "One should not gain at someone else's expense."
- Fourteenth Amendment right not to be deprived of life, liberty or property without due process and equal protection of the law;
- Fifteenth and Nineteenth Amendment rights to vote irrespective of race, color, and sex; and
- Two of what FDR said are our four basic rights:
  1. Freedom from want; and
  2. Freedom from fear of discrimination.

Freedom from Want and Golden Rule of Health Insurance

One of the greatest tragedies has been that the United States is the richest nation on earth but the last industrial nation to insure that everyone has access to Affordable Health Care Insurance. In the 1960s, before and after Medicare and Medicaid were created under the General Welfare goal to provide medical care for 30 million Americans, Satanic Republican tools "bore false witness" and "uttered false reports" that those programs would cause evil, socialized medicine that kills, allegedly as in Great Brittan.

However, during the Affordable Health Care Act (aka Romney-Obama Care) debate, it was clear that England and other nations with socialized medicine had higher standards of care and lower infant-mortality rates than the United States. Every year before President Obama's Affordable Care Act and expansion of Medicaid, tens of thousands died or became disabled because they couldn't afford health insurance or costs of treatment drove them into bankruptcy.

During the 2012 presidential campaign, Satanic Republican Tools counted on Americans not remembering that their predictions in the 1960s about a Medicare/Medicaid-socialized medicine disaster didn't occur. So in 2012, Satanic Tools repetitively lied that Affordable Care Act (ACA) would lead to a socialized medicine catastrophe and high unemployment. They also counted on Americans not remembering that the mechanism to fund the ACA (Individual Initiative) was a Republican concept in the 1990s, but after an Afro-Caucasian-American President Obama adopted "Individual Initiative," Republicans didn't want to play the game anymore.

That's rather childish, is it not? Like children with toys, they play the game until someone else has the ball.

Republican candidate Romney was so intellectually dishonest as to "utter false reports" that the highly successful ACA legislation he signed while governor of Massachusetts wasn't suited for other states. Other Satanic Republican Tools jumped on that bandwagon to espouse "states rights under the Tenth Amendment" to develop their own health insurance system. One fallacy is that no other state has tried. Another fallacy was exposed when ACA increased employment of doctors, nurses, and aids.

In fact Satanic Republican governors (from Governors Walker of Wisconsin to Perry of Texas) and state representatives refused to setup insurance exchange systems and turned down Medicaid expansion even though expansion wouldn't cost those states a single penny.

I can understand why Gov. Perry didn't. Does he get a sadistic pleasure from signing death warrants? I can't help wonder how governors like Walker can sleep at night knowing they're causing thousands of people to unnecessarily prematurely die or become disabled. Whether a governor signs death warrants or allows people to die without medical coverage, "thou shall not kill" is violated.

I remember when Rand Paul was asked during a campaign debate about people being allowed to die in emergency rooms because they didn't have health insurance. Sadistic Republicans in the audience clapped and cheered about that immoral result.

I also remembered something that made my Republican father disgusted during debates about Medicare and Medicaid in the 1960s. A Satanic Republican Tool said, "Rich people and corporations don't want Medicare or Medicaid because they want people on Social Security disability or retirement and welfare to die young so taxes for social safety nets can be cut."

Dad said, "That's outrageous! Those who are on Social Security disability or retirement and Medicare are contractually entitled to those social safety nets because they paid FICA and income taxes."

Those who are receiving welfare and Medicaid are "entitled" to it because they're victims of economic and social repression acts, omissions, and frauds of "One Percent Devils and Their Satanic Tools." Everyone I know who is receiving poverty-level welfare checks would rather work and have more money to spend.

Proposed Golden Rule of Health Insurance

Federal and state Legislatures should "do unto others what they would want others to do to them" if roles were reversed. Therefore, legislatures should ensure that every American has exactly the same health insurance, prescription, *and* dental coverage as they voted to give themselves at taxpayers' expense, coverage Satanic Republican Tools voted to be paid for by:

- Regressive sales taxes on poor, working poor, and middle class;
- Progressive income taxes on working poor and middle class; and
- Cuts of social safety nets for poor, working poor, and middle class;
- But, of course, "One Percent Devils" can avoid income and FICA taxes by hiding income in offshore accounts.

General Welfare Enabling Clause

The means to achieve goals of the Preamble are in Article I, Sec. 8, and Cl. I of the Constitution. The Enabling Clause authorizes Congress to raise taxes:

- "To pay debts";
- "To provide for a Common Defense and General Welfare of U.S.";
- Clause 2 "To borrow money on the credit of the United States";
- Clause 3 "To regulate Commerce with foreign nations, and among the States";
- Clause 4 "To establish uniform Rules of Naturalization, and uniform Laws on the subject of Bankruptcies throughout the United States";
- Clause 7 "To Establish Post Offices and Postal Roads";
- Clause 8 "To promote the Progress of Science and Useful Arts"; and
- Clauses 12, 13, 14, and 15, to pay for an Army (two years per war), Navy, and part-time Militia to suppress insurrections and repel Invasion."

There's nothing in the goals of the Preamble or means of the General Welfare Enabling Clause supporting Satanic Republican policies about:

- Army or navy attacking foreign nations to protect interests of One-Percent Devil kings of industry and finance;
- Not raising taxes to pay for wars in Afghanistan and Iraq; but
- Pay for those wars by cutting social safety net benefits for victims of immorality by One Percent Devils;
- Immigration and Naturalization that violates the Golden Rule: "Do unto others as you would have others do unto you" when:
  1. American Indians didn't handout green cards and work permits at Plymouth Rock to Judeo-Christian Caucasians; and
  2. Mexicans in the Arizona Territory didn't demand an electric fence with moat and alligators on the eastern border to keep out Judeo-Christian Caucasians;
  3. But American, Protestant Judeo-Christians discriminated against and abused Irish, Roman Catholic, Judeo-Christians; and

4. Irish Roman Catholics discriminated against and abused Italian Roman Catholics;

5. Protestants, Irish and Roman Catholics:

   a. Discriminated and abused Jewish immigrants; and now

   b. In the Southwest discriminate and abuse Mexican immigrants.

- There's also nothing in the Preamble or Enabling Clause about:

  1. Causing U.S. Post Office to go bankrupt by forcing it to prepay postal worker pensions for seventy-five years in five years so FedEx and UPS (which didn't exist in the 1700s or 1800s) could have a monopoly that charges five dollars for a postage stamp;

  2. Not repairing and maintaining postal road infrastructure (roads, railroads, bridges, and airports) to keep them safe and efficient; or

  3. Using taxes "to promote science" of warfare to kill but not "to promote General Welfare" by researching cures via:

     a. Medical research;

     b. Alternatives to fossil-fuel pollution and global warming;

     c. Research to develop catalytic converters for smokestacks;

     d. Research to reduce pollution of air, water, land, and food; and

     e. Cutting federal and state general welfare funding of:

        1) Law enforcement, during a period of high unemployment and an increase in property crimes so people can survive;

        2) Firefighters, when bankruptcies cause arson for insurance;

        3) Teachers, in a global, industrial economy when U.S. students rank:

           a. Seventeenth in science;

           b. Twenty-first in math; and

           c. Twenty-fifth in reading comprehension; or

- Providing for Common Defense by cutting general welfare safety nets and taxing the poor, working poor, and middle class to give One Percent Devils (who are already wealthy) tax cuts, subsidies, and deductions for outsourcing U.S. production, jobs, and technology to:

1. An atheistic Communist Chinese New World Order enemy; and
2. Third World nations to exploit their labor and resources, which ultimately leads to U.S. troops protecting interests of One-Percent Devil kings of industry and finance.

As my father wrote on December 24, 1945, "...So who is to blame for WWII? Who put Hitler in power? Who financed him?

"English, French and U.S. industrialists and financiers. They wanted Nazis and Russian Communists, obvious threats to capitalism, to destroy each other, but Hitler fooled them all and attacked in all directions.

"Now in your criticism of any country, do not blame the people. Do not blame English masses or German masses. What is the root of the evil?

"It is not the individual but industrialists throughout the world in all countries. A handful of people who go abroad to invest, looking for cheap labor and mineral resources, to the detriment of their own and our country.

"Then when their toes are stepped on, they influence their own governments to come to their aid to protect their selfish interests. Naturally they do and can because aren't they The Ruling Class?"

General Welfare - Vulture Chart by Ed Schultz of MSNBC

Given that context, wouldn't the Founding Fathers be aghast to see that in the last forty years of One-Percent Devil, Anglo-Saxon New World Order control of the U.S. government:

- Income of One Percent Devils has risen 272 percent and their share of U.S. assets rose from 40 percent to 72 percent?
- While income of their victims, the other 99 percent, has flatlined and their share of U.S. assets dropped from 60 percent to 28 percent; and
- Thirty-three percent of Americans live in poverty?
- But during the last forty years:
  1. Inflation has increased from 9 percent to 2 percent per year;
  2. Gas prices rose from twenty-three cents to over four dollars per gallon;
  3. Cost of housing, cars, and food rose tenfold; and

- Thus both parents have to work or a custodial parent has to have two or more jobs, so children are not properly supervised, don't study, and do poor in school.

Isn't it ironic that Republicans don't want women in the workforce but their social and economic policies force them to work? Those income and asset disparities between "One Percent Devils" and the other 99 percent are a result of several kinds of immoral capitalism:

- One Percent Devils outsourced millions of U.S. jobs, production, and technology of fifty thousand U.S. companies to:
  1. An atheistic Communist Chinese enemy that steals technology;
  2. Third World nations to exploit their resources and labor in ways they're prohibited from exploiting U.S. resources and labor; and
  3. One-Percent Devil immorality is backed up by CIA and United States Military-Industrial Complex;
  4. But One-Percent Devil immorality goes farther with bribes:
     a. To eliminate;
        1) Social safety nets for their victims;
        2) Minimum wage for those who made them rich;
        3) Regulation protections for employees and consumers;
        4) Labor unions and collective bargaining for public workers;
     b. To prevent equal pay for women, who earn 23 percent less than men;
     c. For corporate welfare (tax subsidies, deductions, and cuts) that rewards their immorality; and
     d. To allow tax evasion by "One Percent Devils," who put profits in offshore banks so they don't have to pay taxes for:
        1) Social safety nets for their victims; and
        2) Cost of their Military-Industrial Complex's services;
- One Percent Devils didn't use profits or tax cuts, subsidies, and deductions to expand research and development, production, and hiring in the U.S. Instead they used "corporate welfare" and profits to:
  1. Purchase competitors to create horizontal and/or vertical monopolies to reduce competition and drive up and fix prices;

215

2. Purchase companies in different industries, but when parent company executives and administrators are put in charge of the departments of the purchased company, inevitably expensive mistakes are made and bankruptcy often occurs; and

3. Make profits via layoffs of executives, administrators, and other employees who made "One Percent Devils" rich, and they make:

   a. Remaining workers do the jobs of three to five people;

   b. But without a pay increase; and

4. Instead of buying "Made in USA," those Devils purchase foreign cars, yachts, homes, vacations, furs, jewelry, wine, and caviar.

How Can Republicans Have Moral Authority to Govern?

The United States of America is a multiracial, religious, and culturally diverse nation where over half are female. Republicans not only cannot tolerate dissent within the Republican Party but:

- Are male-chauvinistic, neo-Nazi, racial, religious, and culturally intolerant, biased, prejudiced, and bigoted; and
- Republicans only believe in:
  1. Darwinian "Survival of the Species"; and
  2. Ayn Rand "The strong should take from the weak"; and
  3. Taking bribes from One Percent Devils to allow them to steal; and
  4. Don't believe in Democracy and moral capitalism; and
- But don't obey U.S. Constitution, Bill of Rights, Ten Commandments, Seven Golden Rules, principles of legal and zero-sum outcome equity.

Justice Begins and Ends with U.S. Supreme Court

After the Civil War, the Thirteenth, Fourteenth, and Fifteenth Amendments allowed Afro-American men to vote and have the same rights as Caucasian men, but Republican majorities on the U.S. Supreme Court:

- Allowed Southern states to disenfranchise Afro Americans;

- In Plessy v. Ferguson (1896) and Cummins vs. County Board of Education declared as constitutional "separate but equal":
  1. Facilities for Afro Americans and Caucasians; and
  2. Schools for Caucasians and Afro-Americans.

Yet based upon social science, in Brown v. Board of Education of Topeka, the Warren Court (two Republicans, an independent, and six Democrats) unanimously held that "separate but equal" was inherently unequal and thus unconstitutional. Republican President Eisenhower enforced school integration by sending troops to protect Afro-American students. In 1978 the Supreme Court held in University of California vs. Bakke that universities can admit students on the basis of race in order to reverse poverty and patterns of economic discrimination.

Another unanimous Warren Court (four Democrats, an independent, and four Republicans) found that police officers, instead of using scientific investigation methods to solve crimes, were lazy and violated the Fourth, Fifth, and Sixth Amendments of the Bill of Rights and held:

- In Mapp vs. Ohio (1961) that illegally obtained evidence (via illegal searches, wiretaps, and torture-induced confessions) is inadmissible;
- In Miranda vs. Arizona (1966) that after arrest, police officers should advise suspects: "You have a right to remain silent. Anything you say or do can be used against you in a court of law. You have a right to an attorney, but if you can't afford an attorney, an attorney will be provided for you."

Kerner Commission and Katzenback Commission reports found that racial, religious, gender, and politically biased, uneducated, and unscientific Caucasian law enforcement and criminal justice systems were the cause of racial and other civil disobedience. A National Criminal Justice Commission issued standards and goals to modernize and legalize criminal justice systems.

However by 1975, a Republican Burger Court (five Republicans and four Democrats) and the 5-4 Republican Rehnquist Court decisions whittled down criminal and civil rights. Then an intellectually dishonest 5-4 Republican Roberts Court did what Republicans "bore false witness" about the Warren Court. The Roberts Court didn't strictly construe the Constitution but violated separation of powers by rewriting it:

- In Gore vs. Bush, the Roberts Court overturned a Florida Supreme Court decision to anoint G.W. Bush president despite the fact that:
  1. Bush's brother Jeb was governor of Florida;
  2. Jeb appointed the secretary of state (in charge of elections);
  3. They purchased defective voting machines with hanging chads;
  4. So the Roberts Court enabled Bush (who had fewer votes than Gore) to steal the presidency;
  5. So Bush could aid Anglo-Saxon New World Order plans by:
     a. Giving away the $400 billion budget surplus (created by Democratic President Clinton) through tax cuts (2001 and 2003) that:
        1) Only allowed me to buy two pizzas per week; and
        2) Stimulated outsourcing of U.S. production, technology, and jobs to:
           a) An atheistic Communist Chinese enemy; and
           b) Third World nations; or to
           c) Purchase companies of competitors to create horizontal and vertical monopolies to control and fix prices; and
           d) Purchased companies to diversify financial base; but
           e) Not one U.S. plant or job was created under that failed Republican "trickle-down economic theory or myth" that Pope Francis recently debunked;
     b. Getting the U.S. to go to war in Afghanistan and Iraq;
        1) Without raising taxes to pay for those wars; and
        2) A goal of making the poor, working poor, and middle class pay for those wars by reducing social safety net benefits for victims of One-Percent Devil immorality; and
     c. Not regulating banks and Wall Street but allowed them to gamble on mortgage bundles and derivatives and caused the 2008 Stock Market Crash, where One Percent Devils with insider-trading information got rich:

1) Selling short as the market went down; and
2) After market bottomed out, got richer buying back stock at bargain prices; and

   d. Bailing out bankers and brokers because they're too big to be allowed to fail, they got away with using bailout funds to:

1) Pay multimillion dollar bonuses to the most fraudulent brokers and bankers; and
2) To speculate on oil and gas commodities to drive up the price of gas to over four dollars per gallon; and

   e. While victims of One Percent Devils lost jobs, homes, pensions, medical insurance, and families but got nothing except threats about losing unemployment compensation, Medicare, Medicaid, Affordable Care Act health insurance, welfare, and Social Security;

- A 5-4 Roberts Court also held that:

1. Criminal rights of suspected Muslim terrorists can be suspended under the Patriot Act. So if a Republican president doesn't like Methodists because they disagreed with him/her:

   a. He/she can declare them to be terrorists or communists; and

   b. Suspend their rights without due process under Fourth, Fifth, and Fourteenth Amendments; and

2. Roberts Court also said there was no longer a need for Title V voting right protection for Afro Americans south of the Mason-Dixon Line under the 1965 Civil Rights Act.

Then surprise, surprise, immediately states below the Mason-Dixon Line showed the Roberts Court how wrong they were by enacting voter ID, restricted voting days and times legislation, and gerrymandering to disenfranchise Afro, Asian and Latin Americans; elderly; and college students who tend to vote Democrat. Was the Roberts Court like the Three Monkeys — Blind, Deaf, and Dumb — or merely Satanic Tools?

Didn't the Roberts Court know the Pennsylvania Republican chairman bragged that the voter ID law would assure Romney (a Republican, Dracula, vulture capitalist who outsourced to an atheistic Communist Chinese enemy) would win Pennsylvania and the presidency because Afro and Latin Americans, college students, and the elderly, who tend to vote Democrat, would be disenfranchised?

Didn't the Roberts Court know unconstitutional gerrymandering in Pennsylvania had turned one-person, one-vote into a joke because 60 percent voted Democrat but 60 percent of congressional and state legislative seats went to Republicans?

Didn't the Roberts Court know non-Southern states with Republican governments were trying to disenfranchise Latin, Afro, and Asian Americans, poor, elderly, and college students via voter ID, limited voting hour laws, and gerrymandering?

Didn't the Roberts Court know that once they eliminated Title V, every former Confederate, slavery, racist state would pass the same laws and engage in unconstitutional gerrymandering?

Most importantly, didn't the Roberts Court know the Republican Congress would never hold hearings to determine whether Title V was still necessary below the Mason-Dixon Line? Thus:

- Wasn't the Title V decision intellectually dishonest?
- Wasn't it an antidemocracy and unconstitutional decision?
- Didn't it violate the Nuremburg Doctrine that judges "owe a higher duty to morality than to the laws of a nation and orders of its leaders"?
- Isn't that also true of other Roberts Court decisions?
- Or is the Roberts Court like Nixon, Reagan, Christie, and Walker Monkeys:
    1. I saw nothing in the news;
    2. I heard nothing in the news; and
    3. I read nothing in the news?

A 5-4 Republican Roberts Court also held that:
- Antidiscrimination racial quotas in universities are unconstitutional. Didn't the Roberts Court know:
    1. Universities have those quotas to compensate for racist Republicans in Washington, D.C., and statehouses who, for over one hundred years, voted against:
        a. Equal education opportunities for Afro and Indian Americans?

    b.   Preschool and school lunches for them? and

    c.   Job training for them?

    d.   And any program that would help them move out of a life Of poverty and crime?

  2. Weren't racial quotas in universities designed to compensate for those racist policies intended to keep Afro, Latin, Asian, and Native Indian Americans in poverty and ignorance?

- When the Roberts Court held that segregated charter schools can be funded with tax dollars, wasn't the court saying ,"Go ahead and set up charter schools to segregate and discriminate against Afro and Latin Americans?"

- In "Citizens United" and an even worse subsequent case, the Roberts Court held that freedom of speech includes freedom to secretly bribe politicians with contributions (from Chinese companies and One Percent Devils) to Super PACs, so they can spread:

  1. Orwellian repetitive lies in Republican campaign ads; and

  2. Hitler-Nixon-Machiavellian, Divide-and-Conquer, Wedge-Issue ads;

  3. And even more incredibly, that corporations "as persons" have freedom of speech and freedom of religion rights to impose Roman Catholic St. Augustine's "Rules against Sex" on people of every religion. Even though such rules violate:

    a.   Natural law and thus are unnatural laws;

    b.   Eternal law and thus are anti-eternal laws; and

    c.   Positive law and thus are negative laws.

In "Citizens United," didn't the Republican Roberts Court say it's constitutional for One Percent Devils to bribe satanic politicians in order to violate the following Commandments and Golden Rules:

- "You shall take no bribe, for a bribe blinds the officials, and subverts the cause of those who are in the right";
- "You shall not join hands with a wicked man";
- "You shall not issue a false report";
- "You shall not bear false witness against your neighbor"; and
- "Thou shall not steal" so Republicans can vote to:

1. Eliminate regulations and taxes of corporations and One Percent Devils;
2. Eliminate social safety nets, infrastructure, and education for victims of One Percent Devils;
3. Only fund the U.S. Military-Industrial Complex, domestic spy agencies and SWAT teams in every city to suppress dissent, so "One Percent Devils and Their Satanic Tools" can violate:

- "Thou shall not kill";
- "If you lend money to any of my people…who is poor, you shall not be to him as a creditor, and you shall not exact interest from him";
- "You shall not pervert justice due to the poor";
- "You shall not wrong a stranger or oppress him";
- "You shall not afflict any widow or orphan";
- "You shall help the elderly and disabled";
- "Do unto others as you would have others do unto you";
- "I am my brother's keeper";
- "Help those in need"; and
- "Those who have more should give more to the poor."

Aren't Satanic Republican Tools enabling One Percent Devils to steal from 99 percent of Americans via bribes to achieve One-Percent Devil, New World Order goals that violate the goals of the Preamble of the U.S. Constitution to:

- "Promote the General Welfare";
- "Insure Domestic Tranquility";
- "Establish Justice";
- "Form a more perfect Union";
- "Secure Blessing of Liberty"; and
- "Provide for a Common Defense" when the U.S. Military-Industrial Complex is not for Common Defense but the defense of interests of "One Percent Devils"?

Can Orwellian Lies and Wedge Tactics Be Treasonous?

Article III, Sec. 3 [3] says, "Treason against the United States shall consist only in levying War against them, or, in adhering to their Enemies, giving them Aid and Comfort." So haven't Republicans committed treason by "adhering to and giving Aid and Comfort" to atheistic Communist Chinese, atheist Communist Russians, and Muslim enemies by enabling:

- One Percent Devils to destroy U.S. labor unions by outsourcing U.S. production, jobs, and technology to atheistic Communist enemies;
- One Percent Devils to exploit Third World nation resources and jobs via outsourcing of production until Third World nation people rebel and U.S. troops are sent to protect One-Percent Devil interests; and
- Communist and Muslim enemies can say U.S. government:
  1. Is imperialistic;
  2. Has an immoral democracy;
  3. Is against the rights of U.S. and foreign workers;
  4. Enables immoral capitalism;
  5. Causes wars and uses torture in violation of international law.

In Schenk v. U.S. (1919), Justice Wendell Oliver Holmes said, "Freedom of Speech does not include freedom to shout fire in a crowded theater." Schenk had falsely shouted "fire" and many theatergoers were trampled to death. The Republican Supreme Court said the U.S. can restrict free speech, especially during wartime, when it is shown to present a "clear and present danger." Don't "One Percent Devils and Their Satanic Tools" present a clear and present danger to democracy and moral capitalism and the rights of the other 99 percent?

In Dennis et al. vs. U.S. (1951), the Democratic Vinson Supreme Court declared the Smith Act (which made it is a crime to advocate overthrow of the government by force) constitutional. In Yates vs. U.S. (1957), the Warren Court (four Republicans, four Democrats, and an independent) modified Dennis to apply only to words connected to direct action in this endeavor. Aren't Tea Party Republicans trying to destroy or overthrow the U.S. government by eliminating all federal departments and agencies except the Pentagon, which would be used to suppress insurrection, rebellion, and revolution.

Didn't Orwellian-Hitler-Nixon-style repetitive lies and Machiavellian, Wedge-Issue Tactics stimulate:

- Anti-U.S. government neo-Nazis to assault with guns federal officers who were attempting to seize Bundy's cattle because he refused to pay rent for grazing on federal land?
- Mr. and Mrs. Miller at the Bundy Ranch to advocate armed overthrow of the U.S. government?
- Republican senators, congressmen, and press to declare that anti-U.S. government neo-Nazis on the Bundy Ranch were patriots?
- Republicans to repeat Jefferson's "the price of liberty must be paid for with the blood of tyrants and patriots?"
- Millers to declare war on U.S. government;
- Republicans to praise them as patriots; and
- Millers started their revolution by killing Las Vegas police officers?

Doesn't it appear Republicans in Congress and the Supreme Court want a racial, religious, and gender war to eliminate all who are not Caucasians, Christians, and housewife/mothers?

Wouldn't Holmes also say, "Freedom of speech does not include freedom to tell lies and Wedge Issues to get people to vote against their own social, economic, and physical interests and needs?"

Wouldn't Holmes, Vinson, and Warren Courts find "Citizens United" enables One Percent Devils to overthrow democracy and the rights of 99 percent of Americans by means of repetitive lies and Machiavellian Wedge-Issues?

For Laws to Be Moral, They Must Be Predictable,
and Thus There's a Need to Amend Composition of Supreme Court
For sixty years, Republicans "bore false witness" and "uttered false reports" that they're the Law and Order Party; represented the "Silent Moral Majority"; and strictly construed the words of the Constitution, like fundamentalists believe every word in the Bible was God-inspired.

However, every day in Washington, D.C., and state capitals, Republicans violate Commandments; Golden Rules; the Preamble of the Constitution; Bill of Rights; constitutional law on contraception and/or abortion; and voter, labor union, criminal, and civil rights laws.

Fuller said in "The Morality of Law" that law is an instrument that makes life predictable. However, constitutional law cannot be predictable when it fluctuates depending upon whether there's a Republican or Democratic majority on the U.S. Supreme Court.

Aren't There Seven Other Kinds of General Welfare in the U.S.?

- General welfare of Democrats;
- General welfare of independents;
- General welfare of One Percent Devils and Satanic Tool Republicans;
- General welfare of women;
- General welfare of children;
- General welfare of each race; and
- General welfare of each religion?

If 33 percent of Americans are Democrat, 33 percent are independent, and 33 percent are Republican, there is no way that a Republican or Democratic Supreme Court can represent the interests of a majority of Americans and make decisions consistent with the intent of the Preamble of the U.S. Constitution to:

- "Establish Justice";
- "Insure Domestic Tranquility";
- "Promote the General Welfare"; and
- "Secure the Blessings of Liberty";
- "In order to form a more perfect Union."

The only way to achieve the goals of the Preamble and achieve constitutional predictability is to pass an amendment that reconstitutes the Supreme Court into three Democrats, three independents, and three Republicans. If a Democratic justice dies or retires and a Republican is president, he/she must appoint a Democratic replacement (but likely would appoint a conservative Democrat) and vice versa.

Need to Impeach Justices Thomas and Scalia

First, wasn't it a travesty of constitutional integrity for a Republican president to replace progressive, liberal, and Democratic Afro-American Justice Thurgood Marshall with a regressive, reactionary, conservative Republican Afro-American Thomas who votes against interests of Afro Americans and for "Citizens United" bribery that helps "One Percent Devils" and hurts the other 99 percent, including his fellow Afro Americans?

In Attorney and Judicial Codes of Ethics, "an appearance of impropriety can be as damaging as breaking the law." There are two reasons Thomas should've disqualified himself (due to personal interests or prejudice) from hearing the "Citizens United" case. His Caucasian wife is a CEO of a Republican Super PAC. Thomas and Scalia attended Super PAC conventions. If One-Percent Devil Super PACs can bribe politicians, what makes you think they can't bribe Supreme Court justices with money in offshore accounts and insider, stock-market trading tips?

Need for Constitutional Amendments

The U.S. cannot have majority rule when just one senator of a minority party can filibuster to prevent a vote on legislation and appointment of White House cabinet members unless 60 percent of the Senate overrides the filibuster. No minority party in Congress or the Senate has the right to prevent a president from functioning by not voting on his/her appointments.

Does the U.S. need an amendment to force Congress and the Senate to stay in session until they have a budget the president will sign? Does the U.S. need an amendment to prevent Congress from paying its bills for wars by cutting federal funds for social safety nets? Doesn't "Promote the General Welfare" and "Provide for Common Defense" have an equal rank in the Preamble and General Welfare Enabling Clause?

If the Nuremburg Doctrine is international law, don't U.S. Supreme Court justices "owe a higher duty to morality than to the laws of a nation and orders of its leaders?" Shouldn't U.S. Supreme Court justices apply the tests of morality in "Theory of Law" by St. Thomas Aquinas (Chapter II)?

More Ironies about Republican Dogma

Republican President Nixon's and V.P. Agnew's repetitive lies and Machiavellian, Wedge-Issue immorality caused a transfer of Democratic President Johnson's "War on Poverty" funds (to prevent racial civil war) to the Law Enforcement Assistance Administration for Nixon's "Law and Order" agenda to suppress civil rights, antiwar, and feminist movements and to jail rather than help minorities. However, Nixon and Agnew efforts:

- Drove some civil rights, antiwar, and feminist protestors into revolutionary groups such as the Symbionese Liberation Army, Students for a Democratic Society, and Black Panthers;
- Caused them to commit crimes to finance their revolutions; and
- Then ironically:
  1. Agnew was imprisoned for corruption; and
  2. Nixon resigned to avoid impeachment for burglary of Democratic National Headquarters in the Watergate Hotel and illegal wiretaps and mail openings of over fifty thousand civil rights, antiwar, and feminist activists, press, and 150,000 of their friends and families.

Republican Duplicity

As indicated in the comparative analysis of Chapter IV, when a Republican is in the White House, they love Keynesian borrowing and economic stimulus spending on infrastructure and the U.S. Military-Industrial Complex. It reduces unemployment, budget deficit, national debt, and increases votes for Republicans.

However, when a Democrat is in the White House, Republicans are sore losers, don't believe in The American Way is Fair Play, or care about improving the general welfare of the poor, working poor, and middle class. Instead Republicans continue voting for the U.S. Military-Industrial Complex so it can fight wars for "One Percent Devils" but vote against infrastructure spending to reduce unemployment, deficit, and national debt.

After Republican President Eisenhower, every Republican who has campaigned to become president, starting with Richard Nixon, did so using:

- Hitler-style, Machiavellian, Divide-and-Conquer, Wedge-Issue Tactics to:
  1. Stimulate racial, religious, cultural, and gender bias, prejudice, and intolerance in the uneducated, especially white trash, whose self-concepts are so low that they have a psychosocio pathological need to denigrate and emotionally push others down; and
  2. Stimulate white-trash votes for Republicans who will legislate:

a. Racial, religious, cultural, and gender bias, prejudice, and intolerance; and

a. Elimination of funding social safety nets, education and medical research that helps more poor, white-trash Caucasians than poor Afro and Latin Americans; and

a. Repetitive lies so voters believe Republican lies are true and Democratic truth is a lie; and

- "Satanic Tools" (Republican politicians, preachers, and press) aid and abet by repeating repetitive lies and Wedge-Issue Ploys;

However, Republicans are duplicitous in other ways:

- If a Republican wins the presidency, Republicans say, "Let's put our differences aside and compromise for the best interests of America;"
- If a Democrat wins the presidency:
  1. It's not in the best interest of Republicans to compromise, the word "compromise" became a dirty word; and
  2. Republicans vote against anything that will help the U.S. economy or Americans and stimulate them to vote Democrat;
  3. Especially Caucasian-Afro-American President Obama because after all, Republicans are racists.

Republicans are also duplicitous about President Obama's golf outings, foreign-relations trips, and use of presidential orders and hearings to find impeachable offenses. However, Republican presidents played more golf, took more trips, issued more orders, and actually committed impeachable offenses, especially Presidents Nixon and G.W. Bush and V.P. Cheney.

What's most baffling is why independent and Democratic politicians, Preachers, and press have left President Obama dangling in the wind on every false and immoral issue? Why haven't Democrats and independents used repetitive truth to counter lies and explained that Satanic Republican Tools have been suckering white trash with wedge issues into voting Republican and against their own economic and social interests?

Is it because independents and Democrats are also racially prejudiced against an Afro-Caucasian president? Is it because for forty years, Democratic politicians and press have been intimidated into not opposing Republicans who call opponents communists and aiders and abettors of communists?

Republicans Don't Think Acts and Omissions Are Wrong and Are Elephants Who Don't Forget Who Caught Them Doing Wrong Because, to Them, Immoral Ends Justify the Means

As indicated in Chapter VI on freedom of the press, it took Nixon Republicans forty years to succeed in planting a false story with CBS anchor Dan Rather to get him fired because during White House press conferences he wouldn't allow President Nixon to pull a Nixon (avoid answering a question by changing the subject). Republicans cannot accept responsibility for illegal acts. They've been furious with Democrats for holding hearings to:

- Impeach President Nixon for Watergate and other crimes; and
- Impeach President Reagan for Iran-Gate guns and drugs; so Republicans:
    1. Tried to setup President Carter, Clinton, and Obama for impeachment;
    2. But didn't try to impeach President Bush and VP Cheney, who set up themselves for impeachment via lies that led to Iraq War II, their war crimes against humanity, and war profiteering.

What Do Republican Control Freaks Have in Common?

Watergate, Iran-Gate, Iraq-Gate, Gov. Christie's Bridge-Gate, and Gov. Walker's Campaign-Gate have one thing in common: Nixon, Reagan, Bush, Christie, and Walker are like the Three Monkeys who said, "I said nothing; I saw nothing; I heard nothing."

Role of Universities and Theology Schools

Universities and schools of theology need systemic-analysis centers composed of professors of U.S. history, political science, economics, law, psychology, sociology, medicine, environmental science, and journalism. University centers should rate office holders and candidates for office and newspaper, radio and television reporters, and commentators on factual accuracy, intellectual honesty, objectivity, logic, and morality.

The University of Wisconsin should rate candidates for governor, the Senate, the U.S. House, and state legislators and statewide newspapers, television, and radio news. State universities should rate local politicians, candidates, and news media. Theology schools should rate ministers.

Results should be published and discussed in public meetings.

CHAPTER X

General Welfare and Common Defense Clause
vs.
Outsourcing, Wars, and Four-Dollars-Per-Gallon Gas Prices

At the end of WWII, the United States was the only nation with industries that were not destroyed. After factories converted back to producing consumer goods, they supplied all other nations.

High unemployment caused civil unrest in Europe and Japan and led to fear that democracies would turn communist. Democratic President Truman's Marshall Plan countered the threat by rebuilding industries in those nations.

Technology of U.S. industries was outmoded. Foreign industries were rebuilt with more advanced and less labor-intensive technology, so European and Japanese products cost less to produce. Technology the U.S. didn't give was stolen by Japan and Germany via industrial espionage. Those nations also unfairly subsidized production so their products were less expensive to manufacture and sell than U.S. products. They also prevented imports of American products such as cars. Japan let American produce rot on piers.

By the 1960s, Japan and Germany had a one-third share of steel sales in the U.S. Manufacturing ended for many products in the U.S., such as nails, ball bearings, toys, televisions, radios, stereos, and cameras. U.S. companies either went bankrupt or outsourced production to Japan and Singapore.

Although my father saw television for the first time at the 1936 World's Fair in Chicago, few families had TVs until the mid-1950s. I was seven years old when Dad bought our first black-and-white television. I was twelve when we got a color television console with a radio on one side and a record player on the other side.

Television pictures and sound and radio sound were generated by vacuum tubes. Many American companies manufactured radios and televisions (Philco, Emerson, Magnavox, Sears, Westinghouse, General Electric, and Kodak).

NASA research in the 1960s developed transistors. Transistors required less skilled workers to manufacture. U.S. TV, radio, and stereo manufacturers outsourced production, jobs, and technology to Japan and Singapore until no televisions and radios were Made in USA.

Computer chips replaced transistors. However, production of TVs, radios, and stereos remained in Japan, Hong Kong, and now China.

How Ford, GM, and Chrysler Almost Went Bankrupt
In the 1950s and 60s, most Americans owned large cars with high horse power V-8 engines that guzzled gas at a rate of eight miles per gallon. Four cylinder Japanese car engines sounded like washing machines.

Japanese automakers did what Detroit didn't do.

They "Believe it or not, Ripley" had the audacity to ask Americans what they wanted in cars. They said "safe, reliable, and fuel-efficient cars."

When two gasoline shortages occurred in the mid and late 1970s, Japanese and German automakers had what Americans needed. Suddenly they had a one-third share of auto sales in the U.S.

When I studied management, I read about Japanese management styles that compelled workers to exercise before work and be reliable, efficient, and loyal. When car sales slumped, management and employees shared the loss. Instead of laying off workers, hours, pay, and fringe benefits were temporarily reduced.

However, in the United States, other factors gradually contributed to Japanese and German automakers winning 30 percent of the U.S. auto market. Japan, Korea, and China prevented the import of U.S. cars and trucks.

While Japanese and German manufacturers were making safer, more reliable, and fuel-efficient cars, U.S. manufacturers employed risk analysis and planned obsolescence. Risk analysts calculated how much money could be spent on lawsuits to compensate for injuries and deaths from defects and still make 8 percent or more in profits. That may be the reason for GM's latest scandal for not recalling cars with ignition switch defects.

U.S. auto manufacturers also employed planned obsolescence. They made cars with plastic parts instead of metal parts so cars would break down more frequently. Profits from making replacement parts skyrocketed and so did profits for every dealer's service shop.

United Auto Worker unionists contributed to their downfall in three ways. The rule of thumb became, "Don't buy a U.S. car that was made on Friday or Monday." Too many unionists called in sick on Friday to have three-day weekends and Monday because they had hangovers. As a result, nuts, bolts, and other parts were either not installed or improperly installed.

Labor unionists at GM, Ford, and Chrysler didn't all go on strike to get hourly rate and fringe-benefit increases. Workers at only one automaker went on strike while workers at the other two companies continued working and contributing to a strike fund for the strikers. After they won, the other auto companies followed suit.

Auto Worker unionists had natural law and positive law rights to negotiate in that manner. However, I remember thinking in the 1960s, "They're going to make U.S. cars too expensive. There are no auto-worker unions in Germany and Japan, so wages are lower and their governments illegally subsidize production to keep costs of their cars low."

While Japanese and German auto manufacturers transitioned to robotics to reduce labor costs and eliminate manufacturing mistakes, U.S. labor unions fought and delayed robotics for decades to their detriment.

As the cost of foreign cars went down, the cost of U.S.-made cars rose.

Another great Republican con? Right-to-work laws, which translate into right-to-work-for-less-pay-and-benefits laws. Under those laws, German, Japanese, and Korean automakers built plants below the Mason-Dixon Line. Southern autoworkers earned less than unionized autoworkers.

After the 2008 Republican-created stock-market crash, GM and Chrysler auto and truck sales crashed. Republicans wanted them to go into bankruptcy to totally destroy the United Auto Workers union by outsourcing GM and Chrysler production, jobs, and technology to an atheistic Communist Chinese enemy with a New World Order economic domination plan. Doesn't that amount to treason by "One Percent Devils and their Satanic Tool" under Article III, Sec. 3. [1]:

"Treason against the United States, shall consist only in levying war against them, or, in adhering to their Enemies, giving them Aid and Comfort?"

I applaud President Obama for bailing out Chrysler and GM. However, I must ask, why didn't any U.S. senators, representatives, or governors say, "Until the U.S. economic crisis significantly reverses, it's patriotic to buy Ford, GM, and Chrysler cars and trucks"?

U.S. History of Bailing Out Peter Principle Companies Too Big to Be Allowed to Fail

Republican President Teddy Roosevelt enforced the Sherman Antitrust Act to break up empires of One-Percent Devil robber-baron kings such as:

- King Rockefeller's Standard Oil of New Jersey empire;
- King Carnegie's U.S. Steel empire;
- King Vanderbilt's railroad empire; and
- King J.P. Morgan's bank and Wall Street empire.

Those empires were broken up because their horizontal and vertical monopolies employed merciless, immoral, Darwinian "Survival of the fittest" and Ayn Rand "Strong should take from the weak" capitalism that:

- Drove moral competitors out of business so they could fix prices;
- Bribed governors and mayors to have law enforcement officers assault, batter, kill, and jail labor unionists striking for safer work conditions and more wages; and
- Put unsafe products on the market because:
  1. There was no competition that could make safer products; and
  2. If laws they bought didn't protect them from civil suits by injured customers;
  3. Victims couldn't afford an attorney to go up against corporate law firms.

Those monopolies were also divided into many companies because they were too big to be allowed to fail. If they failed, they'd take down the whole U.S. economy with them.

However, Republican President Richard Nixon reversed Republican President Teddy Roosevelt's policy and allowed companies to buy and merge with other companies within their industry. As indicated, President Teddy

Roosevelt divided Standard Oil of New Jersey into thirty companies. As of now, those thirty companies have been merged into five monopolistic oil and gas companies.

Before and into the 1980s, Chrysler spent profits purchasing other companies instead of investing in research and development of better cars and trucks. To avoid bankruptcy, the U.S. government bailed out Chrysler until it could sell off its tank division to general dynamics.

Penn Central was once the largest railroad company. However, instead of using profits to repair and maintain railroad tracks, engines, and cars and convert to high-speed rail line as in Europe and Asia, Penn Central diversified by purchasing companies in different industries. However, as with other companies that did the same, many purchases were unwise, poorly managed, innately unprofitable, and caused bankruptcies, partly because Penn Central put its executives in charge of companies they didn't know how to manage. To save the U.S. railroad system, the U.S. government put Penn Central in bankruptcy and created Amtrak and Conrail.

A good example of how companies screw up when they purchase companies in other industries occurred in the 1980s. Harold Simons, a vulture venture capitalist who got rich buying companies and selling off their divisions, owned NL Chemicals, which manufactured Titanium Paints (in Hightstown, N.J.). Simons purchased Spenser-Kellogg (S-K) of Buffalo, N.Y., and transferred only twelve of its two hundred employees to NL Chemicals.

I met my now ex-wife, Mary Kay Gentry, an assistant production planner and certified genius, after she was transferred. However, Simons put an NL vice president in charge of the Spenser-Kellogg Division and NL managers in charge of research and development, planning, purchasing, manufacturing, inventory, logistics, and computer departments.

S-K transfers brought along a highly sophisticated online computer program to manage five hundred raw materials used to manufacture three hundred paint products. The vice president and computer department manager wanted to put NL and S-K on the same outmoded batch-card system.

However, after they started transferring S-K to that system, they ran out of storage space and had to wipe-out S-K's program to make more space. One foul-up after another caused the computer to go down and batch-fed updates at night meant no one could determine actual status during work hours of inventory, purchasing, manufacturing, and logistics.

No one except my wife-to-be: Mary Kay Gentry, who graduated from a rigorous English boarding school at age sixteen because she had a genius IQ and a photographic memory. Without a computer, she knew approximate amounts of raw materials available, what and how much was in inventory, being manufactured, and in transit to buyers.

Soon no decisions were made by Spenser-Kellogg VPs or managers without consulting with Mary Kay. For all practical purposes, she was the de facto vice president of S-K Division. She saved the company from millions of dollars of losses. Yet she only earned a poverty-level twenty-two thousand dollars per year. The VP would not promote her to any manager position because she only had an associate degree, and company policy required a four-year degree.

She wasn't earning 87 percent of what men earned for the same job, which led to the Lily Lidbader Equal Pay Act. Mary Kay was earning 13 percent of the income of the incompetent VPs and managers.

After NL transferred production to North Carolina, she managed the S-K Division with a computer and telephone at home. She got jobs with other companies that sold out to other companies. Purchasers also put their executives in charge. Each screwed up. Some companies went bankrupt.

Peter Principle = Republican President Reagan's Incompetence

Peter Principle means "people tend to rise or be promoted until they reach their level of incompetence." I fail to see why Republicans want to claim they're Reagan Republicans.

For months after election, President Reagan didn't issue economic policies to the treasury secretary. He had staff read Reagan's campaign speeches to derive economic policies, which included not regulating banks and brokers.

Reagan's failure to regulate stock brokers and bankers allowed the paper-money and junk-bond scams that caused a stock-market crash, recession, and bailout of banks and brokers. Ironically Republicans are called elephants because they don't forget who hurt them. However:

- After Republican President G.W. Bush was elected, Republicans had amnesia about the consequences of Reagan's lack of regulation of bankers and stockbrokers; and

- After Democrat President Obama was elected, Republicans had amnesia about facts such as:
  1. Republicans causing 2008 Stock-Market Crash/Great Depres-
     sion;
  2. Republican President Reagan raising taxes six times and raising
     debt ceiling twelve times; and
  3. During depressions and recessions, whether the president was
     Republican or Democrat, that they employed Keynesian eco-
     nomic stimulus spending for infrastructure to bring U.S. econ-
     omy back.

So why do Republican presidential candidates want to claim they're Reagan
Republicans? Was Reagan's senile dementia contagious?

Peter Principle = Republican President G.W. Bush Incompetence

Republicans speak with forked tongues. When a Democrat is in the White
House, Republicans demand a balanced budget. However, when Republican
Presidents Eisenhower, Nixon, Ford, Reagan, G.H. Bush and G.W. Bush
were in the White House, Republican forgot their balance-the-budget promises, and the national debt increased each year.

The only president to balance the budget was Democrat Bill Clinton.
He left Republican President G.W. Bush a $400 billion budget surplus.

Given why and how President Bush and Vice President Cheney got the
U.S. into the Iraq War, there's a question whether they ignored intelligence
(or were not intelligent enough to understand the significance of Muslims
getting training to fly airliners but not how to take off and land and other
intel about potential terrorist attacks in the U.S). Did they want the U.S. to
be attacked so they could achieve their selfish financial goals? Could they
have prevented the airliner attacks on the World Trade Center and Pentagon?

If President G.W. Bush read President Franklin Delano Roosevelt's en-
tries in the Presidents "Book of Secrets," he would have seen that FDR sent
a U.S. warship into Japanese waters hoping they'd attack it so the U.S. could
enter WWII. President Lyndon Baines Johnson's entry in the "Book of Secrets" would indicate he sent the U.S. Navy into what the North Vietnamese
considered territorial waters of the Gulf of Tonkin and provoked North Vietnam to attack.

However, according to the History Channel, navy admirals may have lied about U.S. warships being attacked. In any event, LBJ issued the Gulf of Tonkin Resolution declaring war on North Vietnam. Didn't President G.W. Bush send U.S. warships into Iranian and then Iraqi territorial waters hoping their navies would attack?

Republican Trickle-Down Economics Theory Myth

Ever since WWII when a Democrat was in the White House (Truman, Kennedy, Carter, Clinton, and Obama), the Republican campaign platforms included promises to balance the budget and reduce budget deficits. Yet Republican Presidents (Eisenhower, Nixon, Ford, Reagan, G.H. Bush, and G.W. Bush) didn't reduce budget deficits but employed Keynesian borrowing and economic stimulus spending.

Minnesota Democrat Senator Hubert Humphrey in 1968 when he ran for president coined the phrase for Republican economics policies as "trickle-down economics." Republicans advocated that tax cuts, deductions, and subsidies for "One Percent Devils" would result in their hiring more workers and expanding and building of new production and service plants. The obvious flaws in that dogma are that:

- Legislation didn't require companies to reinvest tax cuts;
- Companies only hire and expand plants when demand for products and services exceeds supply; and
- The way to create more demand for products and services is to put more spendable money in pockets of consumers via:
  1. Sizeable tax cuts to working poor and middle class; and
  2. Keynesian borrowing and economic stimulus spending on:
     a. Infrastructure to put construction workers on the job; and
     b. Hiring teachers, nurses, police officers, firefighters, social Workers, and government administrators.

However, in 2001 President Bush's number-one priority was to pay off "One Percent Devils" who gave campaign bribes so he could win reelection in 2004 . He wasted President Clinton's budget surplus by giving most of it to "One Percent Devils" in 2001 and 2003 tax cuts. Yet there's no evidence tax cuts added jobs or caused expansion of production.

My 2001 and 2003 tax-cut rebates were enough to buy two pizzas per week. Instead of "One Percent Devils" using tax cuts and rebates to hire and expand production and services, they were morally unable to show appreciation for American workers and consumers who made them rich:

- They didn't buy Made in USA but bought foreign cars, yachts, vacations, vacation homes, furs, jewelry, wines, and caviar;
- They used tax cuts, deductions, and subsidies to:
  1. Outsource jobs of those who made them rich to:
     a. An atheistic Communist Chinese enemy; and
     b. Third World nations;
     c. So they could immorally exploit foreign workers; or
  2. Used tax cuts to buy other U.S. companies:
     a. To create or expand horizontal and vertical monopolies; or
     b. To expand income base by laying off workers: and
  3. Hurt employees who made companies and stockholders rich:
     a. By laying off employees of companies purchased; and
     b. Forcing remaining workers to do jobs of two to five people; but
     c. Without a pay raise, which means remaining employees were forced to work more hours for the same pay and benefits.

Doesn't that violate "thou shall not steal" and "do unto others what you would have others do unto you?" Isn't that inhumane, a crime against humanity, and inconsistent with God's plan for mankind, ala Chapter II?

Isn't it immoral for "One Percent Devils" to outsource in order to exploit foreign workers in ways they can't exploit U.S. workers? Wasn't it also immoral to outsource knowing that if foreign workers or foreign governments rebelled against exploitation, the CIA and U.S. Military-Industrial Complex would step in and save interests of "One Percent Devils"?

When Americans pay taxes to provide subsidies and deductions for outsourcing or buy products outsourced to China and Third World nations, aren't taxpayers aiding and abetting or coconspirators of immorality and inhumanity of "One Percent Devils"? If the CIA or U.S. military attacks a nation to protect the interests of "One Percent Devils," aren't Americans who buy outsourced products aiding and abetting or coconspirators in the deaths and disabilities of U.S. soldiers and people in those nations?

Vice President Cheney and President G.W. Bush conned America into two unwinnable U.S. Military-Industrial Complex wars but didn't increase taxes to pay for them. Those wars were paid for by:

- Borrowing from an atheistic Communist Chinese enemy, which violates Article III, Sec. 3. [1] "Treason... shall consist of adhering to enemies, giving them aid and comfort;" and
- Cutting social safety net fund for victims of "One Percent Devils";
- But didn't increase taxes to pay for two wars, adding trillions to the budget deficit.

It's been said that President Bush's 2001 and 2003 tax cuts put outsourcing to China on steroids. Did China agree to buy U.S. treasury notes to pay for those wars in exchange for 2001 and 2003 tax cuts that enhanced outsourcing to China?

Within a month of attacking Afghanistan, President Bush knew the location of Osama Bin Laden. Did he chicken out when he didn't take him down? Did President Bush decide not to capture or kill Bin Laden because he wanted to prolong that war to make:

- U.S. Military-Industrial Complex richer?
- President Bush richer because Mideast wars raised the cost of gasoline?
- Vice president richer as former CEO and a large shareholder of Halliburton, a defense contractor?

When questioned about missing the opportunity to take down Bin Laden, didn't President Bush say he wasn't really an important target? If so, then why'd the U.S. go into Afghanistan? Why was it that President Obama got Bin Laden within a year, but President Bush didn't try to get him for seven years?

Was President Bush's attack on Afghanistan a way to give the U.S. Military combat experience for his real target, Iraq, so:

- Value of his stocks and dividends in a U.S. oil and gas company would rise;
- VP Cheney's stocks and dividends in Halliburton, a company hired to supply weapons and mercenaries (to take over jobs of U.S. troops, including torture in violation of Geneva Convention).

Means to those immoral ends started with lies by Bush and Cheney:

- That Iraq had weapons of mass destruction;
- Saddam Hussein had an alliance with al-Qaeda and was going to sell weapons of mass destruction to them so they could attack the U.S. Yet no "Law and Order" Republican suggested impeaching Cheney or Bush for:
- "Adhering to and Giving Comfort" to communist and Muslim enemies;
- An immoral and illegal Iraq War II;
- War profiteering by and from Bush's oil and gas company; or
- War profiteering by Cheney from Halliburton and helping it evade open, public, bidding laws in order to give extremely high profit margins to Halliburton?

Is there any difference between Hitler lying about weak Poland being a threat so Germany could attack and conquer Poland and lies by President G.W. Bush and Vice President Cheney? At least European countries are more moral than Republicans. Bush and Cheney don't fly to Europe because the International War Crimes Tribunal has issued warrants for their arrest.

Those Who Fail to Remember History Are Doomed to Repeat Mistakes of the Past and President Eisenhower's Warning about U.S. Military-Industrial Complex Getting U.S. into Wars

I asked my brother, Warren, who in one year of combat in Vietnam rose from PFC to staff sergeant with a Silver Star, Bronze Star, and Purple Heart and then earned a business administration degree from UW Eau Claire); his son, Jason, (an electrical engineering grad of UW); and daughter, Elizabeth, (who has a BS and MS in biochemical engineering from UW), "What do the American Revolution and Vietnam War have in common with Iraq and

Afghanistan wars?" After no response, I said, "Any time an invading army is opposed by a significant number of the indigenous population, at best the invader can only control cities but is subject to snipers and roadside bombs."

President George H. Bush wrote a book about his presidency. He said, "The Iraq War ended after Kuwait was liberated. We didn't move on to conquer Bagdad and thus the whole country because we had no viable endgame or exit strategy."

After a reporter repeated that, President G.W. Bush was asked if he talked with his dad before attacking Iraq. "Believe it or not, Ripley" G.W. said, "No! I talked with God." I was flabbergasted and said:

- "God told a Judeo-Christian president to attack, murder, and maim thousands of Muslims as if it was some kind of Holy Crusade?
- "Doesn't Exodus say God wanted Hebrews to own Canaan/Palestine?
- "Don't clerics say God wants Muslims to jihad Israel, Jews, and the U.S.?
- "If all three religions believe there is only one supreme god, either:
  1. "Leaders of all three religions are lying about God's will"; or
  2. "Are they inferring that God is psychotic or schizophrenic?"

Remember the Republican Party that claimed it's better at national defense than Democrats but lost the Vietnam War, leaving the U.S. with a 10-1 war record? Remember when G.W.'s dad, President Bush (a WWII hero pilot), ran against Bill Clinton? Republicans criticized him about not volunteering to fight in the Vietnam War. Presidents Clinton and Obama didn't allow Republicans to goad them into wars during their terms in office.

Yet chickenshit G. W. Bush copped out of fighting in the Vietnam War. He joined the Air National Guard but got away with rarely participating in weekend and summer training.

What about chickenshit Vice President Cheney? He also didn't enlist and wasn't drafted for the Vietnam War. How sweet that was for the U.S. Military-Industrial Complex to have two of its members in the White House.

G.H. Bush, G.W. Bush, Bill Clinton, Hilary Clinton, and Barack Obama graduated from Yale. At Yale, Skull and Cross Bones is a secret society whose members are key forces in federal and state governments, no matter which party is in control. Those five Yale graduates were all invited to another secret society, the Hilderburg Group (composed of 102 world leaders, industrialists, financiers, and scientists) who anoint and finance those who become leaders of industrial nations. At Harvard is a secret society named The Illuminati. Freemasons are another society that influences American policies. Some people are members of all three societies with a goal of creating an Anglo-Saxon New World Order that would be no less cruel and inhumane as the Nazi New World Order or the New World Order George Orwell warned about in *1984* and *Animal Farm*. Secret societies set up the U.S. for:

- Wars that will benefit the U.S. Military-Industrial Complex, which include U.S. oil and gas companies; and
- Replacing Democracy and moral capitalism with an Anglo-Saxon New World Order, where 99 percent of Americans would be brainwashed, Mindless, robotic slaves.

Other Failures by President G.W. Bush to Learn History to Avoid Mistakes by Presidents Harding, Hoover, and Reagan

Perhaps G.W. Bush didn't just skip Air National Guard training but also classes at Yale? Should he ask Yale for reimbursement of tuition?

GW's failure to regulate banks and brokers caused the mortgage bundling and derivative scams that caused the greatest stock-market crash and economic depression since Republican Presidents Harding and Hoover's failures to regulate brokers and banks created and caused the:

- "Roaring 20s" for organized crime speakeasies and stock market;
- Greatest stock-market crash on October 29, 1929;
- Great Depression with 13 million people out of work; and
- Great Depression that caused World War II.

President Obama Made One Mistake and One Failure

Except for one failure, I would be the first to start carving President Obama's mug on Mount Rushmore, next to Abe Lincoln. Next to George Washington should be Ike Eisenhower. They were both great generals and great presidents. As Supreme Allied Commander, Gen. Eisenhower was the most powerful military leader in history.

As much as Republicans try to besmirch and impeach President Obama, he's been "like magic." He applies systemic analysis to solve problems, so he doesn't make mistakes. He's never been caught in a lie.

Although he misspoke when he said, "No one will lose their health insurance coverage under the Affordable Health Insurance Act." He should have said, "ACA will prevent health insurance carriers from charging high premiums for grossly inadequate health insurance that doesn't cover preexisting conditions and has coverage ceilings that can still drive families into bankruptcy for unpaid medical bills."

Republicans have failed to find evidence of any impeachable offense by President Obama when a big piece of evidence is right in there faces. Ironically that alleged "Law and Order" Party has said nothing about President Obama's failure to have his attorney general press criminal charges against CEOs and other top executives of major banks and stock brokerage houses that created mortgage bundling and other derivative frauds and caused the second greatest stock-market crash and depression in U.S. history.

Didn't President Reagan's attorney general charge and convict bankers and stock brokers for the junk bond–paper money scams? When President Obama was in the process of bailing out criminal bankers and brokers:

- Was it a mistake or oversight that allowed criminal bankers and brokers to get million-dollar, bailout-money bonuses for their crimes?
- Why didn't President Obama order Attorney General Holder to charge and prosecute those criminals?
- Why didn't President Obama order AG Holder to enforce the Sherman

Antitrust Act to break up those corporations that were "too big to allow to fail" to prevent them from causing another stock-market crash and depression?

- Were those failures a result of a deal Barack Obama made with the Hilderburg Group to get big money contributions for campaigns?

So why didn't Republicans like Assi, I mean Issa, not hold impeachment hearings because President Obama didn't order Attorney General Holder to press charges against bankers and brokers? Is it because congressional representatives and senators have been getting rich off insider-trading tips from brokers and bankers?

Was it because Republicans changed SEC and Banking Commission laws to allow the scams? Did President G.W. Bush tell the SEC and Banking Commission not to enforce laws and regulations? Why haven't Republicans and Democrats been charged for breaking insider-trading laws?

Did they get insider-trading tips to sell short to get rich before stock prices plummeted in 2008? Did they get insider-trading tips to buy stocks when the stock-market crash bottomed out and was about to start rising?

Why Gas Prices Were Twenty-six cents Per gallon in 1948, Twenty-three cents Per gallon in 1971, and Four Dollars Per Gallon in 2008-2014?
WWII ended on V-E Day and V-J Day. German U-boats and battleships in the Atlantic Ocean and U.S. and Japanese submarines in the Pacific Ocean stopped sinking oil and gasoline tankers. There was an oil and gas market glut. Gasoline prices plummeted in 1948 to twenty-six cents per gallon.

For the next seventy years, oil and gas prices were on a roller coaster depending upon whether there was international or civil war in the Mideast.

In the early 1970s at the University of Wisconsin, one of the top three U.S. military history professors said, "Seeds of future wars are laid by how the last war was resolved."

In his farewell White House address, President Eisenhower, who was the former supreme allied commanding general during WWII, warned us, "In the councils of government, we must guard against the acquisition of unwarranted influence, whether sought or unsought, by the Military-Industrial Complex. The potential for the disastrous rise of misplaced power exists and will persist.

"Therefore, we must never let the weight of this complex endanger our liberties or democratic process. We should take nothing for granted. Only a knowledgeable and alert citizenry can compel the proper meshing of a huge Military-Industrial Complex with our peaceful message and goals so our security and liberty may prosper together."

Gen. Washington defeated the greatest army on earth. As president he said something like, "The United States of America must not form alliances with foreign nations that would force the United States into unwanted wars." President Monroe issued the Monroe Doctrine, which told

European nations to stay out of the Americas and the U.S. would stay out of European conflicts.

Isn't it time for Americans to pay heed to President Washington's advice and the Monroe Doctrine? In the movie *Ike*, an audience of allied officers watched a movie based upon a Shakespearean play about a battle at Normandy, France. General Bradley said to Gen. Eisenhower, "It seems like Europeans love wars."

The books *Battlefields of Britain, Atlas of World Military History*, and *The Ancient World of the Celts* seem to support that opinion. In the 1990s, I was in Judge Yaskin's office. On the back of her door was a map of the world showing thirty-two ongoing civil and international wars.

As my dad's 12/24/1945 letter indicates, the U.S. only intervenes in wars when interests of U.S. industrialists are at stake. Why should American soldiers get killed and disabled fighting for their interests?

As to wars, Defense Secretary McNamara (under JFK and LBJ) asked, "How much evil must we do (in war) in order to do good?"

I ask, why should U.S. soldiers get killed and disabled fighting wars for "One Percent Devils" who:

- Don't believe in democracy and moral capitalism;
- Outsourced production of fifty thousand companies and tens of millions of American jobs to:
  1. An atheistic Communist enemy; and
  2. Third World nations;
  3. So they could immorally exploit foreign workers; and
  4. Be defended by the U.S. Military-Industrial Complex?

During the 1700s, the American economy was based upon farming, fishing, mining, and fur trading with European nations. Our Founding Fathers didn't foresee:

- An Industrial Revolution (that began during the Civil War) that would create kings of industry (Carnegie of steel, Vanderbilt of railroads, Rockefeller of oil and gas, and J.P. Morgan of banks and Wall Street); or
- That industrial and financial kings would exploit American workers and cause a need for labor unions, business laws, and regulations;

or

- That there would be world wars that caused a need for the U.S. Military-Industrial Complex; or
- That the U.S. Military-Industrial Complex would fight wars for "One Percent Devils" who exploit foreign workers.

Four important counterforces came about in 1948. Three were contrary to President Washington's advice to avoid foreign alliances and the Monroe Doctrine.

Former First Lady Eleanor Roosevelt ushered in the United Nations (U.N.) to prevent future wars. However, that goal was sabotaged from day one because Communist Russia and China had veto power on the U.N. Security Council. So Russian and Chinese aggression would go unchecked.

The CIA was created to counter the RSU's KGB. However, the CIA's motto was "Fight Fire with Fire." That meant the CIA would have to learn to fight like the KGB, evil for evil. That raised a McNamara-type question: "How much evil should the CIA do in order to do good?" The answers are embarrassing. The CIA developed drugs to make assassination or execution look like death from natural causes. They set in motion the means to topple foreign governments that were allies of Communist Russia, China, or were stepping on the toes of U.S. industrial and financial interests.

The U.S. Military-Industrial Complex had significant negative influences in two other creations of 1948. In case the U.N. was unsuccessful in halting Russian Soviet Union aggression, the North Atlantic Treaty Organization (NATO) was formed. However, that came at a nauseously high price.

America suffered hundreds of thousands of casualties (killed, wounded, and disabled) liberating the French from a Nazi New World Order. After France was liberated, French President De Gaulle blackmailed or extorted the U.S. He threatened that France wouldn't join NATO or the U.N. unless the U.S. supplied weapons, ammunition, food, medicine, and other war materials to the French Foreign Legion so it could reconquer Southeast Asia and return it to the control of an imperialistic French New World Order empire.

Ho Chi Min, who was educated in the United States and grateful that the U.S. liberated Vietnam from the Japanese, pleaded with President

Truman not to assist France. De Gaulle forced President Truman to turn his back on Ho Chi Min. He was forced to seek weapons and supplies from Russian Communists.

Mideast and Northern African Map and Leadership Was Set Up for Future Civil and International Wars

Before WWI the Muslim Turkish Ottoman Empire of Turkey ruled the Mideast and Northern African countries. They were on the wrong side of WWI and lost control of those countries to the British and French. However after WWII, France and Brittan were broke and couldn't afford to keep troops in Northern Africa and the Mideast.

Members of secret societies that advocated an Anglo-Saxon New World Order, U.S., French, and British oil and gas companies, and Military-Industrial Complexes set up the Mideast and Northern African nations for future civil wars and international wars in two ways:

- The Mideast was divided into multireligious nations like Iraq with Indo-European Kurds in the north, Shiites in the south and Sunni in-between;
- Sunni royalty, who were raised to believe Shiites were not "real" Muslims, were anointed as rulers of nations with a Shiite majority and vice versa. That guaranteed high profits for U.S., French and British Military-Industrial Complexes and oil and gas companies with every war and caused other consequences:
- Sunni royalty owed no allegiance and in fact hated the Shiite majority it ruled and vice versa for Shiite royalty. Royalty:
  1. Didn't share oil and gas wealth with the people they ruled;
  2. Used 50 percent of their wealth to purchase jet fighters, tanks, and other war materials, as well as to build massive secret police forces to:
     a. Suppress the Muslim majority in their nation;
     b. Attack neighboring nations or repel an invasion; and
     c. Had no compunction against sacrificing their alien majority in international wars to conquer neighboring nations;
- At first the US-MIC sold fighter planes, tanks, guns, ammo, and other military materials to Shiite and Sunni leaders. However, once

an international or civil war broke out, the U.S. government stopped supplying the aggressor:

1. Russian Soviet Union also had huge stockpiles of weapons left over from WWII and a Military-Industrial Complex primed to make more. So the RSU began supplying aggressors;
2. Soon the French, British, and German Military-Industrial Complexes got a share of the action by selling to nations that didn't want to buy from the U.S. or RSU; and
3. KGB, CIA, French intelligence and British military intelligence destabilized Mideast governments or leadership of Muslim rebel armies; and
4. Some Sunni and Shiite royalty were replaced with equally vicious and immoral dictators."

Each civil and international war drove up oil and gas prices and profits for the benefit of oil and gas companies of the U.S., Britain, and France.

Their Military-Industrial Complexes also got rich. Another major stimulator of Mideast wars was the withdrawal of British troops from the Mideast. (England couldn't afford to pay for armies in the Mideast.) Jewish forces defeated Palestinians and established the nation of Israel.

There's nothing in the Koran or Sunna (Sunnah) law (based upon the words and acts of Muhammad) to support jihads against Jews or Israel. Babylonian King Nebuchadnezzar exiled all Twelve Tribes of Israel in 604 B.C.

Muhammad founded Islam and the Muslim faith in A.D. 604. He only conquered enough of Saudi Arabia to include Mecca and didn't force Jews or Christians to convert to Islam but lived side-by-side in peaceful harmony, traded with, and used skills of Jews and Christians (see *Atlas of World Military History* by Richard Brooks). Furthermore, Muhammad, like Moses and Jesus, were descendants of Adam and Eve, Noah, and Abraham.

When Abraham's wife Sarah couldn't conceive an heir, she, according to tradition, gave her Egyptian slave Hagar to Abraham. Hagar bore Ishmael. Muhammad is a descendant of Ishmael, Abraham, and Noah.

Then Sarah bore Jacob. After he defeated angels in a battle, God renamed him Israel. He founded the nation of Israel. So in the final analysis:

- Muslims and Jews are Semite cousins many times over; and
- There's no historical or religious basis for Muslims, other than Palestinians, to hate or jihad Jews and Israel.

So why do Muslims hate Jews and Israel? Muslim men hate Jewish men and women because:

- They're highly educated and skilled militarists, scientists, doctors, attorneys, architects, and farmers who turned a desert into gardens. However, Muslim men were told by clerics that the only book they needed to read was the Koran; and
- Jewish women are educated, professionals, and owners of businesses and have rights Muslim men won't allow women to have.

Muslim women hate Jewish women because:

- Jewish women wear short sleeves, shorts, sandals, or bikinis, and their hair blows in the wind, but Muslim women must have their faces covered and dress in black from head to toe in one-hundred-plus-degree temperatures;
- Jewish women are as highly educated as Jewish men, but Muslim women cannot go to school;
- Jewish women can vote and run for office, but Muslim women cannot;
- Jewish women can be doctors, attorneys, and scientists and own homes and businesses, but Muslim women can't have a job outside of the home; and
- Jewish women can pick their mate, but Muslim women are sold into marital procreation slavery, and some have to share a husband.

So to divert anger, resentment, and rebellion against rulers of Muslim nations and clerics:

- Clerics, aided and abetted by royalty or dictators, "passed the buck" by "pulling a *1984*" to divert resentment and desire to kill clerics and ruling leaders toward a common enemy: Jews, Israel, and the U.S.;

- Clerics "bore false witness" that Muhammad wanted all Muslims to jihad Jews, Israel, and the U.S. (for providing military and other aid);
- Royalty and dictators ordered forces to jihad Jews and Americans; and
- Of course one path to paradise (heaven) was death in battle for Muhammad and Islam; and
- Of course each resulting jihad war drove up oil and gas prices to the great benefit of British, French, and American oil and gas companies, as well as profits of Military-Industrial Complexes.

Solution?

Why can't America:

- Stop selling oil and gas to China and Japan. Let those countries get gas and oil from the Mideast;
- Tell "One Percent Devils" the U.S. military will no longer fight their wars. So either sell foreign interests or use profits to buy mercenaries to fight their wars;
- Orchestrate North, Central and South American, oil-producing nations to withdraw from OPEC so that oil and gas of the Americas would only be sold to nations of the Americas?
- Work with nations of the Americas to develop:
  1. Methods to prevent carbon (from burning of fossil fuels) from polluting air, water, land, and food and causing global warming; and
  2. Alternatives to fossil fuels before 2030, when there will be more demand for oil and gas than can be produced?
- Only spend foreign-aid money in the Americas to bring American nations up to par with the U.S. in terms of education and training?
- Only outsource to Canada, Mexico, South and Central American nations? (Wouldn't outsourcing to Mexico, Central, and South American nations drastically reduce or eliminate illegal immigrants who come to the U.S. for jobs?);
- Make the Star Wars defense shield impenetrable to missiles and bombers; and
  1. Withdraw all U.S. Naval forces to the western half of the Atlantic Ocean and the eastern half of the Pacific Ocean and Mediterranean Sea (to protect Israel);

2. Withdraw all army, air force, and marines from foreign countries and station them on the east and west coast of the U.S?

Presidents Nixon and Reagan Drove Up Oil and Gas Prices

Gasoline prices three years after WWII were twenty-eight cents per gallon because supply greatly exceeded demand. Four years after the Six-Day War of 1967 drove up prices to over two dollars per gallon, gas prices plummeted to twenty-three cents per gallon because supply again exceeded demand. Major U.S. oil and gas companies manipulated supply to recreate horizontal and vertical monopolies and drive up the price of oil and gasoline by reducing supply so that demand exceeded supply and prices could be artificially increased.

Once major oil and gas companies eliminated competition, their CEOs could illegally fix prices at a golf match or at *The Best Little Whorehouse in Texas*. By increasing supply and artificially lowering prices, they drove thousands of mom-and-pop service stations and dozens of refineries, wholesalers, and oil and gas tanker companies to the point of bankruptcy or having to sellout to a major.

As indicated earlier, trust-busting President Teddy Roosevelt broke up Rockefeller's Standard Oil of New Jersey horizontal and vertical monopoly into thirty component companies. After Israel easily won the Six-Day War of 1967, oil and gas prices plummeted so that everyone in the industry from well to service station were losing money.

President Nixon had two solutions from the Anglo-Saxon New World Order playbook that violated the Sherman Antitrust Act, laws against price fixing, and enabled major U.S. companies to recreate horizontal and vertical monopolies:

- President Nixon and his key aides were attorneys-at-law who ignored the Sherman Antitrust Act and allowed major U.S. oil and gas companies to drive competition out of business with a gas war:
  1. So by 1970, prices at gas stations owned by major oil and gas companies were fixed at twenty-three cents per gallon;
  2. Enough for majors to earn a five-cent-per-gallon profit;
  3. But mom-and-pop gas stations, as well as middlemen, wholesalers, and distributors, had to pay major producers much more than twenty-three cents per gallon;

4. So their customers bought gas at stations owned by major oil and gas companies; and

5. Mom-and-pop gas stations and middlemen either sold out to majors or filed for bankruptcy;

- The winding down of the Vietnam War presented President Nixon with three Anglo-Saxon New World Order plan or goal problems:

  1. The U.S. was using 1 million gallons of fuels each day in Vietnam, and that one million gallons would soon glut the market and keep gas prices down in the twenty-three-cent-per-gallon range;

  2. Major U.S. oil and gas companies would lose their hefty, sweet-deal profits from selling 1 million gallons of fuel per day to the Pentagon; and

  3. U.S. Military-Industrial Complex profits would go down and Military-Industrial factories would have to lay off workers and close plants at a time when:

     a. There were very few jobs open in the U.S.; and

     b. Five hundred thousand soldiers would be mustered out of the military and reenter the job market to compete with millions of college graduates. For example, 300,000 psychology majors graduated with me in 1971:

        1) I went on to graduate school because the only psychology job I found was in an institution for children born with defects. That job only paid $8,500 per year; and

        2) I earned much more during summer-school break doing heavy lifting and carrying in the hottest, stinkiest, and dirtiest job on earth in the Sharon Foundry.

To benefit Anglo-Saxon New World Order goals, the U.S. Military Industrial Complex, and U.S. major oil and gas companies, President Nixon orchestrated a deal to sell Phantom jets and Abram tanks to Iran:

- Officially, said President Nixon, so Iran could thwart a threat from Russian Soviet Union to conquer Iranian oil and gas and have a direct land route from Russia to the Indian Ocean, where the Russian Navy could block access to the Suez Canal to cut off oil and gas flow to Europe. However, even with the jets and tanks, Iran would have been no match for the Russian Army, Navy, and Air Force;

- Unofficially the Sunni Shah of Iran, who ruled a Shiite majority:
  1. Needed jet fighters and tanks to counter threats from:
     a. A Shiite majority who threatened to overthrow the shah; and
     b. From Sunni-ruled Iraq.

However, with gas prices at twenty-three cents per gallon, Iran couldn't afford to buy weapons, and the Koran prohibited borrowing money to pay for them.

Iran and other Mideast, oil-and-gas-producing nations wanted to form OPEC (Organization of Petroleum Exporting Nations) to reduce production and drive up prices. The prince of Saudi Arabia offered to prevent OPEC.

However, President Nixon asked him not to and told Secretary of State Kissinger to hold secret talks with Mideast nations to create OPEC so Iran could afford to buy tanks, jets, and other weapons — weapons Iran used against Iraq in the 1980s. So President Reagan armed Iraq, and it used those weapons against Americans in the Iraq Wars I and II. Now ISIS terrorists are using U.S. weapons against Syria and Iraq.

Similarly in the 1980s, the U.S. armed Afghans to fight a Communist Russian invasion. (see movie *Charlie Wilson's War* about how a U.S. congressman, CIA agent, and Houston socialite armed Afghans to fight against the Russian invasion). Those weapons have been used against Americans in the Afghanistan War. How symmetrical or circuitous!

Also in the early 1980s, President Reagan had Col. Oliver North orchestrate the Iran-Contra, Drugs-for-Guns Deal. The CIA got heroin and marijuana from the Guatemala Contras who were fighting against an atheistic Communist government that had executed a group of U.S. nuns.

The CIA gave drugs to Panama Dictator Noriega for sale in the United States. Was the U.S. Coast Guard in on it and let his planes and ships pass?

Part of the money Noriega received was taken by Oliver North to Iran to buy weapons for the Guatemalan Contras. Those weapons were transported on CIA Air America or Flying Tiger planes to Guatemala.

However, before the Iran-Contra Affair, Shiites overthrew the Shah of Iran, the U.S. embassy was overrun by a mob, and ninety hostages were held for ransom and other concessions. Then two extreme gas shortages resulted from Iran withholding oil and gas from the U.S. market. That caused:

- No one to be able to fill their gas tanks;
- Long lines at gas stations;
- Prices to rise to four dollars per gallon; and
- Economic damage to industries that relied on oil and gas, such as:
  1. Trucking companies;
  2. Airlines; and
  3.. Farms to fuel equipment and because fertilizer is made from oil.

Democratic President Jimmy Carter and a Democratic Congress and Senate spent $750 million per year to fund research and development of alternatives to oil and gas: passive and active solar energy; creating auto fuel from corn alcohol; electric, hydrogen, and helium cars; and more energy efficient cars, homes, and businesses, etc. However, Republican President Reagan and Congress transferred that money to Star Wars missile defense R and D.

Yet even today, twenty-five years later, Star Wars missiles still can't "hit the broad side of a barn." And the U.S. is still almost as reliant on Mideast oil and gas as when Carter was president.

As indicated President Roosevelt split Rockefeller's empire into thirty companies. However, Nixon allowed major U.S. oil and gas companies to drive thousands of mom and pops and small oil or gas companies out of business via The Gas Price War. Other Republican presidents allowed major oil and gas companies to merge. So by 2011 or 2012 congressional hearings, there were only five U.S. oil and gas CEOs to testify about elimination of $400 million in oil and gas subsidies.

At the time, gas prices were over four dollars per gallon. CEOs admitted it only cost eighteen cents per gallon to produce, refine, and sell at the pump. Yet

- Republicans in Congress won't eliminate oil and gas subsidies; and
- Drastically or completely limited subsidies for production of car fuel from grains. My niece, Elizabeth, who has a PhD in biochemical engineering, does R and D of biofuels for a company in Madison.

Other Ways U.S. Oil and Gas Manipulated Gas-Pump Supply
Is it coincidental that oil and gas refinery explosions occur during low demand and high supply of gas and oil? Sigmund Freud said, "There's no such thing as coincidence."

During the Iranian oil and gas embargoes of the mid and late 1970s, fully loaded gas and oil tanker ships were anchored in the Mediterranean Sea and Gulf of Mexico in order to manufacture shortages at the pump so prices could be raised.

Ironic, is it not? "One Percent Devils and Their Satanic Tools" claim or "bear false witness" that they want a laissez-faire, open, free market system when in fact their acts and omissions indicate they want an economic system that can be manipulated via price fixing so they can violate the commandment "Thou shall not steal."

Question is, how much money do "One Percent Devils" of U.S. oil and gas and the U.S. Military-Industrial Complex spend to bribe "their Satanic Tools" to get the U.S. military involved in Mideast and North African wars. "One Percent Devils" such as the Koch Brothers are able to reap (steal from U.S. taxpayers) $7 billion for every $1 billion in bribes.

Nauseating Oil and Gas Company Propaganda Commercials
Is anyone else sick of TV commercials about how products they make or contribute to making and people they employed to con Americans into believing they do more good than harm and evil. What they leave out is:

- How many thousands of people lost their gas stations or other business, including businesses that relied upon those who were driven out of business;
- Their purchases of large shares of stocks in GM, Ford, and Chrysler to prevent them from manufacturing fuel-efficient cars and trucks;
- Their bribes to Republican and Democratic politicians to prevent or eliminate funding for research and development of alternatives to fossil fuels; and
- Instead of wasting billions on TV commercials and bribes to Republican Super PACs, why don't major oil and gas companies diversify by investing in alternatives to fossil fuels?

- Most of their oil and gas was pumped out of federal lands and from offshore drilling and other land owned by all Americans:

  1. Yet none of them get or share a percentage of profits of oil and gas they own; and

  2. By bribes to politicians, they make sure that the U.S. will always be significantly dependent on Mideast oil and gas so that every few years, a Mideast civil or international war will inflate prices to four dollars per gallon and more;

  3. Even though five major U.S. oil and gas company CEOs said it only cost eighteen cents per gallon to pump, refine, and sell;

  4. Isn't that highway robbery without a Chinamen's chance that CEOs would be prosecuted for any of the above?

Solutions

Boycott U.S. Oil and Gas Companies, One at a Time

As indicated, the United Auto Workers Union didn't strike Ford, General Motors, and Chrysler all at the same time:

- Sometimes they struck the most financially sound and wealthy company so workers at the other two automakers continued contributing to the strike fund for the workers on strike;

- Other times they struck the weakest and poorest automaker that would crack or break faster to avoid more financial losses.

Which U.S. Oil and Gas Company Should Be Boycotted First?

The company with the highest profits and most to lose. Don't boycott the weakest first. It's likely that President Obama or a Republican president would only allow it to be merged with another of the Big Five.

So tomorrow, everyone stop buying gas at Exxon-Mobil.

Boycott until they make a commercial saying, "We will reduce prices of gas to two dollars per gallon. Future gas prices will fall as fast as they rose for each Mideast crisis."

If the other four majors don't follow suit within a day, boycott Shell.

Oh! By the way, make sure you buy Exxon-Mobil stocks and bonds as their value drops:

1. Start buying when prices drop 25 percent;
2. Keep on buying more as it drops 5 percent to 10 percent at a time; and
3. Eventually Americans will own enough stock to force Exxon-Mobil to stop violating commandments such as:
    a. "You shall not join hands with a wicked man";
    b. "You shall not offer or give a bribe for a bribe blinds the officials and subverts the cause of those who are in the right";
    c. "You shall not steal";
    d. "You shall not kill" to make profits;
    e. "You shall not wrong a stranger";
    f. "You shall not afflict widows and orphans";
    g. "You shall not bear false witness" and "utter a false report;" and
    h. Commandments for restitution and retribution.

North, Central, and South American Oil-Producing Nations Should Withdraw from OPEC

- North, Central, and South American nations must withdraw from OPEC. Then:
  1. Oil taken from American land and seas should only be sold in the Americas; and
  2. All American nations should coordinate research, Development, and use of:
      a. Grains, sugarcane, and sugar beets to make fuels; and
      b. Passive and active solar technology;
      c. Electric, hydrogen, and helium vehicles;
      d. Hydroelectric irrigation dams and scoop dams;
- Let Japan:
  1. Purchase oil and gas from Malaysia and Mideast; and
  2. Let their carrier task forces and marines protect shipping lanes from the Mideast because:
      a. Japan attacked Pearl Harbor because the U.S. cut off oil because of Japan's brutal invasion of China; and
      b. After Japan's industries were rebuilt by the Marshall Plan:
          1) Japanese companies engaged in industrial espionage to

steal more U.S. technology;

2) The Japanese government unfairly and illegally subsidized the cost of manufacturing so products could be sold for less;

3) While the U.S. allowed importation of all Japanese products, Japan wouldn't allow the sale of U.S. cars and other products in Japan;

4) Production of dozens of U.S. electronic products, toys, nails, and ball bearings was outsourced to Japan; and

5) Japan never repaid its WWII or Marshall Plan debt;

- Let China:

1. Purchase oil and gas from Malaysia and Mideast; and

2. Let their carrier task forces work with Japan to keep oil tanker routes open from Mideast to China because:

   a. U.S. supplied to China during WWII:

      1) A squadron of Flying Tigers (P-40 fighter planes) with American pilots;

      2) Weapons, ammunition, medical supplies, and food over the Burmese Mountains to the Chinese Army to fight Japan; and

      3) Provided Merrill's Marauders (U.S. guerilla fighters) to attack Japanese forces; and

   b. After WWII, China:

      1) Became an enemy of the United States, democracy, and capitalism;

      2) Never repaid its WWII debt to the U.S; and

      3) After Republican President Nixon granted China top-level trade status, the Chinese government and "One Percent Devils and their Satanic Tools" found a way to:

         a) Weaken the U.S. industrial base and go to war economically to create an atheistic Communist New World Order where workers are little more than exploited slaves; and

         b) Weaken and destroy labor unions along with elimination of the minimum wage and federal regulation of business to turn American workers into little more than exploited slaves as they were during the robber-baron era;

- Let Europe:
  1. Purchase oil and gas from Mideast and Russia; and
  2. Let European carrier task forces and marines protect eastern Atlantic Ocean, Mediterranean Sea, and Red Sea shipping lanes; and
- U.S. can:
  1. Return all U.S. Army and Air Force from around the world to U.S. soil;
  2. Withdraw all carrier task forces and marines to the:
     a. Eastern half of the Pacific Ocean;
     b. Western half of Atlantic Ocean; and
     c. Leave a carrier task force and marines in the Mediterranean Sea to back up Israel since European nations that abused Jews for centuries and drove them back to Israel won't accept their moral responsibilities to Jews.

U.S. Constitution Preamble Goals of Forming a More Perfect Union by Promoting the General Welfare and Insuring Domestic Tranquility by Establishing Justice
vs.
Fraud By Bankers and Brokers = Bailed Out and Not Punished

After "One Percent Devils" of banks and brokerage houses and their Republican "Satanic Tools" (who didn't enforce Banking Commission and Security and Exchange Commission laws and regulation) perpetrated massive fraud and caused the second-greatest stock-market crash of 2008 and economic depression:

- Criminalized banks and brokerage houses that were too big to be allowed to fail and go through bankruptcy:
  1. Were financially bailed out with billions of U.S. tax dollars and saved from bankruptcy;
  2. Allowed to used bailout money to give the biggest thieving bankers, brokers, and CEOs million- and multimillion-dollar bonuses for their crimes; and

3. Allowed "to add insult to injury" or "to pour salt on wounds" by using bailout money to speculate on oil and gas futures, adding $1.50 to the price of every gallon of gas; and

4. None of those scam-artist thieves were criminally charged, and Republican lawmakers "kiss their rings" or asses; and

- Criminalized banks can borrow from the federal government at a prime rate of one-percent interest and turn around and:

   1. Charge 19 percent to 22 percent interest and late fees on credit cards of victims (of "One Percent Devils and Their Satanic Tools") who:

      a. Lost jobs, savings, investments, pensions, and homes due to:

         1) Banking and Wall Street fraud and 2008 Wall Street crash;

         2) Outsourcing of their jobs; or

         3) Layoffs to improve bottom line and make remaining workers do the work of two to five people; and/or

      b. Are descendants of racial minorities that have been economically, socially, and politically suppressed;

   2. Charge 26 percent interest on loans under five thousand dollars; and

   3. Those who used to live in three- and four-bedroom homes are required to make 60 percent down payments to get a mortgage to buy a condominium, Wausau home or trailer home.

Until the 1980s, such high rates of interest on loans and down payments were illegal under usury laws (aka anti-loan-sharking laws).

Help Victims of "One Percent Devils and Satanic Tools" by Applying Eternal Law to Bankers, Brokers, and Government

- "You (bankers and brokers) shall not covet your neighbor's ox, house, wife, servant, ass, or anything that's your neighbor's (stocks and bonds)";
- "You shall not steal";
- "You shall not pervert justice due to the poor";

- "You shall not wrong or oppress a stranger";
- "You shall not afflict widows and orphans";
- "Love thy neighbor as you love yourself";
- "I am my brother's keeper";
- "Help those in need";
- "Those who have more should give more to the poor";
- "Do unto others as you would have others do unto you"; and
- "If you lend money to any of my people who is poor, you shall not be to him as a creditor, and you shall not exact interest from him."

Since "Satanic Tools" in U.S. and state governments allowed "One Percent Devils" to rip off a vast majority of Americans by violating eternal law and positive law (regulations of bankers and brokers), they should share in the bailout of Americans put into financial distress. If those evil and criminal "One Percent Devils" can borrow from the federal government at a prime rate of 1 percent, their victims should be "entitled" to receive loans at one-percent interest for:

- Schools in neighborhoods of the poor, working poor, and middle class; and
- Student loans for training, bachelor, and post-graduate degrees (to enable victims to rise out of poverty and lives of crime);
- Homes and car loans for middle class, working poor, and poor can afford (which will require long-overdue increases in minimum wage, worker's compensation, unemployment compensation, welfare, and Social Security disability and retirement);
- Buying or starting small businesses;
- Investing in highly rated stocks and bonds or mutual funds; and
- Impoverished counties and cities, caused by outsourcing, to pay for infrastructure repairs.

As with all Keynesian borrowing and economic stimulus spending:
- The poor, working poor, and middle class would:
  1. Be hired or get better-paying jobs:
  2. Have taxable or more taxable income;
  3. Reduce budget deficits; and

4. Have more purchase power, which would result in:
    a. Hiring of more industrial and service workers with;
        1) Taxable income to reduce government deficits; and
        2) Spending power that results in hiring more service and industrial workers, as well as expansions of production and services industries; and
    •   "One Percent Devils" would be earning significantly more income.

What's Wrong with Facts above and below Those Commandments?
One political party repeatedly "utters false reports" about the cause and solutions for political and economic problems. Both parties "join hands with wicked men" who hedge their bets by bribing Republican and Democratic congressional representatives, senators, and candidates.

The U.S. bailed out mismanaged Penn Central Railroad and Chrysler in the 1980s, did it not? After Republican President Reagan failed to regulate, didn't he bail out Wall Street brokers and bankers after their junk-bond, paper-money scam on pension funds, IRAs, and mutual funds ripped off billions from honest, law-abiding, taxpaying Americans?

After Republican President G.W. Bush failed to regulate Wall Street brokers and bankers and caused the 2008 stock-market crash and second-greatest economic depression, didn't Democratic President Obama bail out General Motors, Chrysler, and Wall Street bankers and brokers?

What's missing in this sordid picture? Millions of Americans took a hit on Wall Street. Millions lost jobs, homes, savings, and families.

In other words:

•   "One Percent Devils" were rewarded for violating commandments;
•   Victims of corruption, malfeasance, and malpractice by "Their Satanic Tools" lost everything but got nothing except pain and suffering; and
•   How can a civilized society or nation:
    1. Sentence a man to prison for stealing a loaf of bread due to God-given natural law human instincts to survive and feed a family (ala *Les Miserables*)?
    2. But not even file charges against one "One-Percent Devil" who stole millions and billions via mortgage bundling/derivatives?

- Because "One Percent Devils" can:
  1. Bribe to get laws slanted in their favor; and
  2. Bribe their way out of any other problem.

Other Solutions:

- To deregulation — every time "Satanic Tools" (Republican-oriented politicians, preachers, and press) advocate deregulation of banks and brokerage houses, independent and Democratic politicians, preachers, press, teachers, and professors should repeat over and over and over again the history of stock-market crashes and economic disaster depressions caused by lack of regulation and deregulation;
- Enforce of the Sherman Antitrust Act and related legislation to break up:
  1. Banks and brokerage houses that are too big to be allowed to fail;
  2. The five major U.S. oil and gas companies to increase competition and reduce prices;
  3. Other companies with horizontal and vertical monopolies; and
  4. Since Republicans are regressive reactionaries who want to go back to the Good Old Days, the U.S. should return to:
     a. Banks being barred from being stockbrokers;
     b. Stockbrokers being barred from doing banking business; and
     c. Banks should be allowed to only do business in one state.
- Progressive income taxation (where those who benefit more from the U.S. economic system pay more taxes);
- Replace regressive sales taxation (where the poor, working poor, and middle class pay a much higher percentage of income on sales taxes than upper-middle class and upper class);
- Sales taxes on alcohol and tobacco are the most immoral form of regressive taxation when it comes to those who lost jobs, savings, pensions, and homes due to :
  1. Outsourcing of U.S. jobs; and
  2. Stock-market crash and depression; or
  3. Those who were raised into poverty;

    4. Because they tend to smoke and drink more to ease suffering; and

- Boycotts of companies until they reform:
  1. Fast-food restaurants that will not:
     a. Hire employees to work more than thirty hours per week:
        1) So they don't have to provide fringe benefits such as health insurance;
        2) So employees must file for Medicaid and make taxpayers pay for their medical treatment;
     b. Raise wages from minimum wage of $7.25 per hour to $15 per hour, which is what minimum wage would be now if Republicans in Congress had allowed minimum wage to rise with inflation during the past forty years;
  2. Boycott all production (domestic and foreign) of companies that outsource some of their production, jobs, and technology;
  3. Boycott Walmart, Target, Best Buy, and other chains that:
     a. Specialize in selling products where production was outsourced to China and Third World nations; and
     b. Won't raise minimum wage and provide fringe benefits;
  4. Boycott Chase Manhattan, Goldman Sachs, and other companies that caused the 2008 stock-market crash and depression;
- Economic disaster relief fund:

In California devastating earthquakes will cause billions of dollars in damage every decade or so. Based upon the U.S. since the Civil War, greedy robber barons and "One Percent Devils" have caused, on average every twenty years, stock-market crashes and economic depressions.

So when the federal government and state governments have budget Surpluses, instead of giving pitiful tax cuts for working poor and middle class, the federal government and states should put budget surpluses into an economic disaster relief fund, especially since state and federal governments cause and contribute to economic disasters.

Aren't tax cuts during an economic depression or recession "adding more fuel to the flames" of economic fires when government workers must be laid off, governments lose their taxable incomes, and the economy loses its purchase power? Why should a small percentage of good, hardworking government employees lose their jobs so that:

- "One Percent Devils" can receive huge tax refunds and buy foreign cars, yachts, vacations, homes, furs, diamonds, wine, and caviar?
- While everyone else's refund only allows families to buy two more pizzas a week? and
- Who lost their jobs because of tax cuts for "One Percent Devils"?
    1. Police officers: They are needed more during depression or recession when crimes of theft increase because laid-off workers must comply with natural law instincts to survive or feed family;
    2. Firefighters: When home and business owners can't sell homes or businesses during hard times, they torch properties for insurance;
    3. Teachers: U.S. students rank low in math, science, and reading comprehension. The U.S. is losing its educational-economic edge; and
    4. Nurses: ERs are filled with unemployed who lost health insurance, are drunks, or are coughers who smoked too much.

Didn't the most moral Supreme Court in U.S. history, the Warren Court, hold in a series of unanimous decisions that a citizen's rights to a job, education, voting, and social safety nets are not and should not be the subject to a majority vote?

What Does Natural Law Say Victims Can or Will Do?
Antiscience "One Percent Devils and Their Satanic Tools":

- May reject Darwin's "Evolution of the Species";
- But believe in Darwin's "Survival of the Fittest"; and
- Are fans of Ayn Rand's philosophy that "the strong should take from the weak."

Didn't President Jefferson say, "From time to time the price of liberty must be paid with the blood of tyrants and patriots?" Didn't Jefferson write the Declaration of Independence based upon natural law? What does God-given natural law based upon God-given instincts and inclinations indicate victims of "One Percent Devils'" theft should or will do?

- When a king or president fails to punish criminals and compensate victims, hasn't the king or president breached his duties?:
  1. Wouldn't victims of thefts have a right to private vengeance?
  2. Isn't there ample historic precedence for that?
     a. During lawless Wild West of the 1800s, victims extracted private vengeance and restitution for murder and theft;
     b. Cattlemen and horse ranchers hung cattle and horse thieves;
     c. Jesse and Frank James, the Cole Brothers, and the Younger Brothers robbed banks and trains of "One-Percent Devil" thieves who rigged the system to steal land; and
- Frankly given the history of slaughters in post offices and others in companies by disgruntled present or former employees, as well as teen murderers of bullies in schools, I'm surprised a military veteran victim of "One Percent Devils and Their Satanic Tools" hasn't executed (with an M-15 or AK-47, APG rocket, or hand grenades):
  1. CEO and board of directors of the bank or Wall Street broker firm that caused him to lose everything; and/or
  2. "Their Satanic Tools" (Republican politicians, preachers, and press).
- I'm also surprised that a veteran hasn't blown the brains out of my congressman, Paul Ryan, and Governor Scott Walker.

CHAPTER XI

Preamble and Enabling Clause Goals of Constitution: Common Defense vs. General Welfare

Again Republicans claim or "utter false reports" that they "strictly construe" the U.S. Constitution like fundamentalists believe the Bible: word-for-word. However, such Republican misinformation propaganda dogma, flies in the face of their words, acts, and omissions.

Doesn't it appear that Republicans haven't read the U.S. Constitution or are intellectually dishonest about its priorities? The goals of the Preamble are:

- To Establish Justice;
- To Insure Domestic Tranquility; *and*
- To Promote the General Welfare;
- In Order to Form a More Perfect Union; *and*
- To Provide for the Common Defense;
- To secure the Blessings of Liberty to ourselves and our Posterity..."

Then the Enabling Clause (Article I, Sec. 8, [1] to [18]) says, "The Congress shall have Power to lay and collect taxes... to pay the Debts and provide for the Common Defense and General Welfare" by:

- Borrowing money;
- Regulating commerce;
- Establishing uniform rules of naturalization...and bankruptcy;

- Coining and regulating money;
- Providing for punishment of counterfeiters of securities and coins;
- Establishing post offices and postal roads;
- Promoting progress of science and useful arts (which include fine arts, liberal arts, and language arts);
- Defining and punishing piracies and felony offenses of the laws of the nation;
- Establishing courts inferior to Supreme Courts; *and*
- Raising and supporting an army but not to appropriate money for the army for more than two years;
- Providing and maintaining a navy (for protection against pirates);
- Providing for, organizing, arming, and disciplining the militia; *and*
- To make all laws necessary for execution of the forgoing powers.

Yet words, acts, and omissions by Republicans imply or infer that every power other than the creation and support of the military is unconstitutional even though five of the six goals of the Preamble and ten of the thirteen powers authorized to Congress address General Welfare, Justice, Domestic Tranquility, and Blessings of Liberty.

Republican lies also imply the following are unconstitutional:

- Regulations of commerce, industry, and finance;
- Social safety nets for victims of "One Percent Devils and Their Satanic Tools";
- Medical, environmental, and alternatives to fossil-fuel research;
- Federal assistance and national standards for preschools, grade schools, and high schools, and college grants and loans; and
- Infrastructure repairs of postal roads, railroads and airports (but only when a Democrat is in the White House); and
- List of what *Republicans are against and for* (found on the third page of the introduction).

In fact Founding Fathers clearly only intended that:

- The navy be permanent and protect shipping from piracy; and
- The army only be called up for two-year durations during war;

- Supported by militia in each state.

That immoral and unconstitutional goal of Republicans to only spend federal money on the U.S. Military-Industrial Complex (so it can fight wars for "One Percent Devils") is exactly what President Eisenhower warned Americans about in his final 1961 White House address:

"...the conjuncture of an immense military establishment and a large arms industry is new to the American experience. The total influence, economic, political, and even spiritual, is felt in every city, statehouse, and office of the federal government.

"We recognize the imperative need for this development. Yet, we must not fail to comprehend its grave implication. Our toil, resources, and livelihoods are involved and at stake. So is the very structure of our society.

"In the councils of government, we must guard against the acquisition of unwarranted influence, whether sought or unsought, by the Military-Industrial Complex. The potential for the disastrous rise of misplaced power exists and will persist.

"Therefore, we must never let the weight of this complex endanger our liberties or democratic process. We should take nothing for granted.

"Only a knowledgeable and alert citizenry can compel the proper meshing of a huge Military-Industrial complex with our peaceful message and goals so our security and liberty may prosper together."

Isn't President Eisenhower's warning becoming facts of life in the United States? Don't "One Percent Devils" of the U.S. Military-Industrial Complex (which includes the five major U.S. oil and gas companies) "and Their Satanic Tools" present a clear and present danger to Democracy when they disenfranchise those who tend to vote Democrat via:

- Unconstitutional gerrymandering;
- Voter ID laws; and
- Laws restricting early voting.

Isn't "the total influence, economic, political, and even spiritual," of the U.S. Military-Industrial Complex, "felt in every city, statehouse, and office of the federal government" when "One Percent Devils" succeed with bribes to eliminate federal funds for:

- State, county and municipal governments so those entities either have to raise taxes or lay off government employees, such as law enforcement officers, firefighters, teachers, nurses, and social workers;
- Infrastructure repair;
- Education;
- Medicare, Medicaid, and Affordable Health Care Insurance;
- Social Security and welfare;
- School lunches and food stamps;
- Federal housing;
- Medical and alternative to fossil-fuels research; and
- Law enforcement, firefighters, teachers, nurses, and social workers.

Doesn't the U.S. Military-Industrial Complex spend:

- Half of the U.S. budget;
- More on defense than all other nations combined;
- More on defense than for the general welfare of Americans; and
- Hasn't the U.S been in more wars since WWII than any other nation?

Is not "our toil, resources, and livelihoods...and very structure of our society involved and at stake..." along with "our peaceful message and goals" when:

- Federal funding is eliminated for states, counties, and municipalities;
- U.S. jobs, production, and technology are outsourced to:
    1. An atheistic Communist Chinese enemy; and
    2. Third World nations so their labor and resources can be exploited in ways that are illegal in the United States in order to destroy:
        a. Labor unions; and
        b. The middle class; and
- When people in those nations complain and the U.S. Military-Industrial Complex protects the interests of "One Percent Devils" and bribe "their Satanic Tools" to reduce funds for a Veterans Administration that treats war casualties; and
- Means to ends of "One Percent Devils and Their Satanic Tools" are:

1. Orwellian *1984* repetitive lies so that voters believe truth is a lie and lies are true; and
2. Hitler-Nixon-type, Machiavellian, Divide-and-Conquer, Wedge-Issue Tactics to:
    a. Stimulate racial, religious, cultural, and gender bias of the uneducated, who have a need to denigrate and put others down to elevate their pathetically low self-concepts; and that
    b. Stimulate them to vote Republican and against economic and social interests of themselves, family, and friends.

Are not the goals and means of "One Percent Devils and Their Satanic Tools" inconsistent with the following on pages thirteen and fourteen of the introduction:

- Thirteen Commandments;
- Golden Rule and seven soul-saving rules; and
- Principles of legal equity:
    1. "One should not benefit from one's wrongs"; and
    2. "One should not benefit at someone else's expense"?

Republican Goals = Inconsistent with Military Needs

"One Percent Devils and Their Satanic Tools" seem to thrive upon paradoxical and oxymoronic contradictions. They need intelligent and strong soldiers but oppose federal funds for prenatal and post natal care; clean water, air, land, and food for children; nutrition for children via food stamps and school breakfast, lunch, and dinner; preschool, grade school, and high school grants and college grants and student loans.

Nixon Republican "Satanic Tools" eliminated the military draft and created a volunteer military system to:

- Prevent future antiwar protests against "One Percent Devils" and their U.S. Military-Industrial Complex wars; and
- Eliminate drafting of college-educated officers who questioned orders and believed U.S. involvement in Vietnam's civil war was wrong and immoral.

So instead of millions of American sons, brothers, and friends sharing responsibility for fighting U.S. wars during one-year combat tours of duty, a few hundred thousand soldiers fought two, three, and four tours of duty in Afghanistan and Iraq. As a result, thousands of soldiers committed suicide in the Mideast or after they were discharged and home in America, in part because "One Percent Devils and Their Satanic Tools" were so grateful for their service that they cut funding for VA hospitals and resisted expansion of treatment to include post-traumatic stress disorder (PTSD), formerly called shell shock and combat fatigue.

Due to those psychological injuries during the Vietnam War, political pressure forced the military to develop treatment programs. When I was studying psychology at the University of Wisconsin, the National Guard medical corps in Madison offered to send me to the Valley Forge Medical Center for neuropsychological training. Chapter XIII will discuss why I turned down that offer and subjected myself to the risk of being drafted to fight in Vietnam.

It's been forty-eight years since my brother Warren's one-year tour of duty in Vietnam (1968-1969), where he rose from PFC to staff sergeant with a Silver Star, Bronze Star, and Purple Heart. Yet he still has severe war nightmares that awaken him in a sweat.

When Warren returned home, he was very thin and said, "I haven't had a solid shit in a year." Before he was drafted, he had a perpetual smile and clever sense of humor. When he returned in August, his face was totally devoid of emotion. He looked like the classic, square-jawed, stone-faced, and steely eyed sergeant of the movies. The best examples of his emotionless face are Peter O'Toole in *Night of the Generals* and in *Lawrence of Arabia* after a disgustingly bloody battle.

For his first week back, Dan De Wolfe and I threw a party every night. However, even bunnies from the Lake Geneva Playboy Club (where I had worked as a trap and skeet shoot instructor in the summer of 1968) couldn't crack his face and make him smile.

That fall Warren went back to UW Eau Claire to finish getting a degree in business administration. However, every other week he drove three or four friends down to Madison for legendary parties Bill Woodard, Jim Quintenz, and I had at #1 Iota Court. In 1969 Playboy Magazine said the University of Wisconsin was the Party School of the Year. We contributed with Wapatooli Parties.

We all worked in sororities for three square meals a day. Our parties had sisters from two sororities. It took three months of parties and Jody (aka Ding-a-ling from the song, "You're My Ding-a-Ling," the funniest girl I have ever known) to bring a smile back to Warren's face.

If one year of combat can do so much emotional damage, think about the psychological damage to soldiers of a volunteer military who fought two, three, and four tours of duty in Afghanistan and Iraq. Ten years of wars in the Mideast have damaged tens of thousands of America's best, discouraged many who'd be good soldiers from enlisting, and weakened the U.S.

That's contrary to a goal in the Preamble of the U.S. Constitution "To Provide for a Common Defense to Preserve our Liberties." A volunteer military is contrary to that goal because now more than then, the U.S. military needs soldiers who are competent in math, science, and computers.

During the Vietnam War, 70 percent of boys at Delavan Darien High School and the rest of Walworth County, Wisconsin, went to a college or university. One-third to half did so to get a college deferment from the military draft in hopes the Vietnam War would end before they graduated. When it didn't, those who could went on to a postgraduate school (law, medicine, MBA, etc.).

Yet many, like first cousin Marvin Olson after he got an MA at the University of Wisconsin, were drafted and shipped off as lieutenants to Vietnam. The average life span of a combat lieutenant was thirty days. If they survived ninety days (aka the basis for Ninety-Day-Wonder Lieutenants), they had a good chance to survive their tours. Fortunately Marvin survived.

The point is that the Baby Boomer Generation was the last generation where boys excelled past girls in high school math, science, and other courses and not only outnumbered but outperformed girls in college and postgraduate schools. Among industrialized nations, U.S. Baby Boomers ranked on top in terms of math, science, and reading comprehension.

Now U.S. high school students rank seventeenth in math, twenty-first in science, and twenty-fifth in reading comprehension. Teacher associations can try to learn teaching methods from Chinese, Japanese, and German teachers. However, that is a waste of effort. We have to get back to fundamental basic causes:

- Without a military draft, high school boys don't have to study hard to get into college and graduate schools to avoid fighting in wars;

- Fifty percent of marriages end in divorce and mothers get custody of sons. That prevents them from excelling in math and science; and
- DWI laws cripple boys and make them dependent upon girlfriends.

The Baby Boomer Generation was the last generation where the vast majority of children lived in traditional families where mom stayed home to socialize kids and make them do homework after school. The next generation was the Feel Good Generation: "If it feels good, do it, but if doesn't, don't" — a philosophy that was applied to marriages. Many Baby Boomers bought into the new marital contract espoused by the feminist movement, which claimed, "Women can become happy whole persons":

- If they have a career, husband, and children;
- Husbands were no longer head of household but shared decision-making, household, and childcare responsibilities;
- It would be in the "best interests of children" to have an equal relationship with both parents; and
- Husband's quid pro quo or tit for tat, so to speak, would be love, respect, and all the sex they wanted or needed.

However, St. Augustine's "Rules against Sex" made that last promise impossible in 60 percent of marriages. Women and men in the same workplace led to illicit affairs. While men were punished for sexual innuendo, puns, and suggestiveness at work, women used their feminine wiles and sex to move up corporate or government ladders.

Baby Boomer Generation wives had often used withholding of sex to force husbands to be civil at home or to achieve goals. However, once Baby Boomer career women attained financial independence, there was no longer joint decision-making. Many used threat of divorce, losing children, and having to pay one-third of their income for child support to get husbands to do what they wanted or to let wives do what they wanted.

Divorce judges aided and abetted by outmoded paternal beliefs that:

- Husbands are the cause of divorce when wives are often the cause;
- Wives need protection from husbands when it is often husbands who need protection from wives;

- Wives are better parents than husbands, but many husbands who shared the household and childcare are better parents;

So misguided judges automatically awarded custody of children to mothers. In doing so, divorce judges ignored:

- Equal gender rights of husband/fathers; and
- Principles of legal equity:
    1. "One should not benefit from one's wrongs";
    2. "One should not gain at someone else's expense"; and
- What was in the "best interests of children," especially sons. As a result:
- Moms made daughters crack the books so they wouldn't have to be financially dependent upon a husband;
- Mothers didn't know how to discipline sons and raise them to be motivated, hardworking, and law-abiding citizens; and
- Most important, sons lost the kinds of daily activities with fathers that enabled them to excel in math and science in high school. Activities that involved application of rudimentary math and science, such as:
    1. Sports;
    2. House renovations and building tree forts, dog houses, and furniture; and
    3. Repairing cars, lawn mowers, plumbing, and electrical appliances.

At this point, I will say this much more.

Common Defense of the United States of America is dependent upon girls and boy being competent in math and science:

- When economically competing against China, Japan, and Germany;
- When U.S soldiers use scientifically sophisticated computers and weapons systems; and
- U.S. schools should not have to import Asians who can barely speak English to teach math and science in grade and high schools.

"Why We Fight" Wars?

My father's December 24, 1945, letter to his parents asked and said,

- "Who is to blame for WWII?
- "Who put Hitler in power?
- "Who financed him?

"English, French, and U.S. industrialist and financiers. They wanted Nazis and Russian Communists, obvious threats to capitalism, to destroy each other, but Hitler fooled them all and attacked in all directions.

"Now in your criticism of any country, do not blame the people, do not blame the English or German masses. *What is the root of the evil?*

"It is not the individual but industrialists throughout the world, in all countries. A handful of people who go abroad to invest, looking for cheap labor and mineral resources, to the detriment of their own and our country.

"Then when their toes are stepped on, they influence their own government to come to their aid to protect their selfish interests. Naturally they do and can because aren't they the ruling class?"

During WWII, Supreme Allied Commander and Five-Star General Eisenhower made it clear to his best tank commander, General Patton, that,

"America didn't send a million of its finest to create an Anglo-Saxon New World Order but to prevent a Nazi New World Order."

However, aren't the goals and means to achieve the goals of "One Percent Devils and Their Satanic Tools" aimed at eliminating democracy, moral capitalism, and the middle class (by eliminating labor unions and public employee unions so no one will be able to afford to give campaign contributions for Democrats and independents), allowing "One Percent Devils" to control federal and state governments via secret "Citizens United" campaign contribution bribes?

Part of the problem is that no congressional representative or senator wants cutbacks on U.S. Military-Industrial Complex. Anglo-Saxon New World Order "One Percent Devils" have cleverly made sure that parts of the Military-Industrial Complex are in every congressional district. No representative or senator wants to cut U.S. MIC components in districts and states of other senators and representatives because they would retaliate by voting for cuts in their state or district.

God's Plan for Mankind Is a Utopia Free of War and Crime where Everyone's Basic Necessities Are Met and Everyone Has Opportunities for Educations, Careers, and God's Gifts

Eternal law (Commandments, Golden Rule and soul-saving rules) and positive law (U.S. Constitution) were not intended only to benefit:

- "One Percent Devils and Their Satanic Tools;"
- At the expense of direct and indirect taxation of the poor, working Poor, and middle class, which is inconsistent with goals of the Preamble of the U.S. Constitution:

Isn't the U.S. Constitution Preamble goal of "Forming a More Perfect Union" the opposite from what Anglo-Saxon New World Order "One Percent Devils and Their Satanic Tools" want and are trying to create?

Shouldn't voters, senators, congressional representatives, and president/commander in chief determine whether going to war passes the three tests of morality set forth in "Theory of Law" by St. Thomas Aquinas:

- Would going to war satisfy a proper balance between natural law, eternal law and positive law;
- Would going to war violate principles of legal equity?
  1. "One should not benefit from one's wrongs"; and
  2. "One should not benefit as someone else's expense"; and
  3. "All transactions should result in a zero-sum outcome"; and
- Shouldn't wars be fought by the senators, congressional representatives, and president who failed to negotiate peace?

CHAPTER XII

Anglo-Saxon New World Order's Antidemocracy and Moral Capitalism Plan of Tyranny Pre-Anglo-Saxon New World Order History

Since 1968 Nixon Republicans have "bore false witness" and "uttered false reports" that:

- They're Christians, but daily they've violated fifteen Commandments, the Golden Rule, and nine soul-saving rules of Christ;
- They represent "The Silent Moral Majority" but actually represent "One Percent Devils and the Silent Immoral Majority" (low-class white trash with racial, religious, cultural, and gender bias/prejudice/intolerance);
- They represent family values, but their acts and omissions have:
  1. Barred increase of minimum wage and equal pay for women;
  2. Outsourced tens of millions of middle-class-family jobs;
  3. Ended collective bargaining and most union jobs;
  4. Caused a 50 percent divorce rate and either forced both parents to work or single parents to have more than one job;
  5. Cut social safety nets and education funding for their victims; and
  6. Left infrastructure in a dangerous condition for families;
- They are the Law and Order Party that strictly enforces the U.S. Constitution while they violate all six goals of the Preamble of the U.S. Constitution, dozens of its provisions, and all ten of our rights under the Bill of Rights;

- They're patriots, but Republicans have developed a half dozen domestic spy agencies and equipped law enforcement and National Guard with combat weapons to suppress the majority when they have had enough and rebel.

"One Percent Devils" are successfully creating an Anglo-Saxon New World Order to enslave the other 99 percent of Americans and Europeans.

"Their Satanic Tools" (Republican politicians, preachers, and press) are aiding and abetting via sophisticated propaganda tactics that include:

- Repetitive lies so voters believe lies are true and truth is a lie; and
- Hitler-Nixon-type, Machiavellian, Divide-and-Conquer, Wedge-Issue Tactics that stimulate racial, religion, cultural, and gender bias, prejudice, and intolerance so anti-Judeo-Christian, unpatriotic and otherwise immoral Americans vote Republican and against economic and social interests of themselves, family, friends, and neighbors.

"One Percent Devils and Their Satanic Tools" are succeeding in destroying democracy and moral capitalism because Democratic and independent politicians, preachers, and press don't know how to counter repetitive lies and Wedge-Issue Tactics because they don't know enough about history, economics, political science, psychology, sociology, and who they have traditionally represented.

Foundation for an Anglo-Saxon New World Order began with a U.S. Constitution endorsement of slavery. Slave owners had support for a right to own slaves in Exodus, which sets forth commandments about the rights and duties of slaves and slave masters.

If a master seduced a virgin slave, he was obligated to marry her. If a master disabled a slave, he was to be set free. Yet such commandments were ignored, as shown in the book and movie *Roots* by Alex Haley.

Female slaves were sexual concubines or courtesans of the master. Perhaps Southern wives didn't care because St. Augustine's "Rules against Sex" had turned them off to making love for fun.

None of my thirteen Puritan ancestral families who arrived in the American colonies before the Revolution owned slaves. Their descendants and the Waltz/Woods's families fought to free slaves and give them equal rights.

Euro-Caucasians were also sold into servitude, including my first colonial Woods ancestor, Jacob Waltz ,who changed his name to Woods. Baron Jacob Waltz of Germany and Switzerland (the original homeland of the first Indo-European Aryans who migrated from India and became Celts) didn't want his eldest son and grandsons to die in wars for Frederick the Great.

So in 1751, Baron Waltz put Jacob Waltz Jr., his wife, and three sons, Jacob, Daniel, and Nathan, on the Phoenix in Holland. They sailed to Philadelphia, where Jacob Jr. sold his three sons into servitude to pay for medical treatment and burial at sea of his wife.

In 1771 Daniel met his brother Jacob near Pittsburgh. For some reason, Jacob had changed his name to Woods. Baptismal records show that he and Katarina Frieth bore my great-grandfather, Jacob Woods, out of wedlock on March 28, 1805. Four of his sons (three of my great uncles and grandfather, Lebbeus Woods) and great-grandfather, Captain Dewitt Clinton Smith, fought to preserve the union and free slaves in the Civil War. They all survived. Dozens of cousins also fought, but a half dozen died.

Doctrine of Manifest Destiny
The doctrine of Manifest Destiny is inconsistent with and violates other Commandments, Golden Rule, soul-saving rules of Christ, U.S. Constitution, and principles of legal equity. It's a doctrine based upon unfettered natural law human instincts and inclinations:

- Social Darwinism "Survival of the Fittest"; and
- Ayn Rand dung that "strong should take from the weak."

The doctrine said, "God wanted Euro-Christians to:

- Turn savage, heathen, godless Africans into slaves and ironically convert them to the Christianity that enslaved them; and
- Take all American lands away from savage, heathen, godless American Indians even though most Indians east of the Mississippi River were descendants of Europeans who began migrating across the Atlantic Ocean glacier to the Americas thirteen thousand years ago and were far more spiritual and complied with eternal law.

After Euro-Caucasians began arriving in the Americas in the 1600s, millions of Indians died because they had no immunity to European diseases. Millions more were killed in wars because Englishmen stopped buying land from Indians and began stealing it. Hitler admired how Euro-Caucasians conquered Indians and the Americas.

After the American Revolution, English Americans violated the freedom of religion of African slaves and American Indians when they were converted to Christianity. Yet there's no biblical support for the doctrine of Manifest Destiny and no mention of Indians or Americas in the Bible.

As a result of the doctrine of Manifest Destiny, my house sits on Potawatomi Indian Land. In 1830 ten thousand Potawatomi lived in one hundred villages in the five states that are adjacent to Lake Michigan (Michigan, Ohio, Indiana, Illinois, and Wisconsin). They didn't overpopulate until there were Indian wars to survive or exhaust natural resources. They were caretakers of the land and food sources God provided.

Potawatomi and Cherokee Indians honored and complied with eternal laws that mirror Commandments, Golden Rule, and soul-saving rules of Christ. They didn't go to war against Euro-Caucasians but helped and warned them when warring Indian nations were going to attack. They were more civilized than Caucasians.

Fontana, Wisconsin, is on the western bay of Lake Geneva. Potawatomi called it Shawneeawkee (Friendly Fontana). They lived in what St. Thomas Aquinas would call a utopia or heaven on earth: rich land to grow vegetables, corn, and tobacco, with plentiful bison, deer, turkey, fish, fruits, nuts, and maple syrup.

Shawneeawkee: Friendly Fontana (by Arthur B. Jensens, Advanced Printing, Delavan, Wisconsin) says in the 1830s, Chief Big Foot's villages of Potawatomi were very spiritual. On the Big Foot Country Club in Fontana are seven pools. Potawatomi deemed those pools "the abode of spiritual beings with power for good and evil. No hunting expedition was begun without their asking for their favor…The Potawatomi were called 'Keepers of the Sacred Fire People.' Their brother and sister tribes were called Ojibwe (Chippewa), 'Keepers of the Faith,' and Odawa (Ottawa) were called 'The Trader People.'

"The chiefs were brothers, and those tribes were part of the Neshname Nation, aka 'Original People.' In 1641, to avoid war with other

Indian nations…according to legend, the three tribes migrated from Canada into Michigan's Upper Peninsula and settled in five states surrounding Lake Michigan."

Jensens says, "One can get an idealistic insight into how they lived by reading Longfellow's, *Hiawatha*, a fictionalized story of a Chippewa Indian living in northern Wisconsin:

'Then the little Hiawatha
Learned of every bird its language
Learned their names and all their secrets,
How they built their nests in summer,
How they hid themselves in winter,
Talked with them whenever he met them,
Called them Hiawatha's chickens,
Of all beasts he learned the language,
Learned their names and all their secrets,
How the beavers built their lodges,
Where the squirrels hid their acorns,
How the reindeer ran so swiftly,
Why the rabbit was so timid,
Talked with them whenever he met them,
Called them Hiawatha's brothers.'"

As to their spirituality, Potawatomi females may have procreated with descendants of angels from heaven or with descendants of Oneida Nation females who procreated with angels from heaven. Oneida Nation arrived in Lake Geneva and Delavan Lake eight thousand years ago.

The Bible talks about Nephilim, a race of giants who were offspring of humans and angels. *Walworth County Sunday* newspaper said May 18, 2014, "Nephilim have been noted by writers like Jewish historian Flavius Josephus as far back as two thousand years. And very large skulls and skeletal remains have been found in archeological digs in England, Peru and the United States… including, as it turns out, Delavan…Ohio and Nevada.

"Native Americans have stories about Nephilim. Paiute Indian elders (Oregon and Washington State) talk about red-haired giants in the land.

Navaho and Cherokee also have stories of a race of giants."

Perhaps Sasquatch (aka Bigfoot) is a Nephilim. In any event, eight thousand years ago, when mastodon (elephants) lived in the area, Oneida Indians (from Asia) arrived. However, lithographs of Potawatomi Indian chiefs in "Shawneeawkee" reveal that they dressed and looked more like Europeans. Oneida men didn't have facial hair but had Asian features. Potawatomi had mustaches, goatees, and European facial features.

Four miles northwest of Lake Geneva is Delavan Lake. On its north shore was an Oneida village and then a Potawatomi village. In the late 1800s, the land was the winter headquarters of the Barnum & Bailey Circus. Now the land is part of a giant resort: Lake Lawn Lodge. It has an airport and golf course.

The *Walworth County Sunday* said in 1911, two Philips brothers uncovered a water and airtight cobblestone pit grave. Inside they found fourteen skeletons that were seven to nine feet tall and had very large skulls.

I'm trying to make a point that Potawatomi and Cherokee Indian nations may be descendants of Nephilim (who were descendents of angels that procreated with humans). That's why I suggest they were far more spiritual and moral than Indian hater and slaughterer President Andrew Jackson and the U.S. troops he ordered to drive Cherokee Indians from their paradise in the Carolinas to treeless and baron Oklahoma.

That trip was called "The Trail of Tears" because Cherokee mourned the loss of their paradise and so many Cherokee died on the way. Potawatomi also walked a "Trail of Tears" but to Council Bluffs, Iowa. U.S. troops were not much better than Japanese troops during the Bataan Death March of American and Philippine soldiers.

Nevertheless, the doctrine of Manifest Destiny is the second element of the Anglo-Saxon New World Order plan. As to the third element, in Article I, Sec. 9, Cl. 8 of the U.S. Constitution, the Founding Fathers said,

"No Title of Nobility shall be granted by the United States; and no person holding any Office of Profit or Trust under them, shall, without the Consent of Congress, accept of any present, Emolument, Office, or Title, of any kind whatever, from any King, Prince, or foreign State."

Based upon Judeo-Christian Commandments, Golden Rule, and soul-saving rules (pages eleven and twelve), the Founding Fathers established a constitutional, Majority-rule democracy "of, by and for the people" with a Bill of Rights to protect the rights of individuals, minority groups, and minority parties.

Founding Fathers didn't intend for King George to be replaced by kings of industry, services, and finance. They expected politicians, press, and preachers would honor and apply constitutional law, eternal law, and positive law to counter natural law human instincts and inclinations of the rich and strong to take from the poor and weak.

However, the Civil War industrial revolution created kings of industry and finance with unquenchable thirsts to become the wealthiest in the world. They didn't care how many workers, consumers, and communities got sick, died, or were crippled so they could achieve their goals.

In the late 1800s and early 1900s, robber-baron kings of industry and finance (Vanderbilt of railroads, Carnegie of steel, Rockefeller of oil and gas, and J.P. Morgan of banking and Wall Street) purchased rights, laws, and police protection against labor unions by bribing presidents, Congress, governors, state legislatures, and mayors.

Republican President Teddy Roosevelt and Congress had lived through three Wall Street stock market and banking collapses that caused economic depressions and enabled robber-baron kings to steal more by purchasing land and businesses for ten cents on the dollar while everyone else in the nation became poorer and poorer.

President Roosevelt used the Sherman Antitrust act to break up horizontal and vertical monopolies of robber-baron kings because they were too powerful, owned too much, and engaged in immoral capitalism. Their monopolies were too big to allow to fail. Their failure could cripple the nation for decades or forever.

However, the second-great industrial revolution of World War II created many more kings of industry and crime. Their children were:

- Educated at the most elite universities: Harvard, MIT, Yale, Princeton, Penn, Michigan, Chicago, Wisconsin, Stanford, Cal Tech; and Smith, Wellesley, and Bryn Mar colleges;
- Members of secret, racist, and religiously bigoted fraternities and sororities; and

Members of even more secret Anglo-Saxon New World Order (AS-NWO) societies, such as Skull and Bones, Illuminati, and Freemasons. Many were members of two or more of the secret societies.

Joseph Kennedy Sr. became wealthy by smuggling Irish whiskey during Prohibition into Canada and across the Great Lakes to cities in the Northeast and Midwest. He trained Joe Kennedy Jr. to be president of the United States and emperor of an Anglo-Saxon New World Order.

Wild Bill Donavan recruited Joe Jr. to be an OSS (Office of Strategic Services) spy. Other sons and daughters of rich and famous members of Skull and Bones, Illuminati, and Freemasons joined OSS and OWI (Office of War Information) because the secret to control of government is control of intelligence and propaganda.

No matter which party controls the White House, Congress, and Supreme Court, there's members of secret AS-NWO societies in office or on staff. Republican members infiltrate offices of Democrats and vice versa.

My mail was illegally opened and laptop computer hacked because my letters to President Obama advised him about how to turn repetitive lying and Machiavellian, Divide-and-Conquer Tactics of Republicans against them by showing how they violate Commandments, Golden Rules, U.S. Constitution, and Bill of Rights.

During WWII General George C. Patton said to the English press that England and the United States would rebuild and rule the world. Supreme Allied Commanding General Eisenhower said to General Patton, "America didn't send a million of its finest to create an Anglo-Saxon New World Order but to prevent a Nazi New World Order."

Sources of Info on Anglo-Saxon New World Order Plan
Sources of information include:

- George Orwell's books *1984* and *Animal Farm*;
- My grandfather, Lebbeus Bigelow Woods, Lutheran minister and attorney-at-law with a PhD in legal philosophy from the University of Chicago and 32nd Degree Freemason;
- My father, Wendell Woods, attorney-at-law and former OWI agent;
- OWI/OSS agents who joined the CIA and FBI and met at our farm;
- President Eisenhower during meetings with Gramps and Dad; and
- Cousins recruited with me by Grandfather Woods to infiltrate secret societies and offices of the federal government.

Means to Achieve Anglo-Saxon New World Order Goals and Plan to End Democracy and Moral Capitalism

Instead of "One Percent Devils" bribing to get what they want, they will use "Citizens United" Super PAC billions to con voters using:

- Repetitive lies so voters believe truth is a lie and lies are truth; and
- Hitler-Nixon-style, Machiavellian, Divide-and-Conquer, Wedge Issues to stimulate racial, religious, cultural, and gender bias so enough vote Republican and against their own economic and social interests;
- Republicans and those who vote for them will then vote to repeal:
    1. Bill of Rights for criminals, not realizing they are voting away their own rights because the Anglo-Saxon New World Order will use criminal and civil justice systems to control, repress, and oppress dissent;
    2. All business laws, regulation, and social safety nets; and
    3. Amend Constitution so that only male, Caucasian property owners and business owners can vote.

You Don't Think that Is Probable or Even Possible?

It could have happened when Republican Richard Nixon was president. He and Vice President Agnew's propaganda:

- "bore false witness" and "uttered false reports" that:
    1. Civil rights, antiwar, feminist, and environmental activists and protestors were leftist, liberal, communist traitors;
    2. Civil rights activists for Afro- and Latin-American rights wanted something (social safety nets) for doing nothing;
    3. Women with careers or jobs who didn't stay home to care for children were destroying American families and society even though they had no choice but to work because:
        a. Some were unwed, uneducated mothers; and
        b. Others were married but the husband died, was killed, or disabled;
    4. Women, Afro, and Latin Americans would take jobs, promotions and bonuses away from male Caucasians

5. Press were leftist, liberal, communist, elitist (Jewish) traitors;

6. Warren Supreme Court justices were leftist, liberal, communist traitors because they ruled in favor of:

    a. Equal racial, religious, cultural, and gender rights; and

    b. Honoring criminal defendants rights they were entitled to under the Bill of Rights; and

- Nixon, Agnew, and other Republicans were so good at antidemocracy tactics that NBC did a *White Paper* report based upon a survey of Americans. NBC paraphrased the Bill of Rights into questions that were something like the following:

    1. Do you believe that civil rights, antiwar, and feminist activists should have a right to protest against government actions?

    2. Do you believe someone who has been arrested for a crime should have a defense attorney, paid by the government, if they are poor?

    3. Should the Lord's Prayer be said in schools?

    4. Should law enforcement use any means to get confessions?

    5. Should police be required to get warrants before searching a suspected criminal's home, car, business, or office?

    6. Should criminal defendants have a right not to testify?

    7. Should government be able to open mail and tap telephones of civil rights, antiwar, and feminine activists and protestors.

Surprisingly and shockingly, NBC *White Paper* reporters found that a vast majority of Americans would be willing to vote to repeal eight of the ten rights in the Bill of Rights. A majority only voted in favor of freedom of religion and right to bear arms. How can that be?

I answered that in a paper in 1972: "Civil Disobedience in a Liberal Society" for "Theory of Justice." In that paper I quoted two legal theorists:

- Criminal Defense Attorney Edward Benet Williams said in a speech, "Traditionally the Bill of Rights has been a repository of minority rights. That is why it was written. It is a safeguard against majoritarian oppression. In all periods of history the majority never used it...except for going to church and bearing arms; and

- Dean Frances Allen of the University of Michigan Law School said,

"Virtually every discretionary power granted to the administration of justice has been employed to harass and suppress the activities of protest groups, regardless of their legal propriety. Powers of arrest, the granting or withholding of bail, revocation of licenses, and even the exercise of the jurisdiction of Juvenile Courts, have been diverted from their own proper and important purpose and converted into instruments of suppression."

If Americans could be induced to vote against the Bill of Rights in the 1960s, history can be repeated. Republican President Eisenhower said in 1961, "We must be knowledgeable and alert to dangers to democracy and our peaceful goals in life."

Composition and Scope of New World Order Government

Each industrial nation would be ruled by a board of directors of thirteen corporations with horizontal and vertical monopolies. The board would chose a CEO emperor. The thirteen corporations would include:

1. Agriculture;
2. Food processing and distribution;
3. Oil and gas, mining, timber, and other natural resources;
4. Steel and other metallurgical manufacturing;
5. Auto, truck, bus, boat, plane, and train manufacturing;
6. Manufacturing of other consumer products;
7. Distribution and retail of consumer products;
8. Finance (banks and Wall Street);
9. Education and training;
10. News and entertainment;
11. Law enforcement and military;
12. Science and research and development; and
13. Medical and psychiatric treatments and drugs to control the masses.

Class Structure of Industrial Nations

Seven classes of people would be ranked in a descending order:

1. Ruling class (CEOs and boards of directors of all thirteen corporations);
2. Professional class (doctors, attorneys, scientists, executives, etc.);
3. News, sports, and entertainment class;
4. Tradesmen and skilled workers class;
5. Law enforcement and military class;
6. Waste and trash collector class; and
7. Unlucky seventh class or 75 percent = mindless, robotic, peasant slaves.

Means to manipulate, manage, and control bottom six classes
- Drugs:
  1. To stimulate problem solving, creativity or performance of artists, professionals, athletes, musicians, actresses, singers; and
  2. To sedate and make 7th class susceptible to brainwashing;
- Television:
  1. To divert attention from problems and disappointments in life;
  2. To allow Big Brother to spy and catch people violating laws; and
  3. For brainwashing to divert anger away from ruling class via:
     a. Repetitive lies;
     b. Hitler-Nixon-style, Machiavellian, Divide-and-Conquer, Wedge-Issue Tactics aimed at stimulating racial, religious, cultural, and gender bias, prejudice, and hatred by blaming women, racial, and religious minorities for their sorry lots in life;
     c. Phony wars where military fire rockets and artillery shells into their own cities but blame China or Russia; and
  4. To provide a cathartic release of anger, and desire to kill ruling class, war, horror, and John Wayne Complex movies.

Procreation
1. Ruling class parents would arrange marriages between sons and daughters in order to increase income, wealth, and power. It would be punishable by death for anyone from the lower six classes to associate with or marry someone in the ruling class;

2. Other classes would only be allowed to mate and procreate with someone within their classes, but couples would be matched based upon potential to enhance mental and physical abilities identified by:
   a. Aptitude tests;
   b. Personality profiles; and
   c. DNA results; and
3. DNA splicing/combination/cloning would be used to make big, fast, strong, athletic, and intelligent athletes, soldiers, and police.

Education and Training
1. Sons and daughters of ruling class would be educated to rule;
2. Other children would be given aptitude, personality profile, and DNA tests to determine into which class they'd be educated or trained;
3. Lower 75 percent of test takers would not receive education or training.

Genocide
After an Anglo-Saxon New World Order takes over control of the U.S., it will order summary execution of politicians, preachers, press, neo-Nazis, and mafias because they cause crimes and wars, and that's bad for business.

How to Prevent Orwell's *1984* and *Animal Farm* in the U.S.
- Chapters II and IV explained how preachers and theology schools can prevent that by teaching:
  1. Commandments, Golden Rule, and soul-saving rules;
  2. U.S. Constitution and Bill of Rights; and
  3. Applying numbers 1 and 2 during sermons to words, acts, and omissions of business people, politicians, government workers, and professionals to show why they're acting immorally and unconstitutionally; and
  4. Theology schools can rate preachers on their sermons;
- Chapter IV explains what universities and theology schools can do;
- Chapter IX explains what press, university schools of journalism/ Media, and citizens (via editorial comments) can do.

What More Can Universities and Colleges Do?

- Major university political science and economic departments can:
    1. Rate national and state level politicians based upon factual accuracy, intellectual honesty, morality, racial, religious, cultural, and gender bias and prejudice;
    2. Report findings in university journals; and
    3. Send copies of reports to news media for mass dissemination to:
        a. Preachers, priests, rabbi, clerics, and monks; and
        b. Newscasters on television and radio and newspapers; and
- Smaller state universities and colleges can do the same for county and municipal government politicians.

Question?

Why do I put so much responsibility on university and college students? Ivy tower intellectuals haven't been ruined by "The Real World."

CHAPTER XIII

Kama Sutra Path to Mankind's Goal: Happiness

In "Theory of Law," St. Thomas Aquinas said God's plan for mankind is a utopia or heaven on earth without war, crime, racial, cultural, religious, or gender intolerance. To assist, God gave humans eternal law. Aquinas also said the goal of mankind is happiness.

While growing up, children seek activities that are fun, exciting, and produce enduring memories through sports, exploration, risk taking, and jokes. After they reach puberty, teenagers find the most stimulating, exciting, fun, and memorable activities revolve around sexual organs or making love. Making love takes their minds off problems, relieves stress or pain, and allows sleep. Ultimate happiness is from making love and procreating with a soul mate who has sexual chemistry and common interests.

Theological texts and legends of several religions say God, gods, or aliens (who were thought to be gods) created humans in their own image. The History Channel shows that ancient people believed gods or Angels procreated with humans around 3000 B.C., and that's the missing link of human evolution. So if creator gods were sexual, humans got that DNA?

Sex, especially Lovemaking, as well as social drugs, are natural law opiates of mankind based on God-given human instincts and inclinations to self medicate to relieve stress, pain, depression, and suffering. However, preachers, priests, clerics, and rabbi cause those emotions by preaching religious, gender, cultural, and racial bias, prejudice, and intolerance that leads to crimes and wars.

As to religious bias against females, one must ask: Don't men and women love their mothers, sisters, and daughters? Shouldn't all females have equal rights with males?

Don't those religions preach that if followers refuse to comply, God will punish them with natural disasters (earthquakes, volcanoes, droughts, famine, pestilence, lightning, and/or floods). They don't want people self-medicating but to suffer, go to religious services, pray for forgiveness of sins and relief, and put 10 percent of earnings or thefts in offering baskets to buy a religious opiate from God.

If everyone believed in gender equality and learned the science, techniques, and art of Kama Sutra, mankind could reach its goal of happiness, and God's plan for mankind could be achieved.

How Religions Have Prevented Happiness
According to Charles Darwin in "Evolution of the Species," humans evolved from apes. The book and movie *Inherit the Wind* is about a Tennessee high school teacher who was criminally charged with violating state law that banned teaching evolution.

His famous defense attorney, Clarence Darrow, an atheist, asked a question about the seven-day-creation myth in Genesis. The prosecutor, William Jennings Bryan (a presidential candidate and expert on the Bible), could not answer, "Which came first, the chicken or the egg?" An equally intriguing question would be "Which came first, man or woman?"

Every religion has an eternal law "Honor thy father and thy mother" and by extension their mother and father ad infinitum. Shouldn't we honor religious beliefs of our ancestors?

For thousands of years, pagan Celts in Europe, Vedas in India, inhabitants of China, Japan, Mideast, and North African Semites (including Hebrews) believed:

- In many gods;
- The creator god was female, and her husband had less power;
- Gods created an Adam and Eve, and since Eve created Adams and
- Eves, women were La Sacre Femme (the Sacred Feminine);
- Making love was a spiritual experience that brought couples closer to God, godliness, heaven, paradise, Shangri-La, or Valhalla; and

- Women and men had equal rights, which included:
  1. Rights to become educated priests and priestesses; high priests and priestesses; herbal healers and surgeons; warriors and warrior kings or queens; and mediators or judges;
  2. Rights to vote for leaders, social and economic issues, and for or against war; and
  3. Right to pick the most attractive, strong, and intelligent mate.

However, each major religion (Hindu, Sikh, Judaism, Buddhist, Christian, and Muslim) dethroned La Sacre Femmes, eliminated their rights, and turned them into marital procreation slaves to produce warrior sons and daughters to be sold to the oldest, ugliest, most disgusting, and brutish men.

The following is how Moses did it. In Genesis 1:26, there's a conversation between gods.

"Then God said, 'Let us make man in our image, after our likeness...' 27 So God created man in his own image, in image of God he created him; male and female..."

Genesis 2:7: "The Lord formed man of dust from the ground, and breathed into his nostrils the breath of life and man became a living being..."

Genesis 2:15-18: "The Lord God took the man and put him in the garden of Eden to till it and keep it. And the Lord God commanded the man saying, 'You may freely eat of every tree of the garden; but of the tree of knowledge of good and evil you shall not eat, for in the day that you eat of it you shall die.

"Then the Lord God said, 'It is not good that the man should be alone; I will make him a helper fit for him...' and while he slept, he took one of his ribs and closed up its place. With flesh taken from the man, he made it into a woman and brought her to the man.

Genesis 2:23: "Then the man said, 'This at last is bone of my bones and flesh of my flesh; she shall be called Woman'"

Genesis 3:22-23: "Then (after Adam and Eve ate the forbidden fruit) the Lord God said, 'Behold the man has become like one of us, knowing good and evil; and now, lest he put forth his hand and take also of the tree of life, and eat, and live forever.' Therefore the Lord God sent him forth from the Garden of Eden..."

In summary Moses presents an Adam and Eve creation story:

- Without any female gods but several male gods who had male and female genitals;
- With a Lord God who directs that man (Adam) be cloned out of dust in the image of bigenital gods;
- Instead of taking Adam's female genitals to clone Eve, gods took one of Adam's ribs to clone Eve, so I guess Adam's female genitals must have disappeared; and
- Even though Adam and Eve are forbidden from eating forbidden fruit, the reader isn't told why gods wouldn't want Adam and Eve:
  1. To know the difference between good and evil; and
  2. To live forever; and
- Despite God-given human instincts and inclinations such as a positive laugh in the face of danger Yin of a Man and conservative negative Yang of Women, Moses claims:
  1. A male serpent coaxed Eve to eat the forbidden fruit first, and she encouraged Adam to join her. However:
     a. God-given natural law based upon God-given human instincts and inclinations indicates Adam's Yin would have driven him to eat the apple first; and
     b. Moses needed a means to dethrone La Sacre Femme Eve;
  2. So Moses said the gods:
     a. Punished Eve and women by making childbirth extremely painful and making Eve subservient to Adam;
     b Kicked them out of the Garden of Eden; and
     c. In Exodus 21 and 22:18, there's commandments:
        1) Allowing fathers to sell daughters into marital procreation slavery; and
        2) "You shall not permit a sorceress to live," which is Moses' means to prevent women from controlling men with herbs;
        3) But there's no commandment banning male sorcerers;
        4) Only men were allowed to become priests and high priests;
        5) And females lost all of their La Sacre Femme rights.

Other religions have similarly subjugated girls and women to men.

St. Augustine's "Rules against Sex"

Mere Judeo-Christianity did not eliminate natural law based upon God-given human instincts and inclinations to find the most attractive, intelligent, and strong mate to procreate. Judeo-Christians still believed in La Sacre Femme and that making love was a spiritual experience that brought couples closer to God, godliness and heaven. St. Augustine's goal was to drive a wedge between spirituality and sexuality when he wrote the following "Rules against Sex:"

"You cannot be spiritual and sexual. so priests and nuns can no longer get married. Sex is only for procreation. So it's a sin to masturbate, use contraceptives, and have fun during sex because that leads to a sinful life and hell."

Except for a tiny fraction of history, the only law was natural law based upon God-given human instincts and inclinations. *Black's Law Dictionary* says, "Natural law grows out of and conforms to the whole mental, moral and physical constitutional nature of humans." So how can human instincts be immoral?

God said, "Be fruitful and multiply" and gave humans hormone-driven instincts for sexuality, mating, and making love to procreate. God made foreplay, intercourse, and after-play the most stimulating, exciting, passionate, enjoyable, and satisfying heavenly experience of life on earth.

God's Goal for Mankind

St. Thomas Aquinas also said in "Theory of Law" that God's goal for mankind is utopia or heaven on earth, free of war and crime. The Baby Boomer Generation of Morality said, "Make love, not war." That's not the first time those words echoed.

In an ancient pagan Greek play, wives, fiancés, and prostitutes (who couldn't earn money) were horny and depressed because men were always away fighting a war where they were serviced by prostitutes who followed an army that raped women in conquered cities.

Finally all the women agreed that when the soldiers return they'd be sexually dressed and perfumed and talk and act sensuously and sexually but not yield to sex. Eventually the men agreed to stop going off to war.

God, gods or aliens from outer space tried to end natural law human instincts and inclinations to go to war by passing on eternal laws to prevent war and crime and achieve God's goal for mankind — utopia:

- "Thou shall not kill";
- "Thou shall not steal";
- "Thou shall not commit adultery"; and
- "Do unto others as you would have others do unto you."

However, misguided religious leaders have prevented utopia by preaching that God wants people to violate eternal laws against cities and nations where people were falsely said to be savage, heathen, and godless.

Puritan Pilgrims Were Not Sexual Prudes

Contrary to evangelical and Republican Tea Party dogmatic propaganda, the Puritan Pilgrim Founding Fathers and Mothers were not sexual prudes and didn't believe in St. Augustine's "Rules against Sex." They risked sailing across the Atlantic Ocean to escape the Church of England's sex patrols because they believed sex was a gift from God to:

- Relieve sexual tension and horniness from testosterone buildup;
- Bring fun, excitement, and joy to life and enhance love;
- Relieve stress, anxiety, and suffering through release of endorphins;
- Allow people to relax, fall asleep, and awaken refreshed; and
- Enable people to "be fruitful and multiply."

Religious leaders want their religion to be "the opiate of the masses," but sex is the real opiate of mankind because of its medicinal properties. Like Celts, Pilgrim Founding Fathers and Mothers were moral Puritans who "obeyed demands of nature in a more moral way." The Nuremburg Doctrine says that, "Everyone owes a higher duty to morality than to laws of a nation."

Again, "how can what is instinctive be immoral?" So in Western civilization, St. Augustine's "Rules against Sex" violates natural law human instincts and inclinations about sex; prevents mankind's goal of Swedish happiness; and causes psychiatric and physical sexual disorders.

Problems with Inadequate Sexual Education

It's been said:

- "Sex is wasted on the young and inexperienced"; and thus

- "Sex can be like the blind leading the blind."

Have you known any Buddhist, Hindu, Sikh, or Muslim husbands and wives whose marriage was arranged with a smile on their faces? Have you noticed couples who've been married five to fifty years don't look at or talk to each other or smile in restaurants or as they drive to and from them and ironically church? I wonder whether they pray for sex.

The happiest and least-depressed nation is Sweden because couples make love three to five times per week. However, in the sexually repressed United States, couples often spend their honeymoon in bed and have sex every night for a week or so. Within a month, sex is down to two or three days per week. Within five years, they're lucky once a month or less, etc.

Would horny boys and men get married if they knew their girlfriend or fiancé faked orgasms and pretended to want to make love every night before marriage but after marriage would use a long list of excuses to avoid sex until the husband gives up trying or expecting sex?

That begs questions. If testosterone in men and women continues to be produced by their bodies and they fantasize about sex on average seven times per day, why don't they have sex every night and every morning before work and twice on Sunday? Why do wives avoid sex by saying, "Not tonight honey. I've got a (head, stomach, back, or neck ache)" or "I'm too tired or stressed out for sex"? What if I said there's a means to alleviating stress, fatigue, and aches and sexually stimulate at the same time via Kama Sutra acupressure reflexology?

If I had a daughter, I would never read her the Cinderella story. It's about girls of all social classes vying for the handsome, rich, and powerful prince. However, that story causes girls to seek a prince of sports, music, movies, law, medicine, or business instead of searching for the magic triad where a couple is in love with their best friend and consummate lover.

Why would a boy or man risk marriage if there's a 60 percent chance his girlfriend or fiancé when seeking a mate placed a higher priority on income, assets, profession, and social status than on love, friendship, mutual interests, and a good sex life? Why would any man want to risk getting married and raising children when there's a 50/50 chance of divorce and losing them, especially sons? Occasionally I have thought, "I'll give to the next gal I could fall in love with tickets to her favorite singer's concert. I'll be there incognito. If she screams and pulls her hair, that will be the end if she hadn't done the same when she first saw me."

If 60 percent of women never or rarely have an orgasm via intercourse, why would they get married to a man who can't bring them to orgasm? Why don't Judeo-Christian women achieve Level 10 orgasms or come close?

That's a result of St. Augustine's "Rules against Sex" and parents who don't explain to children how to make love. Fathers don't explain to sons how to bring a woman to orgasm because they don't know how. Mothers don't explain to daughters what to expect on the way to orgasm or what they must ask their man to do to create orgasms because they never had one. Or parents are too embarrassed to explain "the birds and the bees."

Frankly I don't know whether either of my wives ever had an orgasm. I wonder whether they read romance novels, such as *The Notebook*, *Pride and Prejudice* or *A Good Year*, so they could vicariously experience secondary thrills of romance and passionate love.

If "men are on Mars and women are on Venus" is that why women dream about men they know but men dream about women they don't know?

Why are men sexually on Mars and women on Venice? Why is sex wasted on the young and inexperienced? Why is it acceptable for boys to "sew their wild oats" but girls aren't allowed to get premarital grain? Why do most girls and women have to fake orgasms?

Those phenomenon, statistics, and dozens of psychiatric and physical sexual disorders are caused by more than St. Augustine's "Rules against Sex." Girls and guys are made to feel guilty about sex and sexuality when parents say "sex before marriage is dirty" or "if you masturbate, your eyes will permanently squint and hair will grow on the palm of your hand."

Some fathers take sons to a prostitute to teach them how to be gentle and make love to a woman. Some mothers advise daughters to have their first sexual experience with an experienced man.

However, that doesn't guarantee that sons or daughters will learn what is necessary. Boyfriends or fiancés may have a premature-ejaculation problem and never last long enough for her to achieve orgasm.

Solutions Can Start with Handwriting Analysis, Personality, and Relationship Profile Tests

I learned much about a potential mate, including whether they would be a good lover, via hand writing analysis from an article in *Glamour* or *Cosmopolitan*. After my first disastrous divorce, I read those magazines because I wanted to increase chances of having a mutually beneficial relationship with someone I could love, who could be a best friend with chemistry and common interests, and be a consummate lover.

Articles explain what women wanted and didn't want in a mate, what they liked, disliked, enjoyed, excited or turned them off. Handwriting is like an ocean. If it's calm, writing is smooth. When there's uncertainty or stress, such as a storm, handwriting is choppy, jagged, edgy, and uneven.

Right-handed extroverts slant letters to the right and introverts slant letters left. When letters are equally proportional, round, and vertical, the writer is down to earth with a need to maintain control and be in control.

The way loops of Ys and Gs are shaped indicates sexual tendencies. A perfectly shaped loop where it returns to baseline indicates a mature attitude about sex and sexuality. Open looped Gs and Ys indicate he/she is searching for sexual satisfaction. Fat loops that return to baseline reveal she/he has unfulfilled sexual fantasies. If a wide loop comes to a sharp point, it indicates a person who is sexually aggressive.

Handwriting with a variety of types of loops indicates someone who's hedonistic, rarely makes love the same way, enjoys a variety of types of foreplay and intercourse, and may be bisexual. Those magazines also have personality and relationship profile tests that couples can take separately and compare results to see if they're compatible.

Solution Via the Science and Art of Kama Sutra

St. Augustine drove a wedge between sexuality and spirituality to make them mutually exclusive. Asian philosophies (Confucianism, Taoism, and Daoism) merged into Kama Sutra because sex is a spiritual experience that brings couples closer to God, godliness, and Shangri-La or heaven.

Asian parents put a copy of *Shades of the Jade Bedroom* on the night stand of newlyweds. It explains the science and art of Kama Sutra:

- Foods and herbs that are good and bad for stimulating production of testosterone (in men and women) to increase sexual drive and increase blood supply to genitals;
- Exercises that strengthen genitals to prevent premature ejaculation before simultaneous orgasm;
- Importance of a couple doing and saying romantic, sensuous, and sexual things all day to create a viable mood for making love;
- If a mate is under stress from work or children, has a headache, neck ache, stomachache, backache, or other neuromuscular problem, acupressure charts can show what nerve root endings and pathways to press and stroke in order to both relieve stress or pain and sexually stimulate at the same time;
- Acupressure reflexology and foreplay massage strokes and touches:
  1. Goals of massage and acupressure reflexology:
     a. When body is on stomach and back, stimulate every centimeter of body without touching breasts and genitals;
     b. Prepare mind for sex by pressing nerve endings in tips and circumference of fingers;
     c. Prepare heart, lungs, breasts, and other organs for sex by pressing nerve ending in upper dorsal and palm side of upper half of hands;
     d. Stimulate genitals by pressing nerve endings in circumference of lower hand and wrists;
     e. Similarly pressure point in feet and ankles can stimulate breast and genitals;
     f. From ankles and wrists, press nerve pathways that travel up the arms to T-3 (thoracic third nerve root entrance) and legs to S-2 and S-3 (sacrum second and third nerve root) entrances to spine;
  2. Stroking includes long, slow touches of fingers from head to fingers and toes, dancing like rain or a butterfly;
- Dermatome charts of central nervous system show where to apply pressure with fingertips adjacent to nerve root endings and follow nerve pathways going into spine from peripheral nerve root endings in hands, fingers, feet, and toes to:
  1. Eliminate head, neck, back, and stomachaches or stress;

2. Prepare body for sex by stimulating heart, lungs, glands; and
3. Then stimulate genitals with acupressure of:
   a. T3-T5 nerve roots and pathways to breasts; and
   b. L5-S1-S3 nerve roots and pathways to genitals.
      * Tactile and oral foreplay until orgasms begin; and then
      * There's thirty-seven intercourse positions for making love

Spiritual Sex from Trial and Error Learning Process

A couple must communicate what they like and don't like. They'll gradually learn what sexual turnoffs to avoid and concentrate on stimulating turn-ons. Orgasmic intensity will leap to new heights until Level 10 orgasms are achieved. As Baby Boomers would say, "Make love, not war, and the world will be a better place. Sexual satisfaction is the path to spirituality, godliness, God, heaven, and the goal of mankind — happiness — which is in the best interests of children."

But sex can only be one or two hours a day. What can couples do during the other sixteen or seventeen hours each day?

Those who play together stay together via golf, tennis, canoeing, sailing, biking, hiking, camping, fishing, skiing, playing chess, Trivial Pursuit, and crossword puzzles;

The more common interests couples share (cooking, news, politics, sports, movies, art, music, traveling, restaurants), the more mutually rewarding a relationship becomes;

But likely each couple will have interests that are not shared. Each should support the other's individual interests; and

If both in a couple have careers or jobs, they should share household and childcare responsibilities.

Mother loved to paint, and Father supported that by paying for art lessons and supplies, as well as traveling to scenic places she could paint — fantastic gardens and art museums coast to coast. In exchange Mother learned to love Wisconsin Badger and Green Bay Packer football games and boxing matches.

I learned to enjoy chick flicks and reading novels and discussing them.

www.ingramcontent.com/pod-product-compliance
Lightning Source LLC
Chambersburg PA
CBHW070627290526
45790CB00001B/30